FEMINIST READINGS OF VICTORIAN POPULAR TEXTS

Feminist Readings of Victorian Popular Texts

Divergent femininities

Edited by
Emma Liggins
Edge Hill College, UK
Daniel Duffy
Queen Mary's College, UK

Ashgate

Aldershot • Burlington USA • Singapore • Sydney

Published by
Ashgate Publishing Ltd
Gower House, Croft Road
Aldershot, Hampshire, GU11 3HR
England

Ashgate Publishing Company
131 Main Street
Burlington, VT 05601-5600 USA

Ashgate website: http://www.ashgate.com

ISBN 0 7546 0293 1

British Library Cataloguing in Publication Data
Feminist readings of Victorian popular texts : divergent
    femininities. - (Nineteenth century series)
    1.Popular literature - History and criticism 2.English
    literature - 19th century - History and criticism 3.Women
    and literature 4.Women in literature 5.Women in popular
    culture 6.Feminist criticism
    I.Liggins, Emma II.Duffy, Daniel
    820.9'008

Library of Congress Cataloging-in-Publication Data
Feminist readings of Victorian popular texts : divergent femininities /
edited by Emma Liggins and Daniel Duffy.
        p. cm. – (The nineteenth century)
Includes bibliographical references and index.
    ISBN 0-7546-0293-1 (alk. paper)
    1. English literature–19th century–History and criticism. 2.
Feminism and litature–Great Britain–History–19th century. 3. Women
and literature–Great Britain–History–19th century. 4. Popular
literature–Great Britain–History and criticism. 5. Great
Britain–History–Victoria, 1837-1901. I. Liggins, Emma. II. Duffy,
Daniel (Daniel D.) III. Nineteenth century (Aldershot, England)
    PR468.F46 F46 2001
    820.9'008–dc21

2001022835

This volume is printed on acid-free paper.
Printed and bound in Great Britain by MPG Books Ltd, Bodmin, Cornwall

Contents

General Editors' Preface   vii

List of Contributors   ix

Acknowledgements   xi

Introduction   xiii

Short Stories, Poetry and Periodicals

1   'The False Prudery of Public Taste': Scandalous Women and the   1
Annuals, 1820–1850
Harriet Devine Jump

2   'Too Boldly' for a Woman: Text, Identity and the Working-Class   18
Woman Poet
Margaret Forsyth

3   Every Girl's Best Friend?: The *Girl's Own Paper* and its Readers   35
Hilary Skelding

Popular Fiction

4   Good Housekeeping? Domestic Economy and Suffering Wives   53
in Mrs Henry Wood's Early Fiction
Emma Liggins

5   After Lady Audley: M.E. Braddon, the Actress and the Act of   69
Writing in *Hostages to Fortune*
Kate Mattacks

6   See What a Big Wide Bed it is!: Mrs Henry Wood and the   89
        Philistine Imagination
        Deborah Wynne

7   'Weird Fascination': The Response to Victorian Women's   108
        Ghost Stories
        Clare Stewart

The Popular Stage

8   Feminist Discourse in Popular Drama of the Early- and   126
        Mid-Victorian Era
        Daniel Duffy

9   Women's Playwriting and the Popular Theatre in the Late   147
        Victorian Era, 1870–1900
        Kate Newey

Bibliography   168

Index   172

The Nineteenth Century
General Editors' Preface

The aim of this series is to reflect, develop and extend the great burgeoning of interest in the nineteenth century that has been an inevitable feature of recent years, as that former epoch has come more sharply into focus as a locus of our understanding not only of the past but of the contours of our modernity. It centres primarily upon major authors and subjects within Romantic and Victorian literature. It also includes studies of other British writers and issues, where these are matters of current debate: for example, biography and autobiography, journalism, periodical literature, travel writing, book production, gender, non-canonical writing. We are dedicated principally to publishing original monographs and symposia; our policy is to embrace a broad scope in chronology, approach and range of concern, and both to recognize and cut innovatively across such parameters as those suggested by the designations 'Romantic' and 'Victorian'. We welcome new ideas and theories, while valuing traditional scholarship. It is hoped that the world which predates yet so forcibly predicts and engages our own will emerge in parts, in the wider sweep, and in the lively streams of disputation and change that are so manifest an aspect of its intellectual, artistic and social landscape.

Vincent Newey
Joanne Shattock
University of Leicester

List of Contributors

DANIEL DUFFY teaches at Queen Mary's College, Basingstoke. He has published on Anne Brontë and masculinity and has an article on melodrama in *Nineteenth-Century Theatre* (1999).

MARGARET FORSYTH is in the final stages of completing her PhD thesis on working-class women's poetry of the nineteenth century at Edge Hill College of Higher Education.

HARRIET DEVINE JUMP is a Reader at Edge Hill. Her publications include *Mary Wollstonecraft: Writer* (Harvester Wheatsheaf, 1994) and two edited anthologies for Routledge: *Women's Writing of the Victorian Period* (1999) and *Nineteenth-Century Short Stories by Women* (1998). She has also published articles on Romantic women writers in *Women's Writing* (1998, 1999) and in the *Charles Lamb Bulletin* (2000).

EMMA LIGGINS lectures at Edge Hill. She has published on Mary Braddon in *Journal of Victorian Culture* (1997) and on New Women fiction in *Literature and History* (2000) and *Women's Writing* (2000). She has also co-edited *Signs of Masculinity: Men in Literature 1700 to the Present* (Rodopi, 1998) and has an article on violent women in the *Wilkie Collins Society Journal* (2001).

KATE MATTACKS has just completed her thesis on Mary Braddon and theatricality at the University of Keele.

KATE NEWEY lectures at the University of Lancaster. She has published articles on nineteenth-century popular theatre and melodrama in *Victorian Literature and Culture* (1997), *Journal of Dramatic Theory and Criticism* (1997) and *Journal of Victorian Culture* (2000). Her work on nineteenth-century women playwrights appears in Tracy C. Davis and Ellen Donkin (eds), *Nineteenth-Century British Women Playwrights* (Cambridge University Press, 1999) and in Joanne Shattock (ed.), *Women and Literature in Britain 1800–1900* (Cambridge University Press, 2001).

HILARY SKELDING lectures at Staffordshire University and has published on the historical fiction of Evelyn Everett-Green in *Women's Writing* (2000).

CLARE STEWART has just completed her thesis on Victorian women's ghost stories at the University of Glasgow and is currently lecturing at Aberdeen College.

DEBORAH WYNNE lectures at the University of Keele. Her forthcoming book is entitled *Sensation and the Victorian Family Magazine: the sensation novel in context* (Palgrave).

Acknowledgements

Many thanks are due to staff at Edge Hill and the University of Salford for supporting us on the preparation of this book, in particular Gill Davies and Harriet Jump for their support and encouragement and Antony Rowland, Emma Latham and Peter Wright for assistance with the mysteries of CRC.

Acknowledgements

Introduction

Emma Liggins and Daniel Duffy

It is only in recent years that Victorian popular texts have come to be seen as worthy subjects of academic research. For a long time notions of canonicity and dubious assumptions about aesthetic value, about 'high' and 'low' culture, ensured that popular writing was ignored by academics and edited out of debates on the nineteenth century. Typical of these assumptions about popular writing is Victor Neuberg's belief, articulated in an introduction written in 1977, that 'popular literature can be defined as what the unsophisticated reader has chosen for pleasure. Such a reader may, of course, come from any class in society, although the primary appeal of popular literature has been to the poor'.[1] This exposes a number of common misconceptions about popular texts and their readers, namely that the latter are predominantly lower-class, have no critical faculties, and choose texts that have value only as entertainment. Since popular texts are intended for mass consumption, it was generally presumed that they must be simply formulaic and non-thought-provoking, peddlers only of conservative values. This assumption extended to Victorian popular texts, as R.C. Terry's evaluation of them showed: 'much popular fiction flatters the bourgeois mentality, displaying a depressing tameness'.[2] However, new research into Victorian popular texts and the marketplaces in which they were produced has challenged such limited ways of thinking, paralleling recent redefinitions of the popular in the field of cultural studies. This continuing critical debate about the status of the Victorian popular text and the ways in which it was read and interpreted informs the collection of essays in this volume, which consider both nineteenth-century and current definitions of the popular.

---

[1]   Victor E. Neuberg, *Popular Literature: A History and Guide* (Harmondsworth: Penguin, 1977), p. 12.

[2]   R.C. Terry, *Victorian Popular Fiction, 1860–1880* (London: Macmillan, 1983), p. 54. This is part of a larger argument about the conservative plot resolutions of popular fiction, where texts may range over 'forbidden ground' during the course of the story but will always inevitably conform to 'the moral convictions of the audience' at the end.

Conservative or Radical? The Changing Status of Victorian Popular Genres

Popular culture is now interpreted much more positively than it used to be. Theodor Adorno and Max Horkheimer in the 1940s saw it as an absolutely authoritarian system, 'uniform as a whole and in every part'.[3] Fredric Jameson in the 1970s argued that it incorporates the subversive only to bolster established power; he claimed that it performs 'transformational work on social and political anxieties and fantasies which must then have some effective presence ... in order subsequently to be "managed" or repressed' through 'imaginary resolutions and by the projection of an optical illusion of social harmony'.[4] Today the conservative dimensions of popular culture are not denied, but it is no longer seen as being devoted solely to generating ideological conformity. What Jameson called the 'intolerable, unrealisable' desires of the consumers of popular culture are allowed much greater influence upon it, making for definitions which represent it as genuinely contradictory.[5] Tony Bennett, for example, has claimed that popular culture is 'the terrain on which dominant, subordinate and oppositional cultural values and ideologies meet and intermingle'.[6] These values and ideologies are not seen as equally weighted; rather, as John Fiske puts it, popular culture 'contain[s] both the forces of domination and the opportunities to speak against them, the opportunities to oppose or evade them from subordinated, but not totally disempowered, positions'.[7]

Assessments of Victorian popular culture now appear to approximate to Fiske's model. In the field of Victorian popular drama studies, opinion relating to the conservative/radical issue has followed, on the whole, a similar trajectory to that outlined above. When melodrama, for instance, was generally regarded as featuring what Michael Booth called 'a world of certainties where confusion, doubt, and perplexity are absent', it tended to be seen as politically reactionary.[8] Both Gilbert Cross and Raymond Williams represented the form in Jamesonian ways in the 1970s. Cross surveyed its realization of 'radical

---

[3]   Theodor Adorno and Max Horkheimer, 'The Culture Industry: Enlightenment As Mass Deception' (1946), in Simon During (ed.), *The Cultural Studies Reader* (London and New York: Routledge, 1993), p. 30.

[4]   Fredric Jameson, 'Reification and Utopia in Mass Culture' (1979), in *Signatures of the Visible* (London and New York: Routledge, 1990), pp. 25–6.

[5]   Ibid., p. 25.

[6]   Tony Bennett, 'The Politics of "the Popular" and Popular Culture', in Tony Bennett, Colin Mercer, and Janet Woollacott (eds), *Popular Culture and Social Relations* (Milton Keynes and Philadelphia: Open University Press, 1986), p. 19.

[7]   John Fiske, *Understanding Popular Culture* (London: Unwin Hyman, 1989), p. 25.

[8]   Michael R. Booth, *English Melodrama* (London: Herbert Jenkins, 1965), p. 14.

feelings' only to conclude that while '[p]rotests were permitted' – he noted that 'something of a catharsis resulted', thereby implying the dispersal of discontent – 'conventional moral standards had to be reasserted by the play's conclusion'.[9] Williams argued that melodrama 'touched every nerve of nineteenth-century society, but usually only to play on the nerves and to resolve crisis in an external and providential dramatic world'.[10] More recently, a number of melodrama scholars have come to see it as being 'drawn towards paradox rather than simplification', to quote Simon Shepherd and Peter Womack, and they have produced new estimations of its ideological nature accordingly.[11] Jacky Bratton, for example, has perceived an 'apparent conflict of values' in its rapid juxtaposition of the serious and the comic, finding that in military melodramas the 'anti-heroic comics are centrally important', undercutting the principals' endeavour by 'dramatising an oppositional, anti-imperialist, or at least sceptical view'.[12] In this volume Daniel Duffy and Kate Newey represent stage melodrama as politically ambiguous, focussing their analyses of the form on its relation to nineteenth-century gender issues – a little-explored area. Duffy claims that early- and mid-Victorian melodrama and comedy testify to feminist and to sexist spectatorial conditions of production, arguing that they dramatize and endorse contemporary feminist insights and agencies *and* the patriarchalism 'against which these feminisms formed and fought'. Newey turns to 'the possibilities for multiple readings' in late-Victorian female-authored melodrama, demonstrating that while this 'makes no explicit feminist claims' in the manner of the New Woman plays of the period, it 'calls into question contemporary ideals of femininity ... from within those very conventions'.

---

[9]   Gilbert B. Cross, *Next Week – 'East Lynne': Domestic Drama in Performance 1820–1874* (London: Associated University Presses, 1977), pp. 171, 218.
[10]   Raymond Williams, 'Social Environment and Theatrical Environment: The Case of English Naturalism', in Marie Axton and Raymond Williams (eds), *English Drama: Forms and Development* (Cambridge: Cambridge University Press, 1977), p. 214.
[11]   Simon Shepherd and Peter Womack, *English Drama: A Cultural History* (Oxford: Blackwell, 1996), p. 204.
[12]   Jacky Bratton, 'British Heroism and the Structure of Melodrama', in *Acts of Supremacy: The British Empire and the Stage* (Manchester: Manchester University Press, 1991), pp. 33, 24. See also her 'The Contending Discourses of Melodrama', in Jacky Bratton, Jim Cook, Christine Gledhill (eds), *Melodrama: Stage Picture Screen* (London: British Film Institute, 1994). More negative views of melodrama's ideological nature are still produced, of course. Michael Hays and Anastasia Nikolopoulou, for example, presented some of the essays in their edited collection *Melodrama: The Cultural Emergence of a Genre* (Hampshire and London: Macmillan, 1996) under the title 'Radicalism Contained' and in their introduction established the form as having 'a dissociated consciousness ... betokened by and interpreted through the poverty, rebellion, and popular illegalities adumbrated by the hero or heroine, and another, a "false" consciousness that imposes itself on the first' (pp. xiv–xv).

As Kate Flint's recent examination of Victorian popular fiction and periodical material shows, similar 'disruptive potential' has been detected in other popular genres traditionally perceived to be deeply conservative.[13] Lyn Pykett, whose important work on the sensation novel in the early 1990s was instrumental in provoking a reexamination of popular fiction, has argued that 'the conservative/radical dilemma' is now the 'big question' haunting studies of the cultural history of the nineteenth century, going on to illustrate contemporary approaches to popular authors by concluding that 'Braddon is both a radical and a conservative, and ... she is neither'.[14] Elaine Showalter, one of the first feminist critics to reconsider the women's sensation novel in terms of its potentially subversive content, had argued in the late 1970s that it became a vehicle for 'feminine protest' even though ultimately 'the sensationalists could not bring themselves to undertake a radical inquiry into the role of women'.[15] After her reevaluation of women's popular writing, feminist research into 'forgotten' women writers and neglected genres such as the ghost story and working-class women's poetry and autobiographies was concerned with developing her ideas about the popular writer's relationship with her women readers. However, this prompted some critics to complain that all popular texts were now being indiscriminately celebrated for their latent radicalism. Ann Cvetkovich argued in 1992 that 'there has been a tendency ... to assume that noncanonical texts must be proven subversive to be studied' and that 'feminist critics have also been too willing to celebrate popular culture as a voice for female subjectivity'.[16] There was a general critical consensus in the 1990s that it was more helpful to consider the popular text in terms of its contradictions and to focus more specifically on the cultural context in which it was produced. Critics argued that, rather than simply celebrating female subjectivity, popular texts either 'self-consciously explored or implicitly exposed the contradictions of prevailing versions of femininity'.[17] Emma Liggins demonstrates this in her analysis of Mrs Henry Wood's use of ideologies of domestic management from contemporary household manuals by

---

[13] Kate Flint, *The Woman Reader, 1837–1914* (Oxford: Clarendon Press, 1993), p. 276.

[14] Lyn Pykett, 'Afterword' in Pamela Gilbert, Aeron Haynie and Marlene Tromp (eds), *Beyond Sensation: Mary Elizabeth Braddon in Context* (Albany: State University of New York Press, 2000), pp. 279, 280.

[15] Elaine Showalter, *A Literature of their Own: from Charlotte Brontë to Doris Lessing* (1978: London: Virago, 1982), p. 180.

[16] Ann Cvetkovich, *Mixed Feelings: Feminism, Mass Culture and Victorian Sensationalism* (New Brunswick: Rutgers University Press, 1992), pp. 38, 39.

[17] Lyn Pykett, *The Improper Feminine: The Women's Sensation Novel and the New Woman Writing* (London: Routledge, 1992), p. 5. This argument is linked to the way in which women writers of the popular text operate, though it can also relate to some of the texts published by men in this period.

Sarah Ellis and Mrs Beeton. She argues that Wood's texts allow women to identify with either the conventional suffering wife or more transgressive, independent women, as they promote the joys of domestic femininity whilst highlighting the inadequacy of the domestic angel as a role model for women.

The reexamination of Victorian popular texts also extends to an appreciation of the contradictory nature of magazines, annuals and periodicals, which had a wide readership and tremendous popular appeal throughout the period, not least because they were important vehicles for showcasing short stories, poetry and autobiographical writing. As Margaret Beetham has argued in her study of nineteenth-century women's magazines, texts such as *The Englishwoman's Domestic Magazine* were remarkable for 'the extraordinary diversity of genres and voices' they encapsulated,[18] which again encouraged readers to adopt a variety of different viewpoints and to respond to 'very different models of femininity'. In her analysis of short fiction and poetry in early-Victorian annuals, Harriet Jump has commented on the ways in which contributors were able to appeal to women readers *and* to satisfy the ideals of parents and guardians, offering stories which often 'undermined and deconstructed the very models of femininity and domestic bliss they were overtly recommending'. This diversity of perspectives and voices contributed to the 'radical potential' of periodical writing, opening up a space where it becomes 'possible to challenge oppressive and repressive models of the feminine',[19] though conservative models of domestic femininity are simultaneously reinforced. Hilary Skelding argues in her chapter on *The Girl's Own Paper* that the periodical exhibits 'a frequently baffling tendency to project apparently divergent, or contradictory, notions of femininity, combining the radical with the reactionary' in its approaches to such issues as women's education and work, household management and marriage. Contradictions were also often apparent in the dichotomy between the content of the stories, poems and autobiographies and the 'official' messages of the leading articles, which offered much more conservative views on femininity.

This book, then, seeks to develop the current approach to the 'conservative/radical dilemma' by illustrating ways in which a diverse range of Victorian popular texts appeared both to endorse *and* subvert ideological norms in their representations of femininity. Contributors analyse the non-fictional discourses such as feminist critiques, household manuals, and magazine articles upon which many of these representations drew; deliberately or inadvertently such discourses expose the contradictions of Victorian women's

---

[18]   Margaret Beetham, *A Magazine of her Own?: Domesticity and Desire in the Woman's Magazine, 1800–1914* (London: Routledge, 1996), p. 61.
[19]   Ibid., p. 3.

lives, and so are vital tools with which to illuminate the double-edged nature of their popular texts.

Consumers, Readers, and Marketplaces

The general shift in interpretations of the politics of popular culture has, of course, been matched by changes in the way its consumers have been represented. Happily these consumers are no longer cast as the manipulated, diverted, and degraded dupes of Jameson's implicit assumption.[20] Recent ethnographic research into their actual reading or viewing practices has revealed a much more complex reception phenomenon. While it has been found that some consumers do read texts dominantly, accepting just their conservative values, it has also been found that others read texts ambivalently or oppositionally, only partly accepting or rejecting those values and seeking out critical or subversive ones.[21] Take, for example, Jackie Stacey's fascinating examination of British women's memories of the female Hollywood stars they admired in the 1940s and 1950s. While these stars were read dominantly in that they 'encouraged traditional forms of aspiration' such as feminine beauty and 'attachment to a man', their 'courage, confidence, and independence' were also 'aspired to by spectators who saw themselves as unable to enjoy such admirable qualities'.[22] To sustain this discourse of female energy, spectators had to read selectively:

> Powerful female stars often played characters in punishing patriarchal narratives, where the woman is either killed off, or married, or both, but these spectators do not seem to select this aspect of their films to write about. Instead, the qualities of confidence and power are remembered as offering female spectators the pleasure of participation in qualities they themselves lacked and desired.[23]

Feminist critics have also been reconceptualising Victorian women readers of popular fiction as having the potential to interpret texts and genres oppositionally. As Kate Flint has argued, the woman reader's choice of

---

[20]   Jameson, p. 25. Jameson here writes of 'the mechanisms of manipulation, diversion, and degradation' that he sees as constituting popular culture.

[21]   These reception practices are discussed in Jacqueline Bobo, 'The Color Purple: Black Women as Cultural Readers', in E. Deirdre Pribram (ed.), Female Spectators: Looking At Film and Television (London and New York: Verso, 1988).

[22]   Jackie Stacey, Star Gazing: Hollywood Cinema and Female Spectatorship (London and New York: Routledge, 1994), p. 154.

[23]   Ibid., p. 158.

reading position became 'in the broadest sense, a political choice', involving her in 'an active process of interpretation' and giving her the capacity to resist ideological perspectives which she did not wish to accommodate.[24] According to Pykett, the 'dispersal of narrative identifications' made available in sensation fiction contributed to the creation of 'a space for resistance of the text's "official" morality',[25] thus enabling the reader to choose from a range of possible reading positions and interpretations. Rather than interpreting popular genres in terms of their official messages, as feminist critics we should understand genre as 'a flexible and historically developing set of codes rather than as a fixed formula or category'.[26] Popular writers were constantly engaged in subverting expectations about genre whilst remaining within the broad confines of generic conventions, which helped to give readers more scope for interpretation. In her chapter on working-class women's poetry, Margaret Forsyth discusses the way in which the implied 'threat' of working-class writing could be diminished by the production of texts which appeared to reflect middle-class values, even as they also 'provided [readers with] a means of resisting or re-enacting them in particular class and/or gender contexts'.

The relationship between readers, texts and genres has also been considered in terms of the marketplace, highlighting the demands of consumers and the publication and dissemination of popular texts, such as the serialisation of fiction in periodicals or the circumstances of staging melodramas. Gaye Tuchman has looked at the relationship between publishers, publishers' readers and 'typical library readers', showing how 'the business of publishing, both production and distribution, was increasingly geared towards the establishment of a market' after 1840. In a market determined by industrial forces, readers can be effectively directed towards the consumption of particular genres felt to be appropriate to their gender. By mid-century publishers' readers helped to determine the nature of women's published output by rejecting work in particular genres which might not sell. Women were thus increasingly identified with the 'flutter' of popular culture both as consumers and writers whilst men became associated with the 'high-culture novel'.[27] In her chapter Kate Mattacks argues that Mary Braddon had a profoundly ambivalent attitude to the market she wrote for. While Braddon's status as 'the author of *Lady Audley's Secret*' brought her irresistible fame and success, she resented it for limiting her artistic creativity. However, rather than being 'relegat[ed]' to the popular-culture novel, as Tuchman argues,[28] some female novelists took pride

---

24   Flint, pp. 330, 283.

25   Pykett, pp. 81, 132.

26   Ibid., p. 50.

27   Gaye Tuchman with Nina E. Fortin, *Edging Women Out: Victorian Novelists, Publishers, and Social Change* (London: Routledge, 1989), pp. 67, 69.

28   Ibid., p. 69.

in meeting consumer demand. Deborah Wynne argues in her reading of Mrs Henry Wood that 'she adopted a flexible approach to genre and style, always willing to adapt to the demands of the market', a practice which helped to secure her continuing success. This volume, then, aims to demonstrate an awareness of the ways in which markets could both limit and liberate popular writers, who were able to manipulate generic conventions in order to allow readers to interpret texts oppositionally.

Victorian Debates about Popular Texts and their Reception

Victorian reviews of popular fiction and poetry and observations on the stage offer insights into fears relating to the consumption of popular texts, as well as evidence of that consumption itself. Many of the essays in this volume have analysed the ideological content of such Victorian writings in order to demonstrate prevalent attitudes to specific genres and their readers and spectators. Perhaps surprisingly, conservative commentators often prove very helpful to modern critics, revealing the subversive dynamics of popular genres while condemning them. For example, the decidedly reactionary clergyman Thomas Best may not have been pleased by his discovery of these dynamics in popular drama, but he articulates them much as modern melodrama scholars have. Best wrote of drama 'which maintains a place in popular favour' that 'moral lessons and virtuous sentiments are interspersed here and there', but 'the brilliant passage which shows like virtue ... [is] mixed up with what will most effectually counteract it'.[29] Reviews are also helpful because they point to actual reading practices, and show the power of the marketplace to make or break a writer's reputation. Clare Stewart's chapter on the reception of women's ghost stories makes extensive use of reviews in contemporary periodicals in order to show 'the ambiguity with which the form was received by readers and critics'. She also suggests that unfavourable reviews were often the result of the difficulties in placing supernatural fiction and the attempt to deal with its unfamiliarity, and ultimately contributed to the declining reputation of certain women writers. This section is intended to give a flavour of Victorian debates about the nature and reception of the popular text. Examples given are taken from writings on fiction and drama, though arguments are broadly applicable to other popular genres of the time.

Reviewers of popular fiction assumed that the typical reader was a young, sexually ignorant middle-class woman, which is why they were frequently

---

[29]   Thomas Best, *Sermons on Theatrical Amusements* (London: Seeley, Jackson, and Halliday, 1865), p. 54; *Sermons on the Amusements of the Stage* (Sheffield: George Ridge, 1831), pp. 63, 210–11.

outraged at the ways in which readers might be encouraged to adopt certain attitudes or to identify with supposedly transgressive characters. An article in the *Saturday Review* of 1866 took as its premise that all women read as 'possible wives' in order to be educated about appropriate female behaviour and the kind of man which was suitable husband material. It went on to stress the differences between male and female reading practices, where a woman reader has 'a dangerous habit of identifying the situations of a novel with the circumstances of her own life, and of speaking and acting as she thinks a young lady in a novel would speak and act'.[30] The dangers of reading for women, then, stemmed from the views about sexuality and marriage offered by fiction and their supposed tendency to identify with and emulate fictional heroines, perhaps even those who committed bigamy and adultery. Victorian reviewers such as Margaret Oliphant, famous for her anti-feminist commentaries on popular writers complained that sensation novels depicted heroines who 'marry their grooms in fits of passion' and 'give and receive burning kisses',[31] thereby refusing to conform to contemporary moral codes. Contemporary feminist arguments about the nature of women readers' identification with sensation heroines are clearly relevant here, as discussions of female-authored popular fiction in this volume follow Kate Flint in exploring 'the tensions which are built up between those social assumptions which structure the facts of the plot, and the sympathies which are called out towards the transgressive heroines'.[32] Reviews exposed the fears that women readers would imitate acts of sexual transgression but ultimately reinforced the view that popular texts also tended to redirect women towards a more conservative model of domestic femininity.

Moral warnings were also issued against reading popular fiction because of its cross-class appeal. Reviewers expressed concern about the new marketplace for fiction in which novelists pandered to the public's demands. The resulting commodification of fiction prompted one reviewer, Henry Mansel, to write of the sensation novel, 'A commercial atmosphere floats around works of this class, redolent of the manufactory and the shop'.[33] This precipitated discussions about the cross-class readership of particular genres as increased literacy levels and the changing marketplace ensured that the distinctions between 'the "light reading" of a middle-class and predominantly female public ... [and] the "mass entertainment" of the relatively newly formed

---

[30]   'Novels Past and Present', *Saturday Review*, 14 April 1866, pp. 439, 440.

[31]   [Margaret Oliphant], 'Novels', *Blackwood's Edinburgh Magazine* 102 (1867), pp. 257–80 (p. 267).

[32]   Flint, pp. 292–3.

[33]   [Henry Mansel], 'Sensation Novels', *Quarterly Review* 113 (1863), 481–514 (pp. 482–3).

lower-middle- and upper-working-class readership' were blurred.[34] An often
quoted review of Braddon's fiction claimed:

> The notoriety she has acquired is her due reward for having woven
> tales which are as fascinating to ill-regulated minds as police reports
> and divorce cases ... She may boast, without fear of contradiction, of
> having temporarily succeeded in making the literature of the kitchen
> the favourite reading of the Drawing room.[35]

The best-seller and the conditions in which it was marketed and consumed
blurred the boundaries between distinct, class-based reading cultures, catering
for a socially diverse audience where drawing-room readers shared the reading
habits of those of 'ill-regulated minds'. The 'fascination' of popular fiction
then had an illicit edge, as middle-class women read alongside their social
inferiors, both types of reader enjoying the incorporation of sensational
elements used to titillate the lower classes in the daily press.

Similarly, Victorian writings on the reception of popular drama provide a
picture of an ideologically diverse theatre audience, both trangressive and
conservative in its responses, foreshadowing the cinema audiences revealed by
the ethnographic research referred to above.   Evidence of conservative
spectatorship can be found in Charles Kemble's report to the 1832 Select
Committee on Dramatic Literature that 'I do not think the audience would
suffer anything that was licentious to be said upon the stage'.[36] And when
Dion Boucicault was asked by the 1866 Select Committee on Theatrical
Licenses and Regulations 'what would be a sufficient check to prevent any
improper pieces being produced' in the absence of a censor, he replied, 'the
public themselves are the principal check; there are very many things that the
licenser passes that the public does not'.[37] Modern commentators have tended
to use only this kind of material when reconstructing the Victorian theatre
audience; for example, Janice Carlisle's argument that working-class spectators
were the dupes of a theatre whose 'illusion of freedom fostered the willing
subjection of its inhabitants' is based on similar remarks made by Dickens,

---

[34]   Jenny Bourne Taylor, *In the Secret Theatre of Home: Wilkie Collins, Sensation
Narrative and Nineteenth-Century Psychology* (London: Routledge, 1988), p. 4.
[35]   'Sensation Novels: Miss Braddon', *North British Review* 43 (1865), 180–204
(p. 204).
[36]   *Report from the Select Committee on Dramatic Literature*, (London, 1832), p.
51.
[37]   *Report from the Select Committee on Theatrical Licenses and Regulations*
(London, 1866), p. 142.

among others.[38] But there is also evidence with which one could construct a far from prudish or witless audience, with which one can justify Bratton's call for an overhaul of our 'presentist or elitist' belief that nineteenth-century audiences 'were culturally or theatrically naïve'.[39] This ranges from laments such as the Reverend Best's that '[t]he most dissolute characters are commonly those which excite the interest, or sympathy, or applause of the audience' to reports such as Thomas Morton's to the 1832 Select Committee.[40] This indicates complex oppositional reception: 'I am sure every playgoer would agree with me', Morton told the Committee, 'there is a tendency in the audience to force passages never meant by the author into political meanings. I think constantly I have observed that'.[41]

Crucially, dominant and oppositional sympathies become apparent in records of specifically female reception practices. Consider, for example, the following snapshots of women's responses to the divergent heroines of stage melodrama. In his memoirs, the playwright Edward Fitzball described the response to the realization of the heroine in his Newgate melodrama *Jonathan Bradford* by the famous tragedienne Mrs West at the Surrey Theatre in 1833. He appears to describe women spectators relishing their feminine selfhoods:

> Ann. Oh, my children! my children! What *will* become of *them*?
> The expression, and her look of pale maternal despair, as she uttered the words, were a never-failing signal for universal tears; and how often have I seen females, mothers perhaps, taken out in hysterics.[42]

From later in the century we have another glimpse of a passionate female response to a melodrama, but here the response mirrored a distress on the part of a heroine who was far from passive. Erroll Sherson recalled how, 'In the celebrated Adelphi drama, *The Green Bushes*, Madame Celeste as the heroine has to shoot her husband who has deserted her. In the revival of 1872, a woman started up in the pit and called out, "Serve him right. He's just like my monster!"'[43] Sherson provides another invaluable glimpse of female

---

[38] Janice Carlisle, 'Spectacle as Government: Dickens and the Working-Class Audience', in Sue-Ellen Case and Janelle Reinelt (eds), *The Performance of Power: Theatrical Discourse and Politics* (Iowa: University of Iowa Press, 1991), p. 168.

[39] Bratton, 'The Contending Discourses of Melodrama', p.48.

[40] Best, *Sermons on the Amusements of the Stage*, p. 35.

[41] *Report from the Select Committee on Dramatic Literature*, p. 219.

[42] Edward Fitzball, *Thirty-Five Years of a Dramatic Author's Life* 2 vols (London: T.C. Newby, 1859), I, p. 248.

[43] Erroll Sherson, *London's Lost Theatres of the Nineteenth Century: With Notes on Plays and Players Seen There* (London: John Lane, 1925), p. 15. *The Green Bushes* was written by J.B. Buckstone and first produced at the Adelphi, with Celeste as the Indian huntress heroine Miami, on 27 January 1845.

spectatorial sympathy with an aggressive leading lady of melodrama. T.W. Erle's reminiscences helpfully make clear that the Royal Grecian Theatre's *Catherine Howard; or, Woman's Ambition* was a melodrama in which Catherine was rendered a scheming villainess who 'takes an early opportunity of putting her husband out of the way by a dose of poison' in order that she may marry Henry VIII, but whose 'chuckling ... proves to be disappointingly premature' – her husband miraculously returns to secure her execution.[44] The final scene, Sherson recollected, presented Catherine 'in her shroud': 'This scene was received with the closest attention. Sighs and groans were audible among the occupants of the pit, and one lady next to me, under the influence of strong emotion, muttered under her breath, "Ah! Poor dear, poor dear!"'[45] Perhaps it is not surprising that the Reverend Best felt that in the theatre 'our young females ... learn to regard parental restraints as harsh and burdensome, to cherish thoughts and designs incompatible with propriety, to practise concealment, to conduct an intrigue, and to glory in its success'.[46]

Conclusion

Victorian popular culture was profoundly contradictory in its representation of women and of femininity. To adapt Fiske's words, it incorporated both the forces of patriarchy and opportunities to oppose or evade them, producing as a result divergent femininities – that is, dominant constructions of womanhood together with a range of conflicted and even antagonistic ones. As we point out here, a number of feminist critics have recognised and articulated this. It is the aim of this book to build upon this work, to continue to explore and to offer further accounts of Victorian popular culture's divergent femininities, in relatively well-documented genres such as sensation fiction, as well as in less familiar fields such as popular drama, serialised short fiction, women's magazines and annuals and working-class women's poetry. Contributors also illustrate the ways in which male-authored popular texts can accommodate feminist, or potentially disruptive readings. As feminist critics, we need to continue Showalter's project of rescuing 'lost' women writers and locating their texts in the marketplaces for which they wrote, as well as recognising that what Tuchman referred to as the 'flutter' of popular culture raised much more than a flutter in the lives of Victorian women readers and consumers.

---

[44] T.W. Erle, *Letters from a Theatrical Scene-Painter: Being Sketches of the Minor Theatres of London As They Were Twenty Years Ago* (London: Marcus Ward, 1880), pp. 22–3.

[45] Sherson, p. 363.

[46] Best, *Sermons on Theatrical Amusements*, p. 24.

Chapter 1

'The False Prudery of Public Taste': Scandalous Women and the Annuals, 1820–1850

Harriet Devine Jump

'Few are the modes of earning a subsistence, and those are very humiliating'.[1] So wrote Mary Wollstonecraft of the plight of educated, impoverished women at the end of the eighteenth century. She spoke from bitter experience, having tried for herself each of the limited number of possibilities open to respectable women who were forced to support themselves and their families by their own efforts: lady's companion, needlewoman, teacher and governess. But in the very act of articulating this dilemma she was enacting a fifth way, one which was to provide a living of sorts to steadily increasing numbers of women over the coming decades. Women could also be writers. A generation later, Wollstonecraft's own daughter Mary Shelley, widowed at twenty-three, managed to support herself and her small son by means of all manner of miscellaneous writing, ranging from novels to encyclopaedia articles. A substantial percentage of her income was derived from tales which appeared in various of the newly-founded publications known as the ornamented annuals. The existence of these briefly but immensely popular gift-books, which flourished from the 1820s until the early 1850s, provided work and an income for many of her contemporaries: although precise figures are hard to come by, it has been suggested that writers of short fiction were paid as much as twenty or thirty guineas a sheet.[2] Prominent among the female writers who depended largely on the annuals for their livelihood were the three women who are the subject of this chapter: Marguerite Gardiner, Countess of Blessington, Caroline Norton, and Letitia Landon.

---

[1] M. Butler and J.M. Todd (eds), *The Works of Mary Wollstonecraft*, 7 vols (London: Pickering and Todd, 1989), vol. iv, p. 25.

[2] Carol Polsgrave, 'They Made it Pay: British Short Fiction Writing 1820–1840', *Studies in Short Fiction* 11 (1974), pp. 417–21.

'[The] annuals have grievously hurt the sale of all ... books such as used to be bought for presents', wrote the poet Robert Southey in 1828.[3] He was certainly right: it has been estimated that about one hundred thousand of these beautiful, ephemeral volumes were sold in that year.[4] The first annual, *Forget-me-Not: A Christmas and New Year's Present for 1823*, had appeared in November 1822, closely followed by *Friendship's Offering: A Literary Album* in 1824 and *The Literary Souvenir, or Cabinet of Poetry and Romance* in 1825. The prestigious *Keepsake*, 'the gorgeous watered-silk publication which marked modern progress at that time',[5] appeared for the first time in 1828. The numbers of imitators increased dramatically over the next few years so that by 1832 there were no fewer than sixty-three different annuals in production, some, obviously, more successful than others.[6] Although they all sought to differentiate themselves from their competitors by some means or other – the *Gem* and the *Bijou* were very tiny, the *Keepsake* was always bound in red silk while the *Literary Souvenir* appeared at various times clad in blue velvet, red silk and green morocco leather, the *Amulet* specialised in Christian stories and the *Book of Beauty* in portraits of society women, for example – there was in fact a remarkable homogeneity in the content of the various annuals. All of them contained a mixture of poetry and short stories, and all were lavishly illustrated with attractive and expensively produced prints.

The quality of the literary contributions was decidedly mixed. Editors and publishers were in continuous and heated competition to attract the most celebrated and talented contributors, and were prepared to pay high prices in order to do so. The highest payment on record was one of £500, said to have been paid to Sir Walter Scott for two tales and a sketch published in the first volume of the *Keepsake*, but Wordsworth, despite his contemptuous dismissal of the annuals as 'those greedy receptacles of trash, those bladders upon which the boys of poetry try to swim',[7] accepted a hundred guineas for twelve pages of verse in the *Keepsake*, justifying himself on the grounds that he needed an eye operation. Southey and Coleridge both published poems in the *Keepsake*, and Charles Lamb, despite his opinion of the annual as 'ostentatious trumpery' published in the *Bijou* for 1828 ('I shall hate myself in frippery, strutting

---

[3]   J.W. Warter (ed.), *Selections from the Letters of Robert Southey*, 4 vols (London: Longman, 1856), vol. iv, p. 124.

[4]   R.D. Altick, *The English Common Reader: A Social History of the Mass Reading Public, 1800–1900* (Chicago: University of Chicago Press, 1957), p. 362.

[5]   George Eliot, *Middlemarch* (1871; Harmondsworth: Penguin, 1957), p. 302.

[6]   F.W. Faxon, *Literary Annuals and Giftbooks: A Bibliography: 1823–1903* (Pinner, Middlesex: Private Libraries Association, 1973), p. xi.

[7]   5 June 1830. *Letters of William and Dorothy Wordsworth*, Second Edition V, The Later Years, Part ii. Revised, arranged and edited by Alan G. Hill from the first edition edited by E. De Selincourt (Oxford: Clarendon Press, 1979), pp. 275–6.

along, and vying finely with "Future Lord Byrons and sweet L.E.L.s'").[8] However much they may have protested all the way to the bank, in the final analysis none were rich enough, or proud enough, to resist the temptation.

The fact that it was male writers who felt so distinctly uncomfortable at the prospect of annual publication is revealing. The world of the annual was essentially a woman's world: women were the primary readers, of course, but they were also contributors and, increasingly as the annuals came of age, editors. Women writers, however successful and celebrated they may have been, seem not to have been troubled by considerations of pride and self-respect when offered the opportunity of publishing in these volumes. As in the case of the male writers, financial incentives undoubtedly played a part, although women writers certainly did not earn as much as their famous male contemporaries.[9] Presumably, however, whatever their private opinions may have been, women writers felt less uncomfortable with the public purveyance of the kind of restrictive domestic ideology which was the specialisation of the annuals.

If the annuals' readers were primarily young girls and women, their purchasers must frequently have been parents, godparents and other interested relatives. This fact goes a long way towards explaining the strong element of didacticism which permeates much of the short fiction in these works. A number of writers in recent years have addressed the relationship between conduct or etiquette books and fiction written to be read by young women.[10] The popularity of the conduct books, which reached its height in the late-eighteenth and early-nineteenth centuries, had diminished somewhat by the late 1820s, and, as has recently been pointed out, the stories in the annuals often do 'address, in a fictionalised form, many of the issues considered in the etiquette books'.[11] To argue, however, that such writing 'deserves to be called a conduct book in fictional form ... stuffy, patronizing, and already written',[12] is true only up to a point, however: at times, as we shall see, the short stories undermined and deconstructed the very models of femininity and domestic bliss that they were overtly recommending. This being said, the tales

[8] E.V. Lucas (ed.), *Letters of Charles Lamb*, 3 vols (London: Methuen and Dent (copublishers), 1935), vol. iii, p. 121.

[9] For a discussion of the earnings, from annuals and elsewhere, of the poet Felicia Hemans, see Paula Feldman, 'The Poet and the Profits', *Keats Shelley Journal* 46 (1997) pp. 148–76.

[10] See for example Nancy Armstrong, *Desire and Domestic Fiction: A Political History of the Novel* (Oxford: Oxford University Press, 1987) and Kate Flint, *The Woman Reader, 1837–1914* (Oxford: Clarendon Press, 1993).

[11] Glennis Stephenson, *Letitia Landon: The Woman Behind L.E.L.* (Manchester and New York: Manchester University Press, 1995), p. 145.

[12] Armstrong, p. 108.

had of course to conform, on the surface at least, to ideals which would have met with the approval of parents and guardians while at the same time offering an appeal to the thousands of young girls who read them avidly. Therefore authors had to perform a delicate balancing act, supplying their readers with what they wanted to read, combined (not always happily) with what it was believed they should read. Thus, the fiction would have to fulfil those requirements which young (and not so young) women have traditionally looked for through the ages in their fictional reading: romance, fulfilment, escape. Set against these would have be placed recommendations for conformity to the expectations of society: thoughtfulness, good manners and self-denial came high on the list, but the primary requirement was a total refusal of any kind of sexual permissiveness.

Given the fact that the annuals fulfilled this moralistic, didactic role, it is ironic that so much of the published material was produced or commissioned by Marguerite Gardiner, Caroline Norton and Letitia Landon, all of whom not only wrote for but also edited various of the annuals for a considerable part of their working lives, as we shall see. The irony lies in the fact that each of these three women's personal lives was the subject of scandals of precisely the kind which the annuals sought to persuade their readers to avoid. How well founded the scandals were has been a matter of continuing debate. In the final analysis however this seems almost irrelevant, since in the world of the annuals, as a perusal of many of the tales reveals, to be so much as suspected of immorality is often enough to ruin a woman's reputation or even to end her life.

Marguerite Gardiner was born in Ireland in 1789. Forcibly married at the age of fourteen to a brutal and alcoholic soldier from whom she separated after only three months, she led a somewhat chequered career before her estranged husband's fortuitous death in 1817 freed her to marry the wealthy Irish Earl of Blessington. Rumours of early indiscretions made her less than welcome in London society, and she and the Earl spent most of their married life travelling on the continent before his sudden death in 1829. Finding her income to be much reduced by the peculiarities of his will, she returned to London and set about supplementing it by means of writing. As well as her celebrated *Conversations of Lord Byron* (1834), she wrote numerous travel books and novels, and was an indefatigable editor and journalist. She edited the *Book of Beauty* from 1834 and took on the *Keepsake* in 1841, continuing as editor of both annuals until her departure for Paris in 1849, and contributing prolifically to both as well as occasionally to other annuals as well. She seems to have been good at extracting payment from her publishers, since she is said to have earned between £2000 and £3000 a year for her literary activities.[13]   She needed every penny of it, however, not only to maintain her own luxurious lifestyle but also because throughout her widowhood she was supporting a man with whom her name was inextricably and scandalously linked. He was a handsome young Frenchman, Alfred Count d'Orsay, and was, moreover, her step-daughter's estranged husband. The exact nature of her relationship with d'Orsay has been the subject of much speculation, but the two were certainly inseparable for more than twenty years. The scandal sheets of the day were in little doubt as to what went on behind the firmly closed doors of Gore House in Kensington, and the couple were relentlessly satirised in both *The Age* and *The Satirist* between 1829 and the 1840s: 'The Count makes the most loving of beaux fils to his belle mere ... They are scarcely ever asunder'.[14]

The Honourable Caroline Norton was born in 1808, one of three beautiful sisters whose grandfather had been the dramatist Richard Brinsley Sheridan. She was profoundly unhappy in her marriage to George Chapple Norton, a marriage which had been contracted against her will when she was eighteen. Norton subjected her to mental and physical abuse, and was moreover unable to support her financially, relying on her earnings as a poet and short-story writer to supplement his meagre income. As she wrote in the 1850s:

> The dependence on my literary efforts for all extra resources runs ... through all the letters I received from [my husband] during our union. The names of my publishers occur as if they were Mr Norton's bankers.[15]

Caroline Norton's long poem, *The Sorrows of Rosalie* (1829), was an early success, and she was soon a successful and highly regarded poet. By the 1830s she was boasting that she could earn £1400 a year by her contributions to annuals and periodicals. Like Gardiner, she took on a considerable amount of editing as well as writing: the *Keepsake* for 1835, the *English Annual* from 1834 to 1838, the postage-stamp sized *Schloss's Bijou Almanac* for 1841 and the *Drawing-Room Scrapbook* from 1845 to 1849. She also founded and edited *The Court Magazine and Belle Assemblée*, a periodical which had much in common with the annuals. Her desirability as an editor probably owed something to her title as well as to her literary fame, but again scandal dogged

---

[13]   William Jerdan, *The Autobiography of William Jerdan*, 4 vols (London: Hall Virtue, 1852), vol. iv, p. 132.

[14]   *The Age*, 7 March 1830. Quoted in Michael Sadleir, *Blessington-D'Orsay: A Masquerade* (London: Constable, 1933), p. 140.

[15]   *English Laws for Women in the Nineteenth Century* (Printed for private circulation, London, 1854), p. 25.

her personal life. In 1835 her husband, from whom she had become increasingly estranged, brought an action for adultery against her friend William Lamb, Lord Melbourne, asking for £10,000 damages. The case was dismissed, but her reputation never recovered from the scandal, and *The Satirist* had a great deal of fun with the issues raised by the court case:

> *A Lamb-Poon*
> Though it forever my renown may blot
> I'll still stand up, dear Caroline, for thee
> For Oh! how oft (the marriage vows forgot)
> Hast thou consented to lie down for me.[16]

Letitia Landon was born in 1802. Her family, never wealthy, slid dangerously in the direction of poverty as she entered her late teens, but fortunately she discovered a precocious talent for poetry which in the event enabled her to support a separate household for her mother, to pay for her brother's university education and to buy him a clerical living. She achieved all this, however, at considerable expense to her own health and peace of mind: Germaine Greer has described her life as 'a nightmare of unremitting drudgery broken by bursts of hysterical social gaiety'.[17] Known to her adoring public by her initials ('L.E.L.'), she published prolifically, producing five volumes of poetry between 1821 and 1828. Many of her poems and short stories appeared first in various annuals and gift-books, and by the 1830s she had taken on the editorship of several: she edited Heath's *Book of Beauty* for 1833, *Fisher's Drawing-Room Scrapbook* from 1832 to 1838, and The *New Juvenile Keepsake* for 1838. Editing seems to have been a hard and thankless task, and one for which the remuneration was surprisingly low. If an early biographer can be believed, she earned only £105 per volume, not a very substantial payment considering the fact that she wrote the entire text of each annual she edited.[18] It was presumably her popularity as a writer which made her a desirable property in the editing market, but her position as an arbiter of domestic morality sat oddly with the rumours which surrounded her private life. An attractive, lively, and independent young woman, living alone in London, her name was linked at various times in her life with those of several men: William Jerdan, the editor of the *Literary Gazette*, William Maginn, the editor of *Fraser's Magazine*, and the novelist Edward Bulwer Lytton among

---

[16]   *The Satirist*, 21 June 1835. Quoted in A. Chedzoy, *A Scandalous Woman: The Story of Caroline Norton* (London: Allison and Busby, 1992), p. 115.
[17]   Germaine Greer, 'The Tulsa Center for the Study of Women's Literature: What we are doing and why we are doing it', *Tulsa Studies in Women's Literature* I.I. (1982), pp. 5–26 (p. 23).
[18]   Jerdan, vol. iii, p. 185.

others. Indeed her engagement to Dickens' friend and future biographer John Forster foundered as a result of these various scandals. Once again the rumours were made public, this time in a short-lived scandal sheet called *The Wasp*. This unpleasant publication suggested in 1826, for example, that she had given birth to Jerdan's child:

> it is a singular circumstance, that altho' she was a short time ago as thin and aereal as one of her own sylphs, she in the course of a few months acquired so perceptible a degree of embonpoint, as to induce her kind friend Jerdan to recommend a change of air, lest her health and strength should be affected. She followed his advice, and strange to say, such was the effect of even two months absence from Brompton, that she returned as thin and poetical as ever![19]

Landon's friends and admirers steadfastly defended her virtue and discounted the truth of the rumours. However it has recently emerged that they were not, after all, unfounded. She did in fact give birth to not one, but three, of Jerdan's children between 1822 and 1829, the unlucky consequences of an affair which lasted for fifteen years.[20] Her marriage, in 1838, to the rather disagreeable George Maclean, Governor of Cape Coast, West Africa, was almost certainly a bid for respectability, but it had an unfortunate outcome: Landon was found dead in her room in Africa only months later, a bottle of prussic acid in her hand. Accident, murder and suicide have all been put forward as possible causes.

Three women, supposed arbiters of female morality: three scandalous lives. Each adopted a different strategy for combating the potentially dangerous effects of the rumours which surrounded them. Of the three, Gardiner was perhaps the most enduringly vulnerable, since her relationship with d'Orsay continued from the late 1820s until her death in 1849. It may be no coincidence, then, that she appears as the most rigidly conventional, both in her own writings and in her editing activities. Indeed, letters have survived which indicate that, despite her private views on the matter, she was crucially aware of the need to be more than usually vigilant when deciding what to accept for the annuals. In 1843, for instance, she turned down a story by (Captain) Frederick Marryat on the grounds that 'the ridiculous prudery of a pack of fools compels me to abandon it'.[21] Another letter, to Charles

---

[19] 'Quacks of the Day, No. 2, William Jerdan', *The Wasp*, 7 October 1826, pp. 20–3 (p. 22).

[20] See Cynthia Lawford, 'Diary', *London Review of Books*, 21 September 2000, pp. 36-7.

[21] Quoted in R.R. Madden, *The Literary Life and Correspondence of the Countess of Blessington*, 3 vols (London: Newby, 1855), vol. iii, p. 228.

Matthews, on the subject of a poem which she regretfully described as 'a *leetle* too warm for the false prudery of public taste', is even more explicit:

> I have been for so long a mark for the arrows of slander and attack, that I must be more particular than any one else; and your pretty verses, which in any of the Annuals could not fail to be admired, would in any book edited by me draw down attacks ... What a misery it is, my dear Charles, to live in an age when one must make such sacrifices to cant and false delicacy, and against one's own judgment and taste.[22]

In her own writings Gardiner seems to have taken this approach to what may seem at times to be absurd extremes. Almost all her poems and tales take care to celebrate women 'whose lives are (like their beauty) without spot',[23] and to deplore those who have in some way stepped beyond the pale. In her story 'Remorse: A Fragment', for instance, a 'pale and languid, but still eminently beautiful woman' who has been divorced for adultery returns to her former home. She remembers the happy days she spent there before 'Love, guilty Love! spread his bandage over her eyes, blinded her to the fatal realities of the abyss into which he was about to plunge her',[24] and watches from a distance as her children play happily under the watchful eyes of their new step-mother. Full of regret, she longs to make herself known to them but fears the consequences if she does. Gardiner makes it clear that the fact that the woman is a 'repentant sinner' does not mitigate her punishment, and the tale ends with her collapse and death. This outcome is presumably meant to be read as a result of the strain of living as a social outcast combined with the pain of separation from the children she still loves. The message is clear: disobey the commands of society at your peril.

Gardiner seems, indeed, to have had an undue predilection for killing off women whose lives have proved irregular. In her 'Mary Lester: A Tale of Error', a young woman elopes to Gretna Green with a tubercular young aristocrat. Although she remains physically untouched (the aristocrat is too ill to do more than recline in a corner of the coach, and dies before they arrive in Scotland), her reputation is irretrievably damaged by the episode, and by the end of the story her mother has died of shock, she has been rejected by her fiancé's parents, and shortly thereafter is depicted as 'expiating with her life

---

22   Ibid., p. 353.
23   Marguerite Gardiner, 'The Countess of Wilton', *Book of Beauty* (1835), p. 2.
24   Marguerite Gardiner, 'Remorse: A Fragment', *Keepsake* (1831), pp. 150–55 (p. 151).

her first and last error'.[25]   In Gardiner's tales, even flirts get punished, though not usually by death. 'The Coquette' concerns a young girl who becomes engaged to a worthy suitor but cannot resist entering into an illicit correspondence with another man. Her virtuous sister, who loves the fiancé, allows him to believe that it is she who is responsible for the correspondence, seemingly in order to prevent him from suffering. The narrative commentary encourages the reader to applaud this act of self-sacrifice:

> This is woman's love, when woman is, as nature meant her to be, pure-minded and unselfish; her own suffering appears more easily borne than that of him she loves; at least she is always ready to make the experiment when she thinks it can save him.[26]

Fortunately, the fiancé discovers the truth in time and marries the good sister. The bad coquette, meanwhile, 'continues to exhibit her faded charms at Cheltenham'. She does, at least, manage to remain alive.

Gardiner's strategy for dealing with the scandals that surrounded her private life was, it seems, to remain so scrupulously moralistic in her annual writings that she may be suspected of self-parody: her poetry, as well as her tales, advocates absolute purity of word and deed. In just one poem, published in the *Keepsake* for 1833, she allows herself openly to mock the conventions of the kind of discourse that she demanded from her contributors and that she adhered to herself: she was a guilty as any of her female contemporaries of the clichés she parodied in the poem, which is called 'Stock in Trade of Modern Poetesses':

> Hearts a prey to dark despair,
> Why, or how, we hardly care;
> Pale disease feeds on the cheek,
> Health how feeble – heart how weak –
> Bursting tear and endless sigh –
> Query, can she tell us why?[27]

As we have already seen, Gardiner's own fictional heroines are subject to exactly the kind of wasting – indeed, ultimately fatal – depression that she here depicts as not only useless but also essentially boring from the perspective of the reader. Thus the poem may be said to undermine her own

---

[25]   Marguerite Gardiner, 'Mary Lester: A Tale of Error', *Book of Beauty* (1834), p. 69.

[26]   Marguerite Gardiner, 'The Coquette', *Book of Beauty* (1834), p. 222.

[27]   Marguerite Gardiner, 'Stock in Trade of Modern Poetesses', *The Keepsake* (1834), pp. 208–209.

practice both as an editor and as a writer. However, the satire is mild, to say the least: Gardiner, who was renowned for her racy private wit, kept this side of herself well concealed as far as her literary persona was concerned.

Caroline Norton's tales were almost equally conventional, although her heroines tended not to meet such dramatic ends. She also had a talent for mild social satire: her story 'The Lost Election' published in the *English Annual* of 1835, for example, offers a relatively daring critique of corrupt electoral practices. But Norton was primarily a poet, and her poetry is in many ways more interesting and revealing than her prose. In some of the poems she published in the annuals in the immediate aftermath of the Melbourne case, she alluded to her private situation in terms which surely would have been transparent to those of her readers who were aware of the details of the scandal. It is revealing to compare her private letters to Melbourne, written while the trial was in progress, with the poetry that appeared in the *Keepsake* immediately afterwards. In a letter of April 1836 she wrote, for example:

> I will not deny that among all the bitterness of this hour, what sinks
> me most is the thought of you – of the expression in your eye when I
> told you at D—n–g St – the shrinking from me and my burdensome
> and embarassing [sic] distress … I don't much care how it ends. I
> have always the knowledge that you will be afraid to see much of me
> – perhaps afraid to see me at all.[28]

Whatever may have been the truth of her relations with Melbourne, her letters to him suggest that her deepest regret, both during and after the court case, was the loss of his friendship: as the letter above indicates, he had retreated from her in terror as soon as the scandal broke. Her sonnet 'The Departed Friend', published in the *Keepsake* for 1837, reads like a public enactment of the private hurt, although the last three lines clearly attempt to contextualize the grief into a conventional elegy:

> When life was young, when all the hopes we wove
>   Seemed bright as buds of some unopened flower,
> My friend and I did vow, for very love,
>   Never to be apart in Sorrow's hour.
> How bear I then my sorrow singly now?
>   Why hear I not thy welcome footstep's fall?
> Hast thou forgot that sweet and pleasant vow,
>   Or learn'd to slight my melancholy call?
> Oh! thou, whose kindness never failed at need –

---

[28]   J.O. Hoge and C. Olney (eds), *Letters of Caroline Norton to Lord Melbourne* (Columbus, Ohio: Ohio University Press, 1974), p. 75.

Thou, whose true word was never passed in vain –
What stops thy coming, or delays thy speed?
    DEATH! By the hollow tomb where I complain,
Stands Echo! fiend, whose voice hath no reply
For ever answering Grief with Grief's own bitter cry![29]

Since the Melbourne scandal had ended with a resounding legal victory, Norton presumably felt justified in making her feelings public: she was to do so many times over the coming years, both in her semi-autobiographical novels and in her political pamphlets. Her *English Laws for Women in the Nineteenth Century* (1854), for example, provides a detailed and painful picture of the abuses she suffered during her married life. It is thus interesting to trace the beginnings of this self-justifying self-revelation in the comparatively early writings published in the annuals.

Gardiner's unusual circumstances made her excessively circumspect, and Norton seems to have believed that her best hope for social rehabilitation lay in constructing herself as a wronged innocent. In their annual contributions, both women remained, on the whole, discreetly within the boundaries of the domestic ideology which those publications promoted.   As far as Letitia Landon is concerned, however, discretion is not a term which readily springs to mind: she was often, according to her friend and biographer Laman Blanchard, 'as careless as a child of set forms and rules for conduct'.[30] She did of course manage to be remarkably discreet in the way in which she concealed her pregnancies, disappearing to the country when the evidence became too difficult to hide: few, if any, of her friends and associates were aware of the very tangible results of her affair with Jerdan. But she made undoubted errors of judgment in conducting the rest of her life: moving out of the chaperoned safety of her grandmother's house and into an attic room on her own in the immediate aftermath of *The Wasp*'s scandalous association of her name with Jerdan's was guaranteed to bring accusations of loose living, for example. As far as her writing was concerned, the decline in her personal reputation seems to have precipitated a deliberate reconstruction of her literary persona. In the early 1830s, L.E.L. the sweet and melancholy poetess, whose verse seemed 'the result not of thought but of feeling',[31] was increasingly replaced by an altogether tougher and more cynical literary self. This much is evident in her novels, the first of which, *Romance and Reality*, appeared in 1831, astonishing her devotees by its lively wit and sparkling dialogue which,

---

[29]   Caroline Norton, 'The Departed Friend', *Keepsake* (1837), p. 208.
[30]   Laman Blanchard, *The Life and Literary Remains of LEL*, 2 vols (London: Colburn, 1841), vol. i, p. 52.
[31]   'The Improvisatrice and other Poems', *New Monthly Magazine* (1824), p. 365.

according to a later obituarist, 'in some degree reflect the conversation of their authoress'.[32] It was shortly after the publication of this novel that Landon took on the 'editorship' of *Fisher's Drawing-Room Scrapbook*, for which she continued to produce most of the letter press until her death in 1838.

In common with most of the other annuals, *Fisher's* supplied its editor with pictorial prints to which poems, or occasionally prose pieces, had to be attached. Although some of these engravings were of fashionable young women (a staple of these kind of publications), a surprisingly large percentage showed landscapes and architecture – often from foreign countries – and reproductions of Old Master paintings.[33] While the generality of contributors to the other annuals simply wrote obediently to order, however, Landon seems to have taken pleasure in stripping bare the framework which underlay the surface finery. In *Fisher's* for 1833, for example, her poem to accompany the print she has been supplied with, a view of Macao in China, deconstructs the very practice of writing to order: 'Good Heaven! whatever shall I do?/ I must write something for my readers/ What has become of my ideas?'. Faced with what she finds an uninspiring illustration, she admits that '[i]invention falters'.[34] She continues the theme a few pages further on when she is confronted with a companion print, this one of 'The Chinese Pagoda':

> I sent to Messrs Fisher saying
> The simple fact – I could not write;
> What was the use of my inveighing?
> 'But madam, such a fine engraving,
> The country, too, so little known!'
> One's publisher there is no braving –
>
> The plate was work'd, 'the dye was thrown'.[35]

Landon also makes use of this poem to deconstruct the kind of poetic discourse for which she was arguably responsible, by example, for initiating among her less talented contemporaries: '"the parting look", "the bitter token",/ "The last despair", "the first distress";/ "The anguish of a heart that's broken" – / Do not these crowd the daily press?'.

The most prolific writer of the three under consideration here, Landon's contributions to the annuals were mainly in the form of verse. She did, however, turn increasingly in the direction of short fiction during the 1830s,

---

32   H.F. Chorley, 'Mrs Maclean', *Athenaeum*, 5 January 1839, p. 14.
33   Stephenson rightly observes that among the annuals *Fisher's* was 'most overtly involved in educating the middle classes' (p. 147).
34   *Fisher's* (1833), p. 42.
35   Ibid., p. 49.

producing in all about twenty short stories for various of the annuals.[36] These range from the retelling of historical legends to conventional love stories, and include a sprinkling of gothic tales and ghost stories. Here and there Landon's sense of fun breaks through: an episode in 'Experiments', for example, has the hero entering into an engagement with a mysterious veiled Turkish princess who proves, on removal of the veil, to be:

> so fat, that it was with the greatest difficulty that she could stand; and [to have] an exquisitely tattooed wreath of hyacinths, of a fine blue, [which] began at her chin, meandered over her cheeks, and covered her forehead.[37]

Landon also had a predilection for *grand guinol* horror, which is most evident in 'The Head' in the *Keepsake* of 1834. In this story, set in the France of the 1790s, a young bourgeois, rejected by his aristocratic mistress, becomes a Revolutionary despot who has no compunction in sending his ex-mistress to the guillotine and who, at the end of the story, is revealed to be keeping her pickled head behind a curtain in his study.

It is difficult not to feel, when reading these stories, that Landon is satirising the conventions within which she is forced to work. But nowhere does her 'gallows humour, [her] grim zestfulness in the evocation of human (perhaps universal) triviality'[38] become more evident than in the two prose pieces which she wrote for the *Drawing-Room Scrapbook* in 1834. Supplied by the proprietors with two plates, one depicting 'Grasmere Vale' and the other 'Sefton Church', she clearly set out deliberately to subvert the expectations that would naturally have been raised in her readers by these two illustrations.

For the first tale, the plate supplied to Landon enacts the popular conception of Grasmere as a sublime location of natural beauty, depicting a fine picturesque view of lakes and mountains, with a small group of people in the foreground, some sketching and some reading, presumably from the Lake poets. The story, however, turns conventional sublimity on its head, as even the title indicates: 'Grasmere Lake: by a Cockney'. The tale is intentionally

---

[36]   The fact that contributions to the annuals often appeared anonymously makes it impossible to assess the exact number with any degree of accuracy. Figures here and elsewhere have been taken from Andrew Boyle, *An Index to the Annuals* (Worcester: A. Boyle, 1967).

[37]   Letitia Landon, 'Experiments', *Book of Beauty* (1833), p. 240.

[38]   Tricia Lootens, 'Receiving the Legend, Rethinking the Writer: Letitia Landon and the Poetess Tradition', in Harriet Kramer Linkin and Stephen C. Behrendt (eds), *Romanticism and Women Poets: Opening the Doors of Reception* (Lexington, Kentucky: University Press of Kentucky, 1999), p. 254.

comic, but also rather sad. The narrative persona is that of a male haberdasher who describes himself as 'the victim of an over-excited imagination':

> Some persons have had their happiness destroyed by their wives; others by their children; others, a still more numerous class, by their creditors. Mine has been destroyed by poetry.[39]

Essentially, the story turns on the danger of fulfilling one's fantasies. Having been enabled by a legacy to give up his shop in the Strand and to buy 'a sweet pretty place ... with a porch hung with honeysuckle, [and] roses that looked in at the window', he feels sure of finding true happiness: 'here, I thought, I might copy Wordsworth ... The influence of the Lake poets was on "the haunted air"'. But his dream has turned sour and his experience of rural solitude, far from bringing him fulfilment, is one of miserable boredom and loneliness. In this tale Landon deftly manages to include three separate objects of satire: Wordsworth for setting what the story suggests is an impossible and absurd example; credulous readers for believing in him; and contributors to the annuals, such as Landon herself, who perpetrate the myths. For evidence of the last, one need only turn a few pages of the very same issue of *Fisher's* to find a poem by Landon herself on the subject of 'Coniston Lake':

> Thou lone and lovely water, would I were
> A dweller by thy deepest solitude!
> How weary am I of my present life,
> Its fasehoods [sic] and its fantasies – its noise
> And the unkindly hurry of the crowd! [40]

It is impossible to take this poem seriously in the light of the tale which precedes it by just a few pages.

The same volume of *Fisher's* also contains another prose piece by Landon, written to accompany an engraving of 'Sefton Church, in Lancashire'.[41] Included on the plate, which shows the interior of this pretty medieval church, is a wedding group: the bride in white lace, her eyes modestly cast down, the groom handsome and manly beside her. A clear invitation, a reader might suppose, for a tale of true love and wish-fulfillment. Landon, however, takes

---

[39] Letitia Landon, 'Grasmere Vale', *Fisher's Drawing-Room Scrapbook* (1834), p. 45.

[40] Letitia Landon, 'Coniston Lake' in ibid., p. 54.

[41] All quotations are taken from Letitia Landon, 'Sefton Church' in Harriet Devine Jump (ed.), *Nineteenth-Century Short Stories by Women: A Routledge Anthology* (London and New York: Routledge, 1998).

the opportunity of exploding her readers' expectations, and the accompanying story offers a wittily cynical deconstruction of the ideals of love and marriage which the annuals conventionally sought to perpetrate.

Once again Landon makes use of a male persona, but one who, by contrast, has little time for romantic idealism. It is worth quoting the introductory paragraph at length:

> There are very many devices wherewith we delude ourselves – indeed, human life has never seemed to me anything more than a series of mistakes. It is a mistake to be born – another to live – and a third to die. However, there is one other mistake, more absurd than all the three – and that is marrying – and which is made worse by the fact, that the other three we cannot very well help, but the third we can ... a love match is like that childish toy which consists of a series of boxes enclosed within one another, and yet contains nothing, after all ... I hold that, in marriage, love augments the evil: contrast in such cases is an aggravation of ennui; it is so peculiarly provoking, to reflect how much pleasanter you used to be to each other. Hope and Love are passions of the heart; the difference between them is, that Hope does not come to an end, but Love does. Love has two terminations; it concludes either in profound indifference, or in intense hate. (p. 87).

Already it is clear that Landon's narrator holds views which are diametrically opposed to those generally put forward in the love stories found elsewhere in the annuals. Certainly the prevailing ideology warned young women against making hasty decisions where matrimony was concerned, but matrimony nevertheless remained the ideal to which it was taken for granted they were all aspiring, and love undoubtedly was expected to play a part in their choice of partner. The narrator's bleak perspective is thus in sharp contrast to the norm.

After a long preamble, the story itself finally gets under way. Brief though it is, it serves as a further illustration of the narrator's profound skepticism. He reveals that he has been coerced, much against his will, into attending a wedding, and privately mocks the bride's 'ignorant happiness', which he takes to be largely dependent on her expensive wedding finery. Once again, since the annuals' stock-in-trade was largely composed of illustrations of young women decked up in satin and lace exactly as the bride is in Landon's story, his perspective undermines the conventional ideology of these publications. As time passes and the bridegroom fails to appear, he spends the long hours trying to recall any couples among his acquaintance whose marriages were actually happy: 'at last I recollected one, and they were very happy indeed; she lived at Amsterdam and he in Demerara' (p. 88), thus illustrating his general skepticism as to the possibility of any couple actually living together harmoniously.

Not only is the bride's foolishness illustrative of the dangers of too great a dependence on fine clothes and romantic ideals, but the behaviour of the putative bridegroom too acts to explode sentimental expectations when a messenger, sent to his inn, finally ascertains that 'the recreant lover had taken fright and post horses, and had set off at six that morning, "over the hills and far away"' (p. 89). In a conventional annual story, the jilted bride would then be expected to pine away; it is almost unheard of, in this context, to find stories in which young women, having once been disappointed, are allowed to find happiness with a second suitor, and if they ever do so it is after a decent interval of a decade or so has passed. In Landon's story, however, the absurdity of such an issue is fully demonstrated. The narrator relates how, as the assembled congregation surrounds the bride, attempting to comfort her mainly by abusing the bridegroom, a handsome young sailor steps forward:

> Madam, I could never bear to see a young lady disappointed, that is, if she was pretty. Mr – (hang the fellow, I forget his name, and you will forget it, too), he is off, but I am ready to take his place; and I have been in love with you for a long time, though I did not know it till this morning. (p. 89).

Not only does his speech reduce to absurdity any remaining ideals of romantic love, but the bride's response shows clearly what her priorities are: '"Well", said she, "it is a pity to be drest for nothing – I shall be very happy". And married they were'(p. 89).

Landon, who until very recently has been read as a writer who 'accepted and reflected in her work the dominant views concerning how, what and why a woman wrote',[42] is clearly using these subversive stories to problematize both her own self-presentation and the conventional demands of her readers. It is notable, though, that both these stories come from the same edition of *Fisher's,* which appeared at the end of 1833. Not only is this the only volume of this annual in which she placed any short fiction, but also the poems she supplied to accompany the plates in subsequent editions never again attempted to undermine or deconstruct the expectations of either the proprietor or his readers. Fisher presumably disapproved of what a reviewer of Landon's first novel *Romance and Reality* (1831), had called 'the brave good sense – the sarcasm bitter with medicine, not poison'.[43]

---

[42]   Isobel Armstrong, *Victorian Poetry: Poetry, Poetics and Politics* (London: Routledge, 1993), p. 339.

[43]   *Athenaeum,* 10 December 1831, p. 793.

Much work remains to be done on the annuals, which have too often been dismissed as enacting conventional poetic and fictional models of femininity. The evident self-awareness and the willingness to parody the conventions which has been demonstrated by the writers under consideration here may provide a pointer to new and revealing ways of reading these attractive, if ephemeral, texts.

Chapter 2

'Too Boldly' for a Woman: Text, Identity and the Working-Class Woman Poet

Margaret Forsyth

> I have been told that I write too boldly – that a feminine pen should never have traced such songs as "The Englishman" and "Old Time" … Is there aught condemnatory in the composition? Is there a line offensive to national pride, or reflective morality?[1]

Eliza Cook, in her preface to the second series of her poems, identifies the social and moral concerns associated with nineteenth-century gender politics and writing by women. While the 'feminine pen' has been thoroughly explored by feminist critics as a subject in its own right, it has largely addressed the lives and works of middle-class women writers. I would like to add another dimension to that area by introducing class into the equation; discussing the works of a group of nineteenth-century women poets in relation to their status as *working-class* women who wrote.

However, the whole issue of working-class women writers is complex. Clearly, the transformation of popular culture in the nineteenth century provided opportunities for women poets outside 'the conventionally genteel and polite discourses of literary culture'[2] to publish their works through newspapers, periodicals, journals and as full volume editions. Yet, while popular prints such as these signalled a relative democratization of culture with men and women from socially diverse backgrounds consuming and contributing to a range of printed texts, they were also sites where class and gender identities could be both constructed and contested. As Brian Maidment has argued, the writing of the working classes was often inhibited

---

[1]   Eliza Cook, *Poems by Eliza Cook, Second Series* (London: Simpkin, Marshall and Co.,1845), p. vii.
[2]   Brian Maidment, conference paper: 'Time was...', 'Radical Cultures: From Romanticism to Victorianism', Trinity and All Saints, Leeds (1998).

by middle-class intervention, reflecting concern about the covert political threat posed by working-class writers. I will argue that, for working-class women poets, middle-class fears of female sexuality and the imagined excesses of lower-class, working women compounded this anxiety. The very existence of the employed working-class woman poet ran counter to a bourgeois ideology of 'separate spheres', exposing not only deep seated anxieties about the political challenge of proletarian poetry and prose, but also the potentially deviant nature of female, working-class sexuality. The factory girl, in particular, became the site of these often contradictory discourses of femininity. Subsequently, focusing primarily on the poems and autobiography of the factory-girl poet, Ellen Johnston, I will explore the ways in which she, and her contemporaries, attempted to transcend the limiting discourses of gender and class, and how far their works conform to, or subvert, nineteenth-century codes of femininity.

'The Industrious Muses'

There can be little doubt that the nineteenth century witnessed an increase in working-class literary activity, as W.J. Fox, M.P. noted in 1847:

> There was one peculiar fact which could not but strike every reflecting person at the present day, and that was the number of writers springing up among the working classes.[3]

Similarly, as Stephen Roberts and Owen Ashton point out, *Howitt's Journal* received almost two hundred poems within a few weeks of its publication, forcing its editor, William Howitt, to ask that no more be sent in for twelve months.[4] Overall, developments in the printing process and transport opened up more socially diverse markets for newspapers, periodicals, magazines and journals providing cheap literature for mass consumption. As Fox noted, working-class readers aspired to find a space in these popular texts in which they, too, could contribute to the cultural and creative life of their communities. While Fox gives no indication of gender distribution, there

---

[3] Quoted in John Foster, *Class Struggle and The Industrial Revolution: Early Industrial Capitalism in three English towns* (London: Methuen, 1977), p. 174.

[4] Owen Ashton and Stephen Roberts, *The Victorian-Working Class Writer* (London: Mansell, 1999), p. 1.

were women from a wide range of backgrounds including factory workers,
dairymaids, weavers and servants (most of them self-taught) who published
their works initially through journals, newspapers and periodicals. Of the
women poets central to my discussion, Ellen Johnston's poems were
subsequently published in two editions of her works following success as a
contributor to *The Dundee Penny Post*. Of Johnston's contemporaries, Janet
Hamilton published initially through *Cassell's* before publication of her
poems and essays in volume form, whilst Fanny Forrester published her work
only through the pages of *Ben Brierley's Journal*. What is particularly
striking about Johnston's works is her overt sense of audience and a
willingness to forge relationships with her readers, eliciting responses in verse
from them through the poetry pages of *The Penny Post*. Johnston later
included these in both the first and second editions of *Autobiography, Poems
and Songs*. In the second edition, Johnston also reprinted extracts from
newspaper reviews of her works in addition to a further selection of
contributions from her correspondents. These included 'Lines Dedicated To
The Factory Girl, On The Publication Of Her Works' and the more simply
named 'Fragment' from a regular contributor named only as Edith.

For Johnston and many of her contemporaries, local newspapers were the
starting points for publication as she notes in her autobiography:

> duty called me forth to turn the poetic gift that nature had given me
> to a useful and profitable account, for which purpose I commenced
> with vigorous zeal to write my poetical pieces, and sent them to the
> weekly newspapers for insertion, until I became extensively known
> and popular ... in 1854, the Glasgow Examiner published a song of
> mine, entitled 'Lord Raglan's Address to the Allied Armies', which
> made my name popular throughout Great Britain and Ireland (p.11)[5]

Writing under the pseudonym 'The Factory Girl', Johnston rapidly became a
popular contributor to the pages of the *Glasgow Examiner* and the 'Poet's
Corner' of the Dundee *Penny Post*. Moreover, she established a relationship
with her readers that prompted a series of poetic addresses and responses in
verse from a range of admirers between 1865 and 1866, which were later
included in her *Autobiography, Poems and Songs*. Clearly, as the writer of these
verses suggests, her literary endeavours prompted some readers to take up the
pen:

---

[5]   All quotations are taken from Ellen Johnston, *Autobiography, Poems and Songs*
(Dundee: William Love, 1867).

> The melody of thy sweet muse
>   Has waked my sleeping lyre,
> And in my very heart and soul
>   Has kindled a desire
> To bid my humble muse arise
>   And sing with heartfelt glee
> The praises of the Factory Girl
>   Who dwells in sweet Dundee. (p. 11)

Most of the responses echo this theme of praise, some singling out their favourite poems. One reader, known only as R.H.P. of New Road, Parkhead, writing in December 1865 commends 'We've Parted' and 'The Pleasure Trip'; including with his or her verse a lock of hair and a bible as a token of esteem. Another, a Lanarkshire weaver who signs himself as 'A Friend', responds to Johnston in January, 1866 regretting that:

> Tae her I send nae tuft o' hair
> Nor sacred book wi' Davie's prayer;
> But should she come tae Lanark fair,
>   An' ca' on me,
> I'll tak her, wi' a brither's care,
>   The Falls to see. (p.150)

Apart from the humour in the attempt at one-upmanship in this response, it does indicate that Johnston's readers came from a range of differing economic backgrounds. Significantly, the writers are also clearly responding to each other, as well as to Johnston herself. Obviously aware of Johnston's plans to move into full volume publication, 'A Friend' also offers to 'buy her book if I hae brass/Be't cheap or dear'. This curious three-way communication continues with a response from R.H.P., calling on all of 'Scotia's sons and daughters fair/From out their funds subscribe a share/All those that can a half-crown spare/Will be well paid' (p.149). True to his or her word, R.H.P. also appears in the list of subscribers to Johnston's 1867 edition. Joining this poetic circle, a reader known only as J.H.B.B. commends both Johnston and one of her more regular respondents:

> Had I the gift of thee, or Edith fair,
>   Oft would I sing in classic style to thee;
> For with thy lays I nothing can compare,
>   And nought on earth more sacred is to me. (p. 176)

What is significant here is evidence of what Brian Maidment refers to as
the intimacy of 'local bardic groupings'. Clearly, as Maidment argues, the act
of reading and writing poetry allows the community to assert 'their own
contribution to cultural and artistic life as well as [celebrating] the artistic
endeavours of a fellow poet'.[6] While an increase in the number of newspapers
and journals available to a mass reading public opened up avenues for
publication, Johnston acts as a catalyst; an inspirational local muse for
aspiring poets. This space is more significant for women readers with poetic
leanings. Middle-class women had access to literary circles through their
husbands, fathers or other male relatives. Working-class literary circles,
fostered through institutions such as working-men's clubs, were not open to
women. As Martha Vicinus notes, Isabella Varley, writer of *The Manchester
Man*, hid behind a curtain to hear her poem read out to a (male) literary circle
who met at the Sun Inn, Manchester.[7] Ultimately, as the responses to
Johnston by female readers suggest, newspapers provided an accessible outlet
for literary creativity for those women marginalised or excluded by their
gender and class. This is more evident in 'Lines to Isabel from the Factory
Girl' and Johnston's encouragement, not only to 'Isabel' but also to 'Edith':

> Now, tell me, Isabel, where may I find
> From whence thou cam'st, and who, and what thou art
> For like my sister Edith thou dost bind me
> With chords of melody around my heart. (p. 191)

Consequently, Johnston's request opens a space for 'Isabel's' story, where
she, like Johnston, can re-define herself, and her experiences, in print.

One of Johnston's experiences recorded in print is a very public but poetic
love affair between Johnston and G.D. Russell. It is not clear just how serious
these poems were intended to be, but they kept Johnston's readers interested,
prompting a series of further responses from other contributors applauding
Russell's proposal of marriage and congratulating her on her good fortune.
The marriage, however, did not transpire. Russell emigrated to Australia,
asking her to join him there as his wife. Johnston, an unmarried mother,
declared undying devotion in verse but stayed firmly where she was,
ultimately refusing to accept the more traditional resolutions to the problem of
the fallen woman – emigration and marriage – which would have signalled the
end of her independence and her literary ambitions. Her amazing confidence

---

6   Brian Maidment, *The Poorhouse Fugitives* (Manchester: Carcanet, 1992), p. 161.
7   Martha Vicinus, *The Industrial Muse* (London: Croom Helm, 1974), p. 160.

in her status as a poet is more than evident in 'The Maid of Dundee to her Slumbering Muse'. Here, she reflects that, "'Tis better far that thou shouldst still live single/Than married be, in doubts and fears to dwell' (ll. 61–2) before proclaiming her status as a gifted, poetic individual:

> Go, tell the Penny Post to wave its banner,
>   And bid its minstrels sing thou art free,
> And they shall welcome forth in queen-like manner
>   Thy Factory Girl-the maid of sweet Dundee (ll. 73–76) (p. 227)

While Johnston made clear her ambitions by stating her intention to launch into full volume publication, the transition from publication in newspapers to the more formalized production of volume editions generally required the intervention of middle-class patrons, sponsors, editors and publishers. As Maidment points out, such writing 'would have remained essentially peripheral to bourgeois culture ... an entirely localized phenomenon dependent on local pride' without it.[8] That involvement, however, demanded much more than a sense of local pride or shared community, bringing into force the social and moral concerns associated with nineteenth-century gender and class politics, particularly in relation to the concept of the employed, working-class woman. The title 'Factory Girl', which Johnston used to good effect in creating that sense of shared community through poetry pages of locally consumed papers, was in itself, the site of ideological contention and contradiction.

'Pale Faces over the Loom'

By the time Johnston and her contemporaries were writing as industrial poetesses, the female factory worker had entered a range of medical, social and literary discourses, taking a variety of forms. The figure of the pale, stooping factory worker became a familiar trope of industrial poetry, particularly in those works that supported legislative changes in the working conditions of textile operatives. Caroline Norton, writing in 1833, and Eliza Cook in the 1840s, both used the trope to raise concerns about the nature of urban industrialism. In 'Voice From The Factories', Norton defines 'work' as a physically debilitating form of imprisonment:

---

[8]   Maidment, *Poorhouse Fugitives*, p. 284.

Are they free
Who toil until the body's strength gives way?
Who may not set a term for liberty,
Who have no time for food, or rest, or play,
But struggle through the long unwelcome day
Without leisure to be good or glad? (XIX ll.1–6)[9]

Cook's 'Song of the Haymakers', however, explores the consequences of the separation of the factory worker from her or his natural, 'healthy' rural environment:

We dwell in the meadow, we dwell on the sod,
    Far away from the city's dull gloom;
And more jolly are we, though in rags we may be,
    Than the pale faces over the loom. (ll. 9–12)[10]

While both poets were working to a general moral, reformist agenda, these images of the sickly, debilitated worker were particularly suited to debates centering on specifically female employment. While there was clearly a very genuine concern about the physical effects of industrialization on a large, female, workforce, Lynda Nead points out that 'female dependency was reproduced and guaranteed by the belief that respectable women were inherently weak and delicate'.[11] By constructing the working-class woman within those terms, her potentially threatening sexuality and independence could be contained.

Interestingly, Johnston, Hamilton and Forrester resist the threat to female independence by adopting those images associated with the woman worker, then refiguring them in more enabling terms. In 'The Factory Exile', a poem which relates to Johnston's fight against unfair dismissal, she frames an image of herself 'still bending o'er my loom/ And musing on a lovely form of beauty's sweetest bloom'(ll.7–8) (p. 25). For Johnston, the trope is not patronizingly romanticized, but turned into an act of poetic creativity. At her loom she can disengage her mind from physical labour and find inspiration for much of her work that celebrates her life as a power-loom weaver. Janet Hamilton's woman weaver in 'Lay of The Tambour Frame', 'There, with

---

[9]   Isobel Armstrong, Joseph Bristow and Catherine Sharrock (eds), *Nineteenth-Century Women Poets: An Oxford Anthology* (Oxford: Clarendon Press, 1996), p. 333.

[10]   Cook, p. 168.

[11]   Lynda Nead, *Myths of Sexuality: Representations of Women in Victorian Britain* (Oxford: Blackwell, 1990), p. 29.

colourless cheek/ There with her tangling hair/ Still bending low o'er her rickety frame' (ll. 9–11) is not weakened by the nature of her gender, but by the politics of industrial exploitation.[12] Hamilton's poem subsequently demands union recognition of the woman weaver's skills and the right to equal pay and conditions, not a plea for a return to woman's 'proper', domestic sphere; neither of these poems perceives a contradiction between labour and femininity. Fanny Forrester, however, creates a male speaker for her poem 'The Lowly Bard': a poet who, unlike Johnston, cannot find inspiration for his poems within the confines of the factory. Resorting to the now familiar trope, Forrester's speaker perceives:

> O'er great looms slight figures lowly stoop
> And weary shadows cross their girlish faces
> That like frail flowers o'er stagnant waters droop...
> Toil, toil to-day, and toil again tomorrow: (ll. 22–25)

By concluding 'Yet ne'er were heroines more strong – more brave' (ll. 28), Forrester subverts the conventional representation of the pale, stooping woman worker, endowing her with qualities that were far more threatening to a middle-class ideology of femininity. Susan Zlotnick argues that Forrester:

> destabilizes her own characterization of them by acknowledging their strength and bravery. Enmeshed in a representational system that could only see factory women as victims (frail flowers needing the shelter of the domestic nook), Forrester cannot articulate coherently the lives of millhands like herself, and if she stumbles into contradictions, it is because a working woman in the 1870s was a contradiction, at least ideologically.[13]

While Zlotnick is correct in pointing out that the working woman was an ideological contradiction, I would argue that the position was far more complex. Working-class women were not just defined simply as victims. Female weakness and frailty justified the respectable middle-class woman's position within the private sphere, and by extension, her exclusion from the public realm of work. Similarly, representations of the industrial woman worker as a victim of forced labour affirmed all women's dependency and

---

[12]   Janet Hamilton, *Poems, Essays and Sketches* (Glasgow: James Maclehose, 1880), p. 249.

[13]   Susan Zlotnick, 'Dialect, Domesticity, and Working-Class Women's Poetry', *Victorian Studies* 35 (1991), pp. 7–27 (p. 19).

subsequently, their proper place within the domestic realm. But a more hostile, contradictory perception of the factory girl had already entered the middle-class consciousness. The image of the weak, dependent bourgeois woman was established in opposition to the robustness of the working-class woman, who, at the same time, was perceived more overtly in terms of deviance and disease.

Eliza Cook, writing in the 1850s, subconsciously reflects this middle-class prejudice in an article which attempts to identify the reason for the absence of working-class women poets in the mid nineteenth century:

> The charm of the domestic hearth, the joys of the family circle – these belong to them, and there their particular attributes are best nurtured; but the manufacturing system, where it affects women at all, tends in this respect to unsex them.
> They leave their beds to answer the factory bell, their children are put out to day nurse, or their dame school – they are co-workers with men during their hours of toil; they return at night to the ill-kept, cheerless home, and the poetry of women's writing is too often stifled and deadened.[14]

Cook's concerns subconsciously reflect middle-class cultural fears of a contagious immorality and locates them within the context of the employed, working-class woman poet. While she suggests a seemingly democratic equality in her reference to women as 'co-workers with men', her subsequent reference to 'ill-kept, cheerless home(s)' undermines that notion, fuelling an already established association between working-class women and dirt and disorder. Moreover, the close proximity of male and female workers implied by Cook, together with the image of the 'unsex'd' female (which challenged the orthodoxy of domestic virtue), raised, in middle-class consciousness, the probability of sexual deviancy.

The images of neglect and moral pollution implied by Cook's article conform to what Patricia Ingham calls a 'governing metaphor for the perils of social intercourse between the "Two Nations"'.[15] However, Ingham goes further in her argument, stating that the symbol of pollution gave added power to the rationale behind the divisive class separatism of nineteenth-century Britain:

---

[14]   *Eliza Cook's Journal*, 20 July 1850. Quoted in Maidment, *Poorhouse Fugitives*, p. 308.

[15]   Patricia Ingham, *The Language of Gender and Class: Transformation in the Victorian Novel* (London: Routledge, 1996), p. 24.

> Beliefs concerning the nature of female sexual desire were extremely
> fractured, but these differences could be displaced and a consensus
> reached by invoking a generalized notion of female respectability
> and opposing it to the imagined excess passion and deviancy of the
> women of the undeserving poor.[16]

Ultimately, working-class women who aspired to be taken seriously had to find ways in which their 'female respectability' could be proved to a morally circumspect audience of sponsors, publishers, editors and readers. It is worth noting here that one of the requirements of applications to the Royal Literary Fund, which financially supported poor, but ambitious writers, was evidence of a private life beyond reproach. Without evidence of this, even beyond the demands of the Royal Literary Fund, the working-class woman poet had little chance of recognition or serious consideration.

Caught up in these limiting discourses, working-class women poets who wished to make the transition from contributions of poetry to newspapers, to full volume publication needed to redefine and assert subject positions within and beyond a class context that were both feminine and worthy. This was achieved by the use of introductory prefaces and autobiographical material that affirmed nineteenth-century definitions of femininity. As respectability for working-class women was conferred rather than innate, the idea of respectability could, crucially, be constructed through these texts. In recent years, there has been a significant revaluation of the importance of these introductory texts, or paratexts, particularly in relation to what Maidment calls 'works by authors outside the conventionally genteel and polite discourses of literary culture.'[17] This includes all material that either precedes or follows the main body of the text such as autobiographical material, subscription lists, testimonials and, in some cases, literary reviews of the poet's work. Paratexts, rather than being read casually or separately from the main body of the text, both reveal and engage with the self-conscious class and gender anxieties of textual production.

Working-class women poets were by no means the only people writing autobiographies, indeed it was an increasingly popular genre in the nineteenth century. Yet, like poetry, it was dominated by male writers. Wihelm Dilthey, a nineteenth-century historian who called for a writing of history based on autobiographical documents, pointed out that 'autobiography is merely the

---

[16] Ibid., p. 24.
[17] Maidment, 'Time was . . .'

literary expression of a *man's* reflection on the course of his life (italics mine)'.[18] Dilthey's observation assumes the absence of women's contribution to this field as a matter of course and, at the same time, his description of autobiography as a 'literary expression' identifies it as a genre with its own conventions. Whether 'factually' or imaginatively presented, autobiography as a form of public self-expression allowed men and women to articulate a specific construction of the world and their position or status within it to a readership. This represents, particularly for women, a significant shift away from the oral transmission of personal history as publication immediately opens up a dialogue with a much wider audience that is not confined to either one's family or one's social group. For women poets, autobiography more specifically links their cultural and social background to artistic creativity. However, I should, perhaps, make a distinction between autobiographical prefaces, which provide a more immediate insight into the life of the writer, and 'pure' autobiographies which were published much later than the poems and are more substantial and detailed in content. Although I would argue that they broadly served the same purpose, autobiographical prefaces allowed the working-class woman poet to justify her position from the outset rather than with hindsight.

'The Common Trials of Ordinary Life'

Ellen Johnston's autobiography is arguably one of the most substantial and most self-consciously 'literary' of all the prefaces available to contemporary critics. Addressing the 'gentle reader', she constructs her autobiographical self within the conventions of melodrama. While calling on her peers to confirm the 'veracity' of her life history, Johnston asserts, 'Mine were not the common trials of ordinary life, but like those strange romantic ordeals attributed to the imaginary heroines of Inglewood Forest'(p. 4). The 'romance' continues with a story of abuse at the hands of her stepfather, periods of escape and semi-imprisonment, followed by an astonishing admission of the birth of her illegitimate child:

> I did not, however, feel inclined to die when I could no longer conceal what the world falsely calls a woman's shame. No, on the other hand, I never loved life more dearly and longed for the hour

---

[18]   David Vincent, *Bread, Knowledge and Freedom* (London: Europa, 1981), p. 7.

> when I would have something to love me – and my wish was realised
> by becoming the mother of a lovely daughter. (p. 11)

Johnston's construction of her autobiographical subject as a romance heroine was influenced by her reading of Scott's novels leading Zlotnick to argue that she turned to 'the Romantic tradition of rebellion, a literary mode that encourages the oppositional, confrontational stance Johnston adopts.'[19] While she clearly does not attempt to hide her delight and pride in her daughter, Mary Achinvole, or her love affairs, I would argue that Johnston's attempts to justify herself are continually in tension with her awareness of the prohibitions and limitations of Victorian morality. As ignorance of sexual knowledge was essential to the concept of bourgeois femininity, Johnston's admission represented a significant challenge to her readers. Moreover, in countering charges of immorality, Johnston came as close as propriety allowed to describe her fall:

> I was falsely accused by those who knew me as a fallen woman,
> while I was as innocent of the charge as an unborn babe. Oh! how
> hard to be blamed when the heart is spotless and the conscience
> clear. (p.10)

The same seduction was described metaphorically in more covert terms of bud, bloom and decay in a poem addressed to 'Edith' that was published in the *Dundee Penny Post*:

> Then first love came with golden smiles –
>   Sweet were the vows he did impart,
> And with his false bewitching wiles
>   He stole away my trusting heart.
>
> Then left me with a look of scorn
>   When he the seeds of grief had sown –
> Wrecked in the bloom of life's young morn,
>   Ere scarce her infant buds were blown. (ll. 33–40) (p.158)

In emphasizing her feminine virtues of heart, conscience and purity, Johnston justifies her circumstances within the codes of femininity and not necessarily from the oppositional, confrontational stance of a romantic rebel. From the

---

[19]   Zlotnick, p. 20.

outset, Johnston qualifies the details of her turbulent life with a reminder to her readers that:

> whatever my actions may have been, whether good, bad or indifferent, that they were the results of instincts derived from the Creator, through the medium of my parents, and the character formed for me by the unavoidable influence of the TIME and the COUNTRY of my BIRTH, and also by the varied conditions of life impressing themselves on my highly susceptible and sympathetic nature – physical, intellectual, and moral. (p. 15)

Her pregnancy, she suggests, arose from her encounters with her unnamed false love and her inability to recognise that falsehood, rather than a deviant sexuality on her part. Her dramatic, and at times, melodramatic, plea for respectability anticipates and attempts to counter any adverse response from her readership. In citing 'unavoidable' influences in her defence, Johnston's statement could be read as an oblique criticism of a moral climate that endorsed female innocence to the point of creating the ideal circumstances for its exploitation. Clearly, her resistance to accepted codes and values, and her insistence on asserting her independence and ambition, is, in itself, subversive. Her frank admission of her pregnancy, and her commitment to her literary career, represented something of a challenge to conventional views about the nature of working-class female sexuality. Yet, in also trying to establish her moral credentials, Johnston succeeded in conforming to the negative stereotype of the deviant, promiscuous factory girl. While her admission of love affairs could be legitimated within the acceptable discourse of romance, her lack of shame and rebuttal of guilt arising from her pregnancy could not. That her first edition of poetry, with its controversial preface, was ever published is surprising in itself given our understanding of the Victorian moral climate. It is possible that, having experienced a certain amount of adulation from her *Penny Post* readers, she felt that she could attract similar responses from an equally sympathetic, yet socially more diverse readership; that her poetry offered a means of transcending barriers of gender and class. Ultimately, the uneasy tension between the 'fallen' romance heroine and her audience was resolved for her by the intervention of the publishers of the second edition of her work who censored all references to her love life and illegitimate child.

But intervention took forms other than censorship. As Maidment has pointed out, the poetry of working-class writers was often inhibited or

controlled by middle-class values.[20]   In his exploration of the complex issues
surrounding middle-class responses to the works of artisan and proletarian
poets, he argues that bourgeois intervention contained the political challenge
perceived in working-class cultural advancement.   The articulate poet who
could rally support in the name of literature could equally raise a mob in the
name of politics.   However, Maidment also claims that the 'social and
political threat offered by proletarian or artisan poetic articulacy is constantly
glossed over by focusing the discussion on literary weaknesses apparent in the
texts.'[21] Certainly, George Gilfillan's testimonial to Johnston's works reflects
this anxiety.   He patronisingly commends her attempts, conceding that
'subtracting all the signs of an imperfect education, her rhymes are highly
creditable'.   He concludes his testimonial with the hope that 'she will be
encouraged by this to cultivate her mind, to read to correct the faults in her
style'.   If the quality of working-class texts was found to be deficient,
Maidment argues, 'their potential as a social and political force was thus
diminished or belittled.'[22]

I would argue that this covert anxiety extended equally into the
construction of poetic identity, particularly in relation to the proletarian
woman poet, precisely because it reflected additional concerns about the
nature of working-class, female sexuality.   Subsequently, reviewers and
supporters alike focused not only on issues of class, but also of gender;
defining their 'proteges' in terms of respectability and worthiness.   Alexander
Wallace's review of Hamilton and her works, contained in an essay entitled
'Janet Hamilton at her "ain fireside"' immediately located her safely within
her proper, domestic sphere.   But just in case there were any lingering doubts
about the working-class woman poet's truest, most important credentials,
Wallace stressed to her readers that she was:

> a *gentlewoman*, in the true sense of that term, by instinct, or by a
> delicacy of feeling, and by self-culture. Her ease, self-possession,
> native grace and dignity, all so natural and simple – in short, her true
> *womanliness* – are qualities as remarkable, perhaps, as her poetic
> genius.[23]

Wallace's stress on her '*womanly*' qualities made clear that she was not
just a 'woman' but a '*gentlewoman*'.   That he found these qualities

---

20   Maidment, *The Poorhouse Fugitives*, p. 286.
21   Ibid., pp. 287–8.
22   Ibid., p. 289.
23   Ibid.

'remarkable' is, in itself, a telling sign of the inherent ideological prejudices against 'lower-class' women. In describing Hamilton in culturally feminine terms, beyond those associated with women of the working classes against whom she is covertly defined, she is judged to be morally harmless.

'Playing the Dissembler'

By defining and authenticating Hamilton in terms of bourgeois femininity, Wallace resolves anxieties about her class and gender that she, as a working-class woman, could not. As Nead points out,

> female employment ... it was believed, led to moral degradation and the destruction of family life. Working women transgressed bourgeois definitions of respectability and female dependency; their imagined sexuality and economic autonomy made them objects of threat.[24]

While Nead goes on to argue that the issue of working-class respectability was more complex than simply a straightforward passive adoption of middle-class norms, clearly, the models of femininity available to working-class women were essentially bourgeois. The received images of the factory girl, as I have argued, were constructed either in terms of dependency or disease. The popular text, and its availability to proletarian poets, provided working-class women writers with the opportunity to contest these disabling images by re-figuring the woman worker in alternative terms. But I would also argue that the creation of these alternative identities also highlights femininity as a performance. While outwardly, at least, the factory girls imagined by Johnston, Hamilton and Forrester conform to models of dependency, they are in fact subversively independent. Johnston, particularly, fields more than one model of femininity both in her poems and in her autobiography, a fact recognized by 'Edith' who astutely noted:

> Who that hath seen her loving eye
> Shall e'er forget, in changing scenes,
> That through this shifting folio lie
> Ellen, the lovely actress, leans ? (p. ix)

---

[24]   Nead, p. 31.

Johnston, herself, stated in her autobiography that she was:

> one of those beings formed by nature for romance and mystery, and
> as such had many characters to imitate ... In the residence of my
> stepfather I was a weeping willow, in the factory I was pensive and
> thoughtful, ... when mixing with merry company no one could be
> more cheerful, for I had learned to conceal my own cares and
> sorrows. (pp.7–8)

Johnston's capacity for social role-play is equally as evident in her poems.
While she celebrates life in the factory, constructing herself in terms of
liberation and independence, she also resorts to more melodramatic models of
female behaviour. In 'The Maniac in the Greenwood', for example,
Johnston's heroine is seduced and ultimately becomes insane. While Zlotnick
perceives this madness as reaffirming 'conservative notions of femininity',[25]
the issue of insanity has been reassessed by contemporary feminists who
perceive in female madness the seeds of subversion.

Ultimately, these constructions of femininity highlight the complex nature,
both of the writings themselves, and the texts that carried them. While the
growth of popular texts signalled an increasingly literate population, by and
large, such texts offered conservative models of civilized behaviour and social
virtue that generally reflected bourgeois values. As Maidment suggests,
middle-class fears of the potential for radicalism and revolution in working-
class writing, which were evident in responses to it, could be resolved by
defining working-class writing in terms of cultural advancement, or through
more obvious and direct intervention such as editing or censorship.
Alternatively, focusing on the 'uneducated' status of the poet could diminish
the implied threat of such writing. For working-class women writers, these
processes were further complicated by concerns regarding the nature of
female sexuality. Subsequently, the models of femininity available to them
were re-worked into autobiographical prefaces, or, imposed on them by well-
meaning sponsors or critics in testimonials or reviews. Newspapers, however,
offered a greater degree of freedom from such overt intervention, although
censorship was by no means unknown. Contributions of poetry could be
made anonymously, which circumvented the need for details of class or
gender identity. Certainly there are many examples of this which makes
identification something of a nightmare for the contemporary researcher. By
the 1860s, while a great flood of cheap literature became available to the

---

[25]   Zlotnick, p. 24.

masses, it was not a value-free process. The civilizing social virtues this promoted were ideologically bourgeois. Yet, paradoxically, in reflecting middle-class values, popular texts also provided a means of resisting or re-enacting them in particular class and/or gender contexts. As I have argued, for the women poets discussed here, femininity could be constructed in ways that both conformed to, and challenged, an inherently conservative ideology, particularly in relation to the figure of the factory girl. Johnston flatly rejected marriage as her 'proper' sphere in favour of independence and career; Hamilton challenged dependency as the norm, arguing for equal conditions for the woman worker. Forrester, however, asserted qualities of strength usually associated with the worst excesses of the factory girl in direct opposition to traditional, feminine tropes of weakness and vulnerability. More than anything, perhaps, given the mass of contradictory images against them, the fact that these women found their way into print is, in itself, the most subversive act.

Chapter 3

Every Girl's Best Friend?: The *Girl's Own Paper* and its Readers

Hilary Skelding

Curious, some may think it, curious and perhaps a little ludicrous as well, that the propriety of a young woman earning a certain wage should call for any serious defence. The payment of wages in exchange for services rendered ... is so unquestionably a part of a sound social system, that it may well seem ridiculous to speak of it at this time of day ... It is to the converse side of our modern heresy that I think it more needful to draw attention: the theory that women should take a wage and do no work ... For what many women are being asked to do is to accept board, lodging, and a dress allowance on condition either of remaining absolutely still, or of only making believe to be busy.[1]

Perhaps there is no subject more fascinating to the ordinary woman than that of baby clothes! Of course 'the new woman' finds no charm therein. I am not writing for that modern production, only for those sweet, womanly souls who have the instincts of motherhood implanted in them.[2]

The two extracts above are both taken from articles appearing in 1896 in the Victorian periodical the *Girl's Own Paper*. The first, taken from the issue of 3 October, is from one of two articles on women's employment, 'A Pound a Week: Why Girls Should Earn It', by Margaret Bateson. The second, appearing a month later on 7 November, is taken from a child-care article by Mrs Orman Cooper, 'Queen Baby and Her Wants'. These two examples, appearing in the same year and in consecutive months, serve as an illustration of the paper's frequently baffling tendency to project apparently divergent, or contradictory, notions of femininity; combining the radical with the domestic and reactionary.

---

[1]   Margaret Bateson, 'A Pound A Week: Why Girls Should Earn It', *Girl's Own Paper*, 3 October 1896, p. 14.
[2]   Mrs Orman Cooper, 'Queen Baby and Her Wants', *Girl's Own Paper*, 7 November 1896, p. 92.

Paradoxically, the *Girl's Own Paper* seems to have steered an uneasy course between two extremes. At one extreme are the paper's regular childcare articles and domestic fiction, characterised by the type of domestic sentimentality epitomised by Mrs Orman Cooper. At the other extreme is a range of surprisingly level headed and forward thinking careers and education articles, of which Bateson's article 'A Pound A Week' (discussed in detail later) provides a key example. More confusion is apparent when we consider that some topics, notably that of women's education, are approached from apparently diametrically opposed viewpoints, with 'informative' articles on the physically damaging effects of women's education being followed only months later by positive articles extolling the virtues of women's schools and colleges.

This chapter will attempt to unravel the mystery of this perplexing and contradictory Victorian magazine for girls, and will question the conservative reputation that the *Girl's Own Paper* seems to have acquired. Features such as 'Queen Baby and Her Wants' go some way towards explaining why twentieth-century critical opinion tends to characterise the *Girl's Own Paper* as a conservative magazine, designed to promote the middle-class values of home life, marriage and motherhood, whilst explicitly discouraging any challenge to established versions of femininity. Kimberley Reynolds refers to the paper as 'a placebo', the fiction and features of which cannot be interpreted in a subversive way.[3] Mary Cadogan and Patricia Craig concur with this opinion, referring to the paper's approach during its Victorian decades as 'hardly enlightened'.[4] Indeed, the title of Wendy Forrester's comprehensive and engaging review of the paper's history, *Great-Grandmama's Weekly*, seems to sum up the paper's reputation today; as a domestic-orientated, quaintly old-fashioned example of 'Victoriana'.[5] However, as Forrester herself points out, the paper had far more to offer its readers than cookery tips and fashion advice.

This chapter will question some of the assumptions that most twentieth-century critics have made, by suggesting that the *Girl's Own Paper* (referred to hereafter as the *G.O.P.*) was to promote numerous eclectic, and frequently contradictory, notions of ideal femininity, in response to a late nineteenth-

---

[3]   Kimberley Reynolds, *Girls Only? Gender and Popular Children's Fiction in Britain, 1880–1910* (Hemel Hempstead: Harvester Wheatsheaf, 1990), p. 147.

[4]   Cadogan and Craig further state that the challenge of the *G.O.P.*'s fiction and features 'remained acceptable to the conservative mothers of its younger readers and to the husbands of older ones'. See *You're A Brick Angela! A New Look at Girls' Fiction from 1839 to 1975* (London: Gollancz, 1976), pp. 75–6.

[5]   Wendy Forrester, *Great-Grandmama's Weekly: A Celebration of the Girl's Own Paper 1880–1901* (Guildford: Lutterworth Press, 1980).

century uncertainty surrounding the question of the woman's place. In particular, it will focus upon the nature of the readership of the *G.O.P.*, which may provide the key, not only to the paper's immense popularity, but also to its frequently ambiguous and contradictory presentations of femininity.

The first issue of the *G.O.P.* appeared in 1880. It was published by the evangelical publishing house the Religious Tract Society (R.T.S.), and was the first magazine to specifically target a juvenile, female audience. In addition to being the first, it was also the best-selling and longest-running girls'/women's magazine, beginning in 1880 and running until 1946. By the end of its first year, the *G.O.P.* had a readership of two hundred and sixty thousand, almost double that of its brother publication the *Boy's Own Paper (B.O.P.)*, introduced during the previous year, and was soon outselling its contemporaries in the adult publishing market. It was to prove the R.T.S.'s most successful venture to date becoming, according to contemporary critic E.J. Salmon, 'the best-selling illustrated paper in the land', reaching an estimated quarter of a million readers by the end of the century.[6]

The continued demand for, and success of, the *G.O.P.* throughout the 1880s and 1890s indicated the potentially vast market there was for women's magazines, as well as suggesting a growing demand amongst a juvenile, female readership for a literature of their own. More significantly perhaps, it indicates a growing awareness, amongst parents and educators, of the need to provide a suitably 'feminine' reading matter for girls and young women. The *G.O.P.* was initially introduced in response to an awareness of the growing female readership of the *B.O.P.*. The sisters of *B.O.P.* readers, it seemed, required a magazine of their own. It was partly in response to this potential new audience, and partly to dissuade young women from reading fiction and features intended for their brothers, that the *G.O.P.* was introduced. Certainly, the 1880s and 1890s saw a proliferation of reading matter intended to supply the real, or supposed, wants of a juvenile, female readership.

Twentieth-century critics often perceive the emergence of the girls' literature genre as part of a conservative backlash, in response to the social changes of the late nineteenth century. Such literature, it has been suggested, was specifically designed to promote and enforce traditional 'safe' values and sexual stereotypes, whilst discouraging change.[7] Such criticisms have

---

[6] E.J. Salmon's comments on the *G.O.P.* can be found in 'What Girls Read', *The Nineteenth Century* 20 (1886), pp. 515–29, (p. 520). Forrester estimates that a quarter of a million readers, both at home and overseas, bought the paper every week by the end of the century. See front jacket.

[7] The contention that girls' literature of the late Victorian period was intended to reinforce traditional, or 'safe', feminine stereotypes, as part of a conservative response to

coloured perceptions of the *G.O.P.*, and seem to receive confirmation in the editor Charles Peters' own description of the paper's commitment to the teaching of the domestic virtues. In the Editor's Prospectus, of 1880, he claimed that:

> This magazine will aim at being to the girls a Counsellor, Playmate, Guardian, Instructor, Companion and Friend. It will help to train them in moral and domestic virtues, preparing them for the responsibilities of womanhood and for a heavenly home.[8]

However, an initial reading of the *G.O.P.* gives a confused impression of precisely who the magazine was intended for, and what images of femininity it was attempting to endorse. A bewildering range of articles and features will confront a reader picking up any issue from the first twenty years. Traditional housekeeping and dressmaking articles appear alongside careers advice columns and articles on shorthand and typing, articles on etiquette and on being presented at court next to features on blacking a grate or feeding a large family on a small income. Alongside all these, you may also find serial stories featuring the romantic exploits of young, middle-class women, whose lives revolve around Sunday school classes, church bazaars and housework.

A sample issue will give some idea of the range of articles and fiction included in the paper. The issue of 3 October 1896, already referred to as containing Bateson's article 'A Pound a Week', serves as a typical illustration. It begins with the first instalment of a serial story, 'Doctor Luttrell's First Patient', by one of the paper's regular contributors, Rosa Nouchette Carey. This serial tells the story of a young middle class heroine struggling to cope with her first year of marriage, and follows a typical didactic *G.O.P.* theme as the young Olivia Luttrell struggles to adapt from frivolous young girl to ideal companion and helpmeet for her husband. 'Doctor Luttrell's First Patient' is followed by a page of 'Household Hints', another regular feature of the paper, and an occasional page of music entitled 'Retrospection', composed by one of the paper's more distinguished contributors, H.R.H. Princess Beatrice. A short story, 'Lord Montgomery's Protégé', comes next, followed by one of the informative articles for which the *G.O.P.* was well known, 'Our Girls A Wheel', which details the various merits of the current models of bicycle available for women. In addition to 'A Pound A Week', one further article, a review of two unpublished letters of Sir Walter Scott, also appears.

---

the social changes of the period, is expressed by Reynolds, p. 98, and by Cadogan and Craig, p. 9.

[8]   Charles Peters in the Editor's Prospectus for the *Girl's Own Paper*, quoted in Forrester, Frontis.

The edition ends, as always, with a page of correspondence including a regular careers advice column. Queries include 'Augusta', who enquires about the possibility of becoming a stewardess on a liner, (the editor advises her that 'posts as stewardesses are rather hard to obtain for persons who have no previous connection with the shipping companies' and suggest that it would 'be better to obtain some knowledge of nursing that would enable you to become a district nurse'). Other queries include 'Chip', who enquires about wood carving as a possible career, and 'Kathleen', who asks for advice on nursing in hospitals and is told:

> Twenty-five is the earliest age to be admitted to several of the most important London hospitals, but in some institutions girls are accepted as probationers at twenty-one.[9]

This eclectic mixture of domestic fiction, informative articles, household tips and careers advice raises an interesting question: who was the paper intended to be read by? This question is central to an understanding of the G.O.P. and its aims. It is a difficult point to resolve. Phrases such as 'every girl's magazine' or 'every girl's best friend' frequently recur throughout the pages of the G.O.P.. Both the editor, Charles Peters, and the contributors were keen to stress the universal appeal of the magazine, which deliberately targeted a wide audience. Whilst twentieth-century critics often overlook the significance of the ambiguous and wide ranging nature of the paper's audience, I suggest that the paper's ambitious attempt to be 'every girl's magazine' may have contributed to its many ambiguities and inconsistencies.

Central to an understanding of the magazine is an understanding of the terms 'boy' and 'girl', which seem to have had widely different applications within the context of Victorian literature. The G.O.P.'s brother publication, the Boy's Own Paper, had a clearly defined, school-going audience, aged approximately between eight and eighteen, and had fiction and features of a predominantly juvenile nature: articles on sports and hobbies predominate, with fiction characterised by adventurous themes or school stories. The Boy's Own Paper exhibits a clear sense of boyhood as a definite period distinct from the nursery and from manhood, during which boys were allowed a period of license and could enjoy escapist fiction and entertaining articles. However, there is no accompanying rationale for girls, who seem to have been expected to move from infancy to adulthood with virtually no transitional period.

In an article on 'What Girls Read', appearing in the journal the Nineteenth Century in 1886, E.J. Salmon praised the G.O.P.'s housekeeping and domestic

---

[9]   3 October 1896, p. 15.

articles, and its encouragement of charity and religious fervour in young women, claiming that:

> Probably the best feature of the paper is its prize competitions. These are made the medium of much charity ... Its great merit is that it does not depend wholly upon fiction for its success, but gives interesting articles on all kinds of household matters.[10]

It is significant that Salmon sees the great merit of the *G.O.P.* as being its ability to instruct and inform its readers, but plays down the paper's fiction, despite the fact that fiction made up two thirds of every issue. Fiction, on the other hand, was seen as the greatest strength of the *Boy's Own Paper*. Essentially, whilst boys' literature treats boys as boys, and is primarily entertaining, girls' literature is primarily didactic, focusing on informative, domestic articles and fiction, and treating girls as embryonic wives and mothers. This is certainly true as far as the *G.O.P.* was concerned. The title **Girl's Own Paper**, is deceptive and implies a distinct juvenile audience which was not, in fact, the case. The tone of fiction and features suggests that the paper was actually targeting an older audience, with readers' letters from women in their twenties, thirties, even forties and fifties making appearances. Fictional heroines were nearly always of a marriageable age, often with children, and articles on childcare and housekeeping were common.

Thus, within the pages of the *G.O.P.*, the term 'girl' appears to include women of virtually any age, married or single. Peters deliberately fostered the notion that the *G.O.P.* appealed to all generations of women. Contributions from girls as young as six, and from married mothers and even grandmothers, frequently appear. The *G.O.P.*'s policy was to publish only the replies to reader's letters, and all correspondents were urged to use either initials or a pseudonym. However, from the editor's published responses, it is possible to infer a vast cross-section of ages in the correspondents. In 1897, the *G.O.P.*'s seventeenth year, Charles Peters requested readers to write in with their comments and suggestions on the paper. Selections from these letters were published and a small sample from them serves to illustrate that, by 1897 at least, the *G.O.P.* had become established as a magazine for women:

> Having been married at the age of eighteen, three months after leaving school, I consider the 'G.O.P.' the means of my becoming a capable housewife.

---

[10]   Salmon, p. 521.

Though long past girlhood, it is now, and always has been, my favourite periodical. I have been a reader for nearly eighteen years.

I have taken the 'G.O.P.' for eighteen years, and hope to do so for another eighteen.

I have received from the G.O.P. for the past eighteen years. I am in my 58th year.[11]

More significant, perhaps, than its appeal to several generations was the paper's apparently wide cross-class appeal. The paper appeared in two versions: a weekly issue, priced at one penny and intended for a working-class audience; and a monthly compendium issue, priced at six pence and intended for a middle-class readership. When asked to define the paper's readership, in 1880, Peters said:

> Anyone, with half an eye, can see that "THE GIRL'S OWN PAPER" is intended for girls of all classes. Girls of a superior position ... should read everything, and be well up in *every* matter upon which we give instruction ... Servant-maids communicate to us well-written letters, and by their tone we can see that our magazine has indeed helped them to an intelligent carrying out of their humble work; that it has been a companion to them in their isolation and a counsellor in times of sore temptation ... From our daily letters from girls, written upon coronetted notepaper by those of noble birth, and by others from the kitchens of humble houses, we gather that there is help needed by all.[12]

The idea that copies of the *G.O.P.* filtered down through all layers of society, with young mistresses passing them onto their serving maids and vice versa, is perhaps romanticized by Peters. However, it was frequently upheld as one of the paper's greatest achievements. In 'Servants and Service', an article from 1882, Ruth Lamb claims to be writing specifically for young women in service. She argues that the *G.O.P.* is:

> a friend whose face is seen everywhere. I know some mistresses, not young ones either, who read it in the drawing room and then send it down to the kitchen, daughters of the household who take it and then pass it to their waiting maidens with comments on such portions of its content as are likely to interest them in turn, and what is if anything more pleasant still, I know more than one handsome,

---

11   'The Editor Acknowledges a Favour', *G.O.P.*, 22 May 1897, p. 539.
12   Charles Peters, *G.O.P.*, 2 October 1882, p. 15.

well-appointed home in which a young servant lends her G.O.P. to her mistress![13]

In 1881, Peters printed a letter from one such servant under the title, 'A letter from the Kitchen'. The letter was signed Janet Cooper, a general servant. She praises the housekeeping articles as invaluable to her everyday life:

> There's many pieces in it very nice to read, and useful, no doubt, to the ladies as have not got to work all day, but that poor folks might pass by, with – "Oh, that isn't suited for the likes of us; however could we do all that's written down here?" That's what I thought when mistress made me a present of the first few numbers, and advised me to take it regular.[14]

Janet Cooper's comment that many pieces are nice to read but 'not quite suited to the likes of us' raises an interesting question. It suggests that some working-class readers may have read selectively, taking the paper for its housekeeping tips but ignoring the fiction, which seemed largely middle-class orientated. Charles Peters made the same point in answer to a reader's query in 1880, when he suggested that working-class women should primarily read the housekeeping articles, whilst their middle-class mistresses should read more widely. Girls belonging to:

> the 'upper ten thousand' – should read everything ... Their money, time, and superior intelligence admit of this. For girls of a less high position there are papers on economical cookery, plain needlework, home education and health.[15]

This kind of selective reading may have been common amongst *G.O.P.* readers. Peter's claim that the paper deliberately targeted a broad class spectrum is certainly in evidence in the issue of 12 December 1896. It begins with an article on 'How I was Presented at Court' in which a reader, signing herself 'La Petite', describes how, along with some hundred other debutantes, she was presented to the Princess of Wales. It ends with two prize essays, submitted by a lace maker and a general servant, for a competition that invited working-class women to write about their lives and their jobs.

Whilst readers may have been encouraged to read selectively, it also seems clear that the *G.O.P.* may have deliberately promoted some kind of cross education between the classes, giving working-class women a glimpse of

---

[13]   Ruth Lamb, 'Servants and Service', *G.O.P.*, 9 December 1882, p. 150.
[14]   Janet Cooper, 'A letter from the Kitchen', *G.O.P.*, 1 January 1881, p. 215.
[15]   Charles Peters, *G.O.P.*, 2 October 1882, p. 15.

middle-class life, and vice versa. Certainly, a working-class reader finding entertainment and escapism in an article on 'How I was Presented at Court' seems just as plausible as her upper class mistress taking an interest in the everyday life of a lace maker or a factory worker.

This is clearly the case with 'Sackcloth and Ashes', a serial story from 1892. It features a working-class heroine, but is clearly directed at middle-class readers, with the aim of raising a social conscience at the plight of their less fortunate working-class sisters. Note, for example, the moral tone of scenes such as that in which the working-class heroine, a shirt maker, overhears a conversation between two middle-class young ladies discussing the cheap price of the work she has laboured to produce:

> "They are so ridiculously cheap. It is certain they were never made for the money."
> "That is just what I object to," said Aileen. "I like the articles very much, and I am sure my mother would. But I should be miserable every time I put them on, if I were to think that they were not properly paid for. Fancy all the stitches that have gone into each, the wearing effect on the worker's sight and health, and the miserable price paid in return for time and labour".[16]

It seems clear that the *G.O.P.* was attempting to be a type of 'universal' women's magazine by catering to the real, or supposed, wants of a broad spectrum of women of all ages and classes. Further significance is attached to the *G.O.P.* when we consider that its first two decades of publication coincided with the last two decades of the nineteenth century, a period frequently identified as one of social ferment. At this time, the possibility of education and employment for women had undermined the previously domestic-orientated version of the woman's role, and generated a sense of anxiety as to the precise nature of the woman's sphere. The 'New Woman' has also appeared on the scene as a challenge to the 'Angel in the House'. During this period, the *G.O.P.* was virtually the only magazine available to both women and girls, and claimed to speak to, and on behalf of, all women, seeking to offer advice on all aspects of their lives.[17] Bearing all this in mind, perhaps it is no surprise that, in its ambitious attempt to cater to such a vast audience, the paper seems confusing or contradictory.

---

[16]   Ruth Lamb, 'Sackcloth and Ashes', *G.O.P.*, 2 July 1892, p. 628.

[17]   Other girls' magazines were published during this period, notably the *Girl's Realm* (1899), the *Girl's Own Messenger* (1895) and the *Girl's Best Friend* (1899). However, these magazines were not introduced until the late 1890s and, unlike the *G.O.P.*, cater to a distinctly juvenile audience.

I have already mentioned that most twentieth-century, and contemporary nineteenth-century, critics seem to view the paper as being essentially conservative and domestic-orientated. These accusations of conservatism need to be addressed. It is the paper's consistent commitment to the teaching of the domestic arts that is largely responsible for this reputation. Domestic articles were certainly a common feature. Throughout the 1880s and 1890s, the *G.O.P.* featured a regular page of household hints giving recipes, advice and tips for young housekeepers. Regular cookery articles by Phyllis Browne (pseudonym of Sarah Sharp Hamer) were also a feature, along with informative fictions such as 'The Difficulties of a Young Housekeeper and How She Overcame Them' (1880).

Non-fiction articles on child care were also common. Mrs Orman Cooper's, at times unbearably sentimental, series of articles on 'Queen Baby and Her Wants', has already been referred to and typifies this type of non-fiction. Another regular contributor of such articles was Ruth Lamb, whose earlier domestic series, 'How to Wash and Dress the Baby', paints a vivid picture of the ideal Victorian girl as the 'little mother':

> From her very infancy she loves her doll as a true mother loves her child, and should an accident befall her wooden or waxen darling, she grieves and moans over it, not as a broken toy, but as a wounded baby.[18]

Such features not only give advice on how to survive in the domestic sphere, they are also a celebration of the woman's role within that sphere, and often contain an implied criticism of any woman who sought to step outside of that role. Lamb, like Mrs Orman Cooper, uses her celebration of motherly instincts in young girls to explicitly criticise the modern woman and modern education, hinting that the 'little mother', trained in the arts of child care, is more feminine and more attractive to men than the modern public school or college girl:

> Bless the loving little woman! She is not without a reasonable liking for schoolwork, and loves reading as well as most. But her great charm is her delightful motherliness, even as a child, a quality which is, I fear, insufficiently cultivated at home, and never thought of at all in schools, or supposed to have any place in the so-called 'Higher Education of Women'. Yet, when I see these sweet feminine qualities in the lassie, I often think to myself that if I were a youth –

---

[18]   Ruth Lamb, 'How to Wash and Dress the Baby', Chapter 1, *G.O.P.*, 23 April 1881, p. 475.

a good one, mind – I should watch the growing into womanhood of such a 'little mother' as I have described. I should value the development of these heaven-bestowed womanly instincts as something more precious than any amount of certificates won for Latin or advanced mathematical knowledge. And though I might have a choice between such a little damsel as I have described and a feminine senior wrangler, I would do my best to win the little mother as the mistress of my future home.[19]

Such articles represent the *G.O.P.* at its most sentimental and reactionary. However, at the other extreme, there are articles on politics, education and careers. I have already referred to Margaret Bateson's two articles, from 1896, in which the author argues for a minimum wage for women. She urges the paper's readers to resist the arguments of the 'old fashioned and the sentimental' who discourage young women from entering the job market:

> Everyone must be familiar with the usual line of attack. It takes the form of an appeal to a girl's generosity and to her fellow feeling for other girls. The individual girl is reminded that if she remains living at home tranquilly and quietly (for movement is of itself expensive), she can just manage to subsist. Then why should she insist in doing work for pay? It is sordid of her to wish it. Moreover – and it is at this point our tender-hearted girl succumbs – she must infallibly deprive other girls of a wage who need it more. Some person I have know to be so possessed by the force of this reasoning that they will gravely argue that a responsible post should be filled by the poorest candidate.[20]

In the first article, Bateson challenges a society that forces women to be reliant upon the financial support of men. In the second, she offers practical careers advice to young women.

In stark contrast to Lamb's account of the 'little mother', Bateson's articles are an assertion of the woman's equal right to sell her labour at a fair price, and of the need to challenge and break down the restrictive ideologies that prevent her from doing this. The closing paragraphs of the first article strike a note of hope for the future of women on the brink of a new century:

> Indeed what we term the 'Woman's Movement' means, if we regard it from one point of view, the creation of many demands. Who is it, for instance, who employs the expert woman shorthand-writer? It is

---

[19] Ibid.
[20] Bateson, 'A Pound a Week: Why Girls should Earn it', p. 14.

in many cases, the woman-lecturer, the woman of business, or the woman doctor. Who requires the woman accountant? The society for promoting some reform in which women are interested, or the governing body of a public girls' school. The employment of girls in the Civil Service leads to the engagement of a woman-doctor to attend them, and the factory whose labour machinery so largely utilises, need women inspectors to safeguard their conditions of work. And though in London and our large towns we are slowly waking up to the fact that the capacities of women of the educated middle and upper class are not wisely allowed to atrophy, the country at large still wastes much useful labour.[21]

Bateson even seems to hint at the desirability of some kind of organised movement to assert women's rights:

I regard a pound a week as the average beginning salary of the middle-class girl. To the girl who in the factory or the workshop is earning less, and by very hard labour, I have no need to appeal. My only word to her is one of inducement, to try, by superior training, by *combination*, by whatever fair means lie in her power, to win more adequate pay [italics mine].[22]

Bateson was not alone in demanding equal pay for women. An 1897 series of articles, entitled 'Girls at Work', stresses the same message. This earlier series of articles opened with an attack on the notion that women's work renders them 'unladylike':

No work is degrading! Cast behind you all false ideas about gentility. Utilise each of you, those talents which God has given you. Choose to be a good cook rather than a bad teacher, a thorough parlour maid rather than an incompetent hospital nurse. The time will come and you will be helping to bring it nearer, when the whole world will recognise that, no matter what work you may undertake, you are 'ladies', if not strictly speaking genteel.[23]

This series encouraged women in the adoption of a wide range of careers, including medicine, urging them to avoid what the author referred to as the 'inevitable trio' of 'suitable' jobs for ladies: governess, nurse or companion.

---

21   Ibid., p. 15.
22   Ibid., p. 15.
23   'Girls at Work', *G.O.P.*, 10 April 1897, p. 441.

This message was not simply confined to the paper's non-fiction. In December 1881, the *G.O.P.* ran a three-part serial story, 'The Other Side of the World', which featured the adventures of two middle-class heroines who, faced with limited opportunities at home, emigrate to Australia. Despite criticism that they will compromise their gentility, the two women take jobs as domestic servants and build for themselves a more liberated life overseas. 'The Other Side of the World', by regular contributor Isabella Fyvie Mayo, highlights the increased problem of female unemployment and offers a radical solution. The story is an informative fiction, apparently intended to offer advice to the paper's readers who may have been contemplating a similar course of action. The narrative dwells in detail on the formalities and procedures involved (the address of the Women's Emigration Society is printed in full) as well as giving a realistic account of the cramped and lengthy sea passage and the discomfort and lack of privacy experienced by the two genteel heroines. 'The Other Side of the World' offers a realistic summation of the chances for women emigrants, and points to the need for middle-class ladies to overcome sexual and class-based stereotypes in order to take on hard physical work:

> I could not advise any girls to come out here to fight their own battle, except those who know the world thoroughly and are able and willing to turn their hands to almost anything. It is not fancy-work lady-helps who are wanted, but women who can really take a servant's place, scrub, wash and cook ... I feel sure, even among the prejudices of English life, that whatever work ladies did would soon become lady-like![24]

The *G.O.P.* did on occasion touch upon politics. In 1890, a solicitor wrote on the 'Married Women's Property Acts', and, in 1895, an article on 'Politics for Girls', prophesied the enfranchisement of women 'within ten or twelve years'. Whilst Peters continued to give space to writers of domestic articles and fiction, such as Mrs Orman Cooper and Rosa Nouchette Carey, he was also consistent in giving space to articles on education and careers. The paper openly acknowledged that a large number of its readers were either already within full-time employment or seeking a means of earning their independence. The careers advice column soon became a regular feature and, throughout the 1890s, a variety of articles giving employment advice appeared. A typical example is 'The Girl's Own Shorthand Class', a series of

---

[24]   Isabella Fyvie Mayo, 'The Other Side of the World', *G.O.P.*, 4 February 1882, p. 290.

articles from 1891. Thus, whilst continuing its commitment to the promotion of the domestic arts, the *G.O.P.* also seems to have had a definite policy to confront new ideas, as well as an awareness that not all of its readers were confined exclusively within the domestic sphere.

It certainly seems that the paper's editor and contributors were aware of the changing world in which its readers were living, and were willing to confront the issues raised by these changes. However, there is often a sense of confusion over the treatment of some aspects of change for women. The subject of women's education, for example, generates huge confusion, with *G.O.P.* education articles ranging from the reactionary to the enlightened. One of the less enlightened articles, 'Thoughts on the Higher Education of Women' by 'A Man', from 1891, advises readers not to compromise their femininity by undertaking 'masculine' subjects:

> The tendency of mathematics for women is to make them narrow, and creatures of only one idea ... Depend upon it, ladies, the judgment of the Cambridge undergraduate represents fairly the judgment of English manhood upon your sex; and if there is anything he hates and ridicules, it is a masculine unwomanly woman...He wants to find sympathy in his pursuits – true womanly sympathy; a helpmeet, not a lady who understands differential and integral calculus, who will discourse learnedly and drearily upon one everlasting subject[25]

February of the following year witnessed an even more reactionary outburst in an article on 'The Disadvantages of Higher Education for Women'. The author, using the initials M.P.S., utilised the language of eugenics to suggest that women were physically unsuited to mental exertion, and rendered themselves physically ill, unfeminine, and ridiculous in the eyes of men, by persisting in pursuing such studies:

> We hear a great deal nowadays about the advantages of higher education of women ... Is this altogether advisable? ... It is well known that a woman's physique is not equal to a man's, and the brain power depends very much on the physique which nourishes the brain – ergo, the average woman will never equal the average man on his own ground ... Woman was created as a helpmeet for

---

[25]   'A Man', 'Thoughts on the Higher Education of Women', *G.O.P.*, 10 October 1891, p. 20.

man, not as his equal or rival; and woman nowadays is very apt to forget that fact.[26]

Yet, an article on 'The North London Collegiate School for Girls' appearing only a month later, on 29 April 1882, begins with an enthusiastic note of welcome for opportunities in higher education for women, as well as a marked scorn for the type of 'old-fashioned' opinions expressed in the previous articles:

> Perhaps among the many and various phenomena of nineteenth-century civilisation none is more curious and interesting than the sudden springing into life and rapid vigorous growth, all over the country, of large public schools for girls. Twenty years ago even, if the daughter in an ordinary English household had twice the intellect and capacity of her brother, his head it was that Latin, Greek, and mathematics must at any cost be made to fill, or at least to seem to fill, while if she had aspirations for anything beyond her piano, some acquaintance (often the slightest) with the French and Italian languages, and such knowledge of English history and literature as could be gained from an accurate verbal acquaintance with "Mangnall's Questions" such unfeminine desires were not to be mentioned in a well-regulated family.[27]

The article was accompanied by a line drawing of students in the gymnasium swinging on parallel bars and ropes.

Of course what the average *G.O.P.* reader, whoever that may have been, must have made of the paper's contradictory stance on education is difficult to assess. It was magazine policy not to publish readers' letters. On occasion, however, this rule is breached. Following the publication of 'The Disadvantages of Higher Education for Women', a reader's letter appeared in an occasional page of amateur contributions, published on 8 April 1882. The letter, which occupied two columns, was signed Bertha Mary Jenkinson, who gives her age as fourteen years and seven months. The writer complains in irate terms about the dangerously reactionary opinions expressed by M.P.S. whom she wrongly, if understandably, identifies as a man (the editor assures her that 'M.P.S. is *not* a man but the daughter of an illustrious dignitary of the Church of England'):

---

[26]   M.P.S., 'The Disadvantages of Higher Education for Women', *G.O.P.*, 18 February 1882, p. 333.

[27]   'The North London Collegiate School for Girls', *G.O.P.*, 29 April 1882, p. 494.

> It is unmistakably written by a man, and one who has certainly never
> had a wife who has been highly educated, or he would never have
> wasted his time in penning the article before mentioned. He says a
> woman's physique is not equal to that of a man's, and therefore the
> brain power of a woman can never equal a man's. That may be; but
> is it necessary, does it follow that a woman after she has learnt to
> read and write, to sew, clean a house, and cook a dinner, should
> allow her brains to lie dormant? ... If God had intended woman to
> be merely man's slave he would never have furnished her with
> reasoning powers. She need not have had even a tongue, for she
> could have cooked his dinner and mended his shirt quite as well
> without one ... Some women cannot be wives and mothers. They
> have their living to earn and must go out in the world, and if they are
> not educated, and highly educated too, I think the right word to
> apply to them would be incapables.[28]

That Peters should have taken the decision to print such a critical letter is
surely significant. Could it be that M.P.S.'s article had generated such a large
number of complaints that he felt it could not be ignored? This might be
surmise on my part, but Bertha Mary Jenkinson's letter remains one of the
very few readers letters that Peters allowed to be published, and is perhaps a
significant indication that at least some *G.O.P.* readers objected to its
frequently reactionary tone.

What emerges from an overview of the *G.O.P.'s* education articles is a
sense of on-going debate. Not only are both sides of the argument, both for
and against, represented, but Peters also seemed willing to open up the debate
to his readers. What the *G.O.P.* may have been attempting to provide then,
was a forum for the discussion of contemporary issues affecting young women
and girls. I have tried in this chapter to give some idea of the readership,
scope and significance of what I consider to be a unique women's magazine.
Rather than to describe the *G.O.P.* as either overtly reactionary or overtly
radical, it might be more accurate to say that its pages were used as a medium
to wage contemporary debates about the woman's place in society. It was the
first magazine intended exclusively for women, and whose contributors were
largely female. It gave women the opportunity to read about contemporary
issues and even, on occasion, air their own views. It was capable of extreme
conservatism as well as moments of radicalism, and although the overall effect
can be one of confusion and ambiguity it became, I suggest, a reflection of a
contemporary climate of confusion and ambiguity surrounding the question of
the woman's role in society.

---

[28]   *G.O.P.*, 8 April 1882, p. 444.

The wide readership, which the paper's editor stressed with such pride, may perhaps provide the key to the frequently confused images of femininity it projects. Certainly, the *G.O.P.*'s apparent attempts to cater to such a vast cross section of the female world make the paper unique amongst its nineteenth-century contemporaries and twentieth-century descendents. In her study of twentieth-century girls' magazines, 'Jackie: An Ideology of Adolescent Femininity', Angela McRobbie has suggested that girls' and women's magazines are designed to isolate a specific phase in a woman's life, defining how that phase should be dealt with, and encouraging women to see themselves in terms of particular stereotypes: hence schoolgirl magazines, teenage romance magazines, bridal magazines, magazines on motherhood, homemaking, child care etc.. She suggests that girl's/women's magazines use a variety of techniques to 'frame' the world of their readers addressing women and girls as monolithic groupings and thereby asserting a kind of 'false sisterhood' by obscuring differences such as age and class: 'having mapped out the feminine "career" in such all-embracing terms, there is little or no space allowed for alternatives'.[29]

What makes the *G.O.P.* significant is that it *does* allow space for alternatives. It does not project one view of women but many views. It seems, whether by accident or by design, to avoid targeting specific phases in women's lives, or specific groupings of women. Thus, in its attempts to cater to all classes and all ages, the *G.O.P.* may well have been quite deliberate in its projection of several versions of femininity and the female role.

Perhaps the most useful way to view the *G.O.P.* is as an index of the roles available to women during the latter stages of the nineteenth century. It offers a wide range of divergent female roles from, at one extreme, the sweet uneducated 'little mother' and, at the other, the female college graduate or the woman emigrant. It caters for the modern, rational, healthy, educated woman, keen for employment and for an active role in society, as well as the modest middle-class girl content to wait within the safe haven of home for a husband and children. Which of these versions of femininity it endorses, and which it rejects, varies from issue to issue, sometimes from page to page, and frequently it will attempt, with varying degrees of success, to offer amalgamations of these differing roles.

The *Girl's Own Paper* was as much concerned to express as to allay the anxieties and confusions generated over a crucial twenty-year period that witnessed major changes in women's lives. At a time when the woman's role,

---

[29]   Angela McRobbie, 'Jackie: An Ideology of Adolescent Femininity', reprinted in Bob Ashley, *The Study of Popular Fiction: A Source Book* (London: Pinter, 1989), pp. 203–206.

within and without the domestic sphere, was the subject of controversy and confusion, it is perhaps not surprising that the largest-selling women's magazine, which reached such a vast cross section of the female world, should become a focus and expression of that controversy and confusion.

Chapter 4

Good Housekeeping? Domestic Economy and Suffering Wives in Mrs Henry Wood's Early Fiction

Emma Liggins

At mid-century, debates around household management and the prescribed role of the middle-class housewife were a significant feature of advice literature, periodical articles and popular fiction. In her discussion of the rise of the domestic woman in the early-nineteenth century, Nancy Armstrong has argued that the young middle-class woman made herself desirable by reading conduct books, where 'her desirability hinged upon an education in frugal domestic practices'.[1] In the 1860s Mrs Henry Wood picked up on the contradictory nature of this feminine ideal, borrowing from key texts on household management and the fulfilment of marital duties by writers such as Sarah Ellis and Isabella Beeton in order to expose women's dissatisfactions with domesticity. Whilst acknowledging 'the role that the novel played in sustaining mythologies of the middle-class homemaker', Elisabeth Langland has addressed the key issue of the differences between fiction and domestic discourses, suggesting that the latter:

> tend to emphasize the bourgeois household manager more consistently than literary representations do, perhaps because the former carry the burden of explicitly addressing class issues, of at least acknowledging that middle-class life depends upon successful management of a servant class. Literary works – particularly domestic novels directed at middle-class audiences – have the luxury

---

[1]   Nancy Armstrong, *Desire and Domestic Fiction: A Political History of the Novel* (Oxford: Oxford University Press, 1987), p. 59. Armstrong claims that this new model of womanhood was then placed at the centre of the evolving tradition of the nineteenth-century domestic novel, which came to celebrate woman's managerial role in the Victorian household. Her discussions of the domestic novel only extend up to the late 1840s and the fiction of the Brontës, so do not take account of fictional representations of the household manager at mid-century.

of ignoring or obscuring that fact, often burying it in the romance
plot.[2]

Clearly novels and advice literature do have separate agendas, but I would
suggest that most domestic fiction *did* carry the burden of addressing class and
that Wood's romance plots effectively facilitate a critique of the household
manager rather than obscuring her significance. Wood's treatment of the
domestic woman bears out Lyn Pykett's claim that sensation novels of this
period simultaneously reproduced 'culture's stories about femininity' and
'exposed the contradictions of prevailing versions of femininity'.[3] Women
readers are urged to admire good managers, and to participate in the suffering
of wives who neglect their duties, whilst the novels also provide a covert
critique of domestic ideologies. Wood's novels may appear conservative in
their criticisms of women for failing to accommodate themselves to the role of
bourgeois home-maker, but they simultaneously expose the contradictions and
inadequacies of the icon of domestic woman.

Contemporary Advice on Household Management

Wood was beginning to establish her reputation at the same time that advice
about running the home and domestic economy was being distributed in Mrs
Beeton's successful *Book of Household Management* (1861), first published in
the pages of the widely read *Englishwoman's Domestic Magazine*, from 1859–
61. This publication testified to women's continuing demand for advice on
domestic matters; Sarah Ellis' hugely influential works of the late 1830s and
1840s, particularly *The Wives of England*, were still being used to educate
women readers at mid-century. According to Margaret Beetham, the 'new
feminine genre' of women's magazines was instrumental in 'the
reinterpretation of the ideal of domestic management' so that Beeton's readers
were constructed primarily 'in terms of a universal womanhood centred on
home-making'.[4] In her Preface Isabella Beeton explains that what prompted

---

[2]   Elizabeth Langland, *Nobody's Angels: Middle-Class Women and Domestic
Ideology in Victorian Culture* (Ithaca and London: Cornell University Press, 1995), pp. 12, 60.
This forms part of a broader argument in which she claims that the role of the bourgeois
manager is 'mystified' in both non-literary and fictional domestic discourses. The novel is
also able to expose the mythology it sedulously portrays, contributing to the contradictory
discourses on household management.

[3]   Lyn Pykett, *The 'Improper Feminine': The Woman's Sensation Novel and the
New Woman Writing* (London: Routledge, 1992), p. 5.

[4]   Margaret Beetham, *A Magazine of her Own? Domesticity and Desire in the
Woman's Magazine, 1800–1914* (London: Routledge, 1996), pp. 64, 62.   Beetham's

her to write was 'the discontent and suffering which I had seen brought upon men and women by household mismanagement', going on to point out that mistresses should cultivate the 'arts of making and keeping a comfortable home' which included practising her recipes in order to 'compete' with the attractions of male domains such as 'clubs, well-ordered taverns, and dining-houses'.[5] According to both novelists and advice writers, men spent their leisure hours elsewhere in order to escape a badly-run home. As in Ellis' vision of the domestic woman, the position of Beeton's mistress of the house was contradictory; she could build up her power by regulating her servants, acquiring a 'knowledge of household duties' and the authority of a 'commander of an army', yet she must never 'let an account of her husband's failings pass her lips'.[6] By the 1860s the wife's skills in economy were more pronounced, as practical advice such as how to deal with trades-people personally in order to purchase smaller quantities of food was included alongside more abstract prescriptions about dealing with servants and husbands.[7] In a *Saturday Review* article analysing 'Domestic Autocracy' in 1864, this performance of wifely duties was seen as part of a woman's training for life beyond her husband's death, as the woman whose husband 'orders her dinners, and adds up her housekeeping books every week' is promoting a 'disastrous' 'condition of helplessness' which detracts from equality in the home.[8] Men's purposes were no longer served by feminine helplessness, as women who knew how to order meat cheaply were to be valued for their capacity to maintain economic security.

Ellis' projections of the ideal marriage were predicated on the woman's ability to recognize and act on the seriousness of her position. This involved turning away from the deceptive images of women in fiction towards the realities of the Victorian household: 'young women of England should be educated not to imitate the heroines they read of; but to plunge into the actual

---

discussion of the 'different models of femininity' made available by the 'extraordinary diversity of genres and voices' of the *Englishwoman's Domestic Magazine* is very useful in the context of changes in perceptions and images of domestic women, as she argues that domestic knowledge had become something to be learnt, rather than passed on through generations of women (p. 66).

[5]   Mrs Isabella Beeton, *The Book of Household Management* (London: Chancellor Press, 1982; first published 1859–61 as monthly supplements to *Englishwoman's Domestic Magazine*, 1861 one volume), Preface.

[6]   Ibid., pp. 7, 1, 4.

[7]   This has been pointed out by Beetham in relation to the *Englishwoman's Domestic Magazine*. She suggests that it provided an alternative kind of advice for readers than that on offer in 'the earlier ladies' magazines and the popular conduct books by Sarah Ellis' (p. 66).

[8]   'Domestic autocracy', *Saturday Review*, 25 June 1864, p.778.

cares, and duties, and responsibilities of every-day existence'.[9]   Sexuality remained unacknowledged in the domestic space, though as Catherine Hall has pointed out, 'middle-class women ... provided sex on demand for their husbands along with preserves, clean linen and roast meat'.[10]   Ellis stressed the importance of maintaining a husband's desire through scrupulous attention to personal appearance, as well as cultivating 'a feeling of contentment with your home, your servants and your domestic affairs in general'.[11]   Married women's 'business' in life was 'to soothe and cheer', which included both managing servants and looking desirable.   Husbands were not to be reproached for transgressions such as intemperance nor unduly involved in the trials of household management; wives should try not to complain but 'to make all her domestic concerns appear before her husband to the very best advantage'.[12]   The dutiful, desirable uncomplaining wife then guaranteed the smooth running of the home and was able to manage or endure her husband's problems through her 'strength and patience'.

Given such utopian images of household harmony, it seems unsurprising that both Ellis and Beeton were forced to acknowledge flaws in their prescriptions for wedded bliss.   Leonore Davidoff and Catherine Hall have highlighted the 'contradictory demands' placed on domestic women, arguing that Ellis' popularity can be explained by 'the tension between the notion of women as "relative creatures" and a celebratory view of their potential power' in her writing.[13]   A. James Hammerton has argued that readers found Ellis' advice difficult to follow, establishing that 'the heightened emotional expectations of marriage' tended to increase the focus on men's marital misconduct as the century progressed.[14]   In her reading of Ellis' vision of women's work, Langland has contended that women's supervisory role is constantly downplayed as 'Ellis yokes a patriarchal ideology of idealized womanhood with a bourgeois ideology of class regulation in ways that simultaneously expose and disguise the role of the middle-class housewife'.[15]

---

[9]   Sarah Stickney Ellis, *The Women of England: Their Social Duties and Domestic Habits* (1839; London: Fisher, Son & Co., [nd]), p. 205.

[10]   Catherine Hall, *White, Male and Middle-Class: Explorations in Feminism and History* (Cambridge: Polity Press, 1992), p. 61.

[11]   Ellis, *The Wives of England*, p. 179.

[12]   Ibid., p. 181.

[13]   Leonore Davidoff and Catherine Hall, *Family Fortunes: Men and Women of the English Middle Class, 1780–1850* (London: Hutchinson, 1987), p. 183.

[14]   A. James Hammerton, *Cruelty and Companionship: Conflict in Nineteenth-Century Married Life* (London: Routledge, 1992), pp. 2, 3.

[15]   Langland, p. 75. Her view is that Ellis is less concerned with 'the skills necessary to manage a bourgeois household' than the notion of 'womanly sympathy' which

She suggests that like the domestic novel, Ellis 'obscures the material and political reality of domestic life' producing 'a justification of the status quo and a concealment of the class issues as gender ones'.[16]

Yet even from an early stage Wood's brand of domestic fiction tended to focus very specifically on material and political realities and the class implications of domestic management. In her short story 'Rushing Headlong into Marriage' first published as one of a series in *Bentley's Miscellany* of 1858, she gives detailed information on the economic pitfalls of marriage, including the payment of bills, monthly expenses and the expected costs of bringing up children. Annis' struggle to manage monthly expenses on her husband's fixed salary of 300 a year is contrasted with her sister's negligence of all financial matters and reliance on her husband's property. Whilst Augusta's husband squanders his money on opera and his club as his wife turns a blind eye to domestic economy, Annis manages with only one servant, helps with the cooking and dusting, goes to market to buy cheap meat and tries to learn how to iron. However she is accused of 'bad management' by her sisters when her cook answers the door, and her 'scheme of economy' seen to be 'degrading' as she stands on the boundary between wife and servant.[17] Wood seems to be drawing directly here on ideas articulated by Ellis, who included a diatribe against the perils of 'domestic drudgery' and the misguided women who 'plunge head, heart and hand into the vortex of culinary operations'.[18] Annis' key speech defending her position demonstrates the potential dangers of both neglecting and embracing household management:

> There are notions abroad ... that for people in our pretentious class of society ... all participation in, all acquaintance even, with domestic duties is a thing to be ashamed of ... I don't know which is the worst: a woman who entirely neglects to look after her household, where her station and circumstances demand it, or one who makes herself a domestic drudge. Both extremes are bad, and both should be avoided ... It would have been well for me, I think, had Mamma brought us up in a more domestic manner. There is another fallacy of the present day: the bringing up young ladies to play and dance, but utterly incapable as to the ruling of a household. (p. 343)

---

allows middle-class women to regulate the behaviour of their servants and thus to instil conservative class positions.

[16]   Ibid., p.76.

[17]   All quotations are taken from [Mrs Henry Wood], 'Rushing Headlong into Marriage', *Bentley's Miscellany* 43 (1858), pp. 338–51.

[18]   Ellis, *Wives of England*, p. 261.

Whilst household management is then linked to women's need to recognise their limited economic resources, 'where her station and circumstances demand it', they must also learn to position themselves between the extremes of domestic· drudge and neglectful wife. Middle-class education is also blamed for gearing women towards finding a suitable husband rather than 'ruling' a home, suggesting that marital tensions can be traced back to cultural formations of ideal femininity. The 'barbarous picture of domestic economy' (p. 351) used by Aunt Clem to frighten Augusta also blames the wife for her economic problems. Augusta is 'no manager' and 'knew literally nothing of practical domestic details when she married' whereas her husband is far too 'accustomed to his clubs and their expensive society' (p. 344). It is acknowledged that 'all men are not calculated *by nature* to economise in domestic privacy' (p. 349, my italics), suggesting that women's nature should guarantee these skills. Wood's early story then sets the scene for her later fiction in which women's ignorance of economy will be seen as a far more serious cause of marital breakdown than men's refusal to 'give up [their] social habits'.

The importance of women's managerial role was also stressed in the periodicals of the time, where fulfilling the criteria for the perfect wife was discussed alongside anxieties about the bachelor lifestyle, the late age for men marrying and the inadequacies of women's education in domestic matters. In a *Saturday Review* article of 1863 advising men on their choice of marriage partner, it is claimed that there are three classes of wife: 'the wife dominant, the wife co-operative and the slave wife'.[19] Whilst one version of the cooperative wife seems to be another rendition of the household manager who ideally shields her husband from 'the minuatiae of household management' and 'squabbling housemaids', the slave wife is driven by a 'restless anxiety to please her lord' so that he is elevated to the status of a 'divinity'.[20] This negative role-model is offered as a warning to readers who may allow desire to cloud their sense of responsibility; wives who displayed their sexuality or allowed their husbands to flirt with other women were seen as inadequate.[21]

---

[19]   'Wives', *Saturday Review*, 19 December 1863, p. 779.

[20]   Ibid., p. 780.

[21]   One article suggested that, rather than conforming to the 'old-fashioned idea ... that a young lady married was a young lady shelved', social conditions had ensured that 'a youthful matron is no longer a withdrawn competitor for the attentions of the male sex, but a dangerous, almost irresistible rival, released from all the disabilities under which young ladies live, and armed with new powers to dazzle and enslave'. Far from spending time ordering meat and pandering to their husband's wishes, 'frisky matrons' have achieved a 'new position ... in society', where they 'desert the duties of their station, to lead the van of frivolity and excess'. Again this is blamed on limitations in female education and seems typical of

The articulation of women's desire within marriage appears problematic, as 'the management of female sexual ignorance was central to the discourse of the domestic'.[22] Marital sexuality was perceived to be one of 'the trials of married life' by Ellis, which was reflected in the increased emphasis on fears of sexual rejection in the home in mid-Victorian novels. The responsibilities of the mistress of the house, which could become 'very substantial' as wives became 'indispensable' in running men's homes,[23] ran from managing servants and ordering meat to meeting the sexual and emotional needs of husbands, placing women under tremendous pressure in their fulfilment of the role of household manager. Hall's contention that at mid-century women were 'beginning to articulate the limitations of their "separate sphere"'[24] is illustrated in Wood's writing which repeatedly shows women finding domestic ideologies inadequate to their sexual needs.

'Household Mismanagement' in Wood's Fiction

Wood's fiction showcases for the reader the possible causes and effects of household mismanagement, focussing specifically on the trials of women who neglect their duties and the difficulties of being both desiring subject and domestic.woman. The popularity of her writing is uncontested, though where to place it generically is perhaps more difficult. It does not fit comfortably into the sensation genre, bearing more resemblance to what we now refer to as family sagas: Pykett refers to her novels as both 'sensation-influenced' and as 'dynastic narratives'.[25] Bracketed with Dinah Muloch as being in 'the lower range of feminine fiction', her work was rarely perceived to have been on a level with Mary Braddon's fiction, either in sensationalism or in terms of control of plot.[26] Although she did portray deviant and criminal women in

---

contemporary fears about the unconventional behaviour of married women. See 'Frisky Matrons', *Saturday Review*, 4 July 1863, pp. 10, 11.

[22]   Beetham, p. 65.

[23]   Hall, p. 183. Responsibilities were particularly heavy when the home doubled as the man's workplace so that the wife was also involved in running the business.

[24]   Ibid., p. 190. This was partly due to the rise of feminism in the 1850s and the demand for more employment opportunities for women.

[25]   Pykett, pp. 114, 115.

[26]   'Authoresses', *Saturday Review*, 10 October 1863, p. 483. Typically in this article Wood is compared unfavourably with writers such as George Eliot and Harriet Martineau, who were praised for tackling serious issues like political economy. Whilst *East Lynne* was generally agreed to be 'one of the best novels published for a season' despite its sensational content, the reviews of Wood's 1860s' fiction were generally lukewarm and sometimes vitriolic.

some of her novels, in general her work was not nearly so escapist as the more popular sensation texts so that the experiences and desires of the heroines perhaps chimed more with readers' own sense of lived femininity, particularly in the concentration on the trials of married life. Pykett comments particularly on the 'woman-to-woman address' in her work and the way in which 'both Braddon and Wood employ a complex manipulation of point of view, and offer their readers a variety of perspectives and positions within the text which permit a dispersal of narrative identifications'.[27] Identification with infamous sensation heroines such as Wood's adulterous Isabel Vane or the homicidal Lady Audley clearly left the reader on dangerous ground but identification with bad household managers was more a recognition of the demands and contradictions of the role.[28] Even as her novels work to remind married women of their duties and reposition them within domestic ideology, however, transgressive women who reject the role of home-maker are quietly celebrated and offered as alternative role models to wives struggling to follow the advice of Ellis and Beeton.

Wood's most famous novel, *East Lynne* (1861), notorious for its adulterous heroine, clearly offers a critique of bourgeois marriage, locating Isabel Carlyle's desertion of her husband in her debilitating experience of home life. Comparing Wood to Braddon, Elaine Showalter has claimed that Wood is 'equally adroit in tapping female frustrations',[29] and this is borne out by Isabel's frequent complaints that 'there's nothing to do' (p. 179) in the bourgeois home.[30] Her dissatisfaction with her domestic role is signalled in her complete ignorance of household economy, a situation made worse by the presence of Cornelia, her husband's sister, an 'extremely active housekeeper' who belittles Isabel's lack of domestic skills. In one significant scene her inadequacy as a housewife is exposed when she is unable to give orders to the butcher: 'Totally ignorant was she of the requirements of a household; and did not know whether to suggest a few pounds of meat, or a whole cow' (p. 157). Isabel's failure to assume the position of mistress of the house, or to challenge her sister-in-law's authority, makes her susceptible to illness; she is also depressed by her husband's absences from the home and the decline of his sexual interest in her. Feminist critics have been divided in their reactions to

---

27   Pykett, pp. 32, 80–81.
28   Kate Flint has argued that readers of sensation novels are typically 'implicated, placed in a position of complicity with a heroine's transgressive, yet highly understandable desires' as she is drawn into a recognisable contemporary world. See *The Woman Reader, 1837–1914* (Oxford: Oxford University Press, 1993), p. 282.
29   Elaine Showalter, *A Literature of their Own: from Charlotte Brontë to Doris Lessing* (1977; London: Virago, 1982), p. 171.
30   All quotations are taken from Mrs Henry Wood, *East Lynne* ed. Fionn O'Toole (1861; Stroud: Alan Sutton, 1993).

her flight with Levison and consequent suffering when Carlyle remarries. Showalter picks up on the fact that 'fantasies of pure escape had a great deal of appeal',[31] whereas more recently feminist critics have tended to emphasise Wood's conservatism; Pykett argues that the process by which 'the family becomes for Isabel (and by extension the reader) the object of desire rather than the cause and focus of discontent ... works to defuse women's discontent and reposition them as domestic creatures'.[32]   Arguably, the novel is typical of Wood's contradictory attitudes to domesticity; although the text may ultimately work to reposition women as domestic creatures, the signalling of women's discontent remains high on the agenda, as one of the covert messages is that the 'glad sensation of security' experienced by the married woman cannot accommodate her sexual impulses, rendering home life unfulfilling. The satisfaction of Barbara, Carlyle's second wife, an excellent household manager and 'the unmistakable mistress of the house and children', seems illusory, given the patterns of illness, discontent and sexual frustration mapped out by Wood as symptomatic of the bourgeois marriage. In Wood's lesser-known fiction of the 1860s, women's discontent appears to be championed more strongly as the model of domestic woman is shown to be vulnerable; domestic skills alone cannot guarantee female fulfilment.

Mrs Henry Wood's first novel, *Danesbury House* (1860), which won first prize in a competition by the Scottish Temperance League for a novel dramatising the evils of drink, typically focuses on the inadequate domestic skills of young wives and their inability to control their husbands. Hammerton has argued that by mid-century conjugal unhappiness was no longer to be exclusively pinned on women's domestic failures as described by Ellis but increasingly to 'men's tyrannical dictation, insistence on literal obedience and lack of sympathy with women's burdens in the domestic sphere',[33] and to a certain extent this is reflected in the novel which dwells on men's neglect of their wives and children for evenings spent in gin-palaces and men's clubs.[34]   There are frequent scenes of young women left in the house whilst sons and fathers routinely go out to drink with their friends. Isabel's aristocratic husband nearly dies in a duel following one of these evenings of debauchery, whilst Eliza Danesbury is unable to prevent her sons from experiencing the pleasures of city entertainments; the men's gambling

---

[31]   Showalter, p. 173.

[32]   Pykett, p. 127. She goes on to argue that this then offers women 'a potentially empowering fantasy in which the family is reclaimed as a revitalised women's space'.

[33]   Hammerton, p. 166.

[34]   Though the novel does quickly become tiring in its tirades against alcohol and its effects on family life, Wood does seem to have a particular interest in men's cultures which feature in her other fiction.

and expenditure on alcohol then constantly threaten the economic security of the middle-class home. The separate spheres ideology is endorsed throughout as men exclude their wives from their business concerns and spend their time predominantly in the company of other men. However, as men's shortcomings and absence from the home are increasingly referred back to women as 'bad managers', women readers are urged to reflect on their capacity to prevent such problems by correcting their own behaviour. With a nod to Ellis, we are told that 'Isabel's daily influence would do much' (p. 136) to reform her errant husband, whilst Eliza fails to make her home into a place of entertainment and leisure to rival the atmosphere of men's clubs as advised by Mrs Beeton.[35] Yet the novel also demonstrates the breakdown of this model in its articulation of women's dissatisfaction with their domestic roles. The bad-tempered Eliza's refusal to play the happy housewife is signaled by her striking one of the servants and the shocking declaration 'I hate children' when faced with the prospect of her new step-children. The novel then advocates the practice of good household management but implies that women's domestic authority may not be sufficient to moderate men's behaviour.

This analysis of the drawbacks of the separate spheres ideology is developed in a later novel, *The Shadow of Ashlydyat* (1863), which is much stronger in its punishment of the inadequate wife, despite its acknowledgement of the husband's crimes. George Godolphin's gambling which is kept secret from his wife Maria is inadvertently sanctioned by her failure to pursue matters about the payments of servants and tradespeople; bowing to her husband on the handling of household bills, she also neglects to assume her position of domestic power, beginning the slide into helplessness rather than assuming the position of 'commander of an army'. Bowing to a wife's domestic authority appears anathema to men who have also been brought up in ignorance of marital responsibilities: George is said to prefer living 'in a separate home where he can be entirely *en garçon*', rather than suffering female management. However, in the first argument they have about money, the masculine challenge to women's domestic authority is displaced onto women's expression of her sexual desire, thus diffusing tensions by diverting economic issues onto emotional ones. Ann Cvetkovich has argued that this is typical of the popular text, where readers are encouraged to dwell on the emotional rather than the economic problems of women so that 'what are effaced are the historical conditions that determine

---

[35]   All quotations are taken from Mrs Henry Wood, *Danesbury House* (1860; London and Glasgow: Collins Clear-Type Press, [nd]) and Mrs Henry Wood, *The Shadow of Ashlydyat* (1863; Stroud: Alan Sutton, 1994).

women's lives'.[36]   George's angry reply to his wife's pleas about saving money is set against signs of their continuing physical attraction to each other so that the argument about money shifts to centre on Maria's emotional state:

> She put up her hands, as if absorbed in reading, but her tears were falling. She had never had an ill word with her husband; had never had any symptom of estrangement with him; and she could not bear this. George lay on the sofa, his lips compressed. Maria rose, in her loving, affectionate nature, and stood before him. [they make up with kisses] She fully resolved that it should be the last time she would hint at such a thing as economy ... of course her husband knew his own business best. (pp.178–9)

The estrangement produced by disagreement over economy can then be alleviated by the exchange of kisses, as Maria's desire to be loved triumphs over her need to fulfil her duty as household manager.[37] Sexual desire then precludes communication over household matters, as woman's emotional satisfaction is privileged over her pleasure in running the house. This may form part of Langland's vision of 'a changing conception of bourgeois woman', where woman's role as consolidator of middle-class values takes second place to her sense of herself as a sexual subject.[38]

Even as the novels seek to present a more balanced view of household tensions than advice literature, then, they do appear to be repeatedly punishing the heroines for their domestic failures and their incapacity to maintain desire and romance. Although homosocial cultures and men's infidelities do have an impact on marital relations, women are blamed for their failure to live up to prescriptive images of ideal wives. Marital estrangement is linked to female emotional states, obscuring the details of men's neglect and expenditure. Maria's forced confession of her ignorance of her husband's gambling and fraud is repeatedly referred back to her neglect of her wifely duties and her

---

[36]   Ann Cvetkovich, *Mixed Feelings: Feminism, Mass Culture and Victorian Sensationalism* (New Brunswick: Rutgers University Press, 1992), p. 122. Her argument about Isabel Vane's position in *East Lynne* is that it 'dramatises for the reader the emotional costs of women's dependence, which forces them to accept hardships without complaint' (p. 101). By extension the reader is then educated into accepting her own hardship by responding emotionally to the heroine's suffering. Foregrounding the emotional rather than the economic problems of women is a way of co-opting readers into believing that if women could only articulate their pain, their problems would be solved.

[37]   Women's 'moral degradation' of neglecting their personal appearance can also precipitate 'symptoms of estrangement' according to Ellis who suggests that women who do not dress well for their husbands do not deserve 'sympathy or commiseration'. See Ellis, *Women of England*, p. 260.

[38]   Langland, p. 11.

inadequacy in comparison to better household managers such as her sister Grace, who proclaims: 'Maria has not paid her housekeeping bills for ever so long. *Of course* she must have known what was coming!' (p. 313). Had the situation arisen in her own well-managed household, Grace is quite sure that she 'would have deemed her state of contented ignorance to be little less than a crime' (p. 313). And yet the criticism of ignorant wives does not entirely preclude sympathy for the young housewife who is 'bound by an unacknowledged and mystified agenda'.[39] In *East Lynne*, the narrator urged readers to '*resolve* to bear [the trials of married life] ... pray for patience; pray for strength to resist that demon that would urge you so to escape' (p. 309), repeating Ellis' philosophy of endurance. Nevertheless, in his reading of uncontrollable husbands in Anne Brontë's *The Tenant of Wildfell Hall* (1847), Daniel Duffy points out that Ellis *did* acknowledge 'a distinctly unmanageable masculinity' that women were powerless to control, needing 'supplies of strength and patience beyond what any earthly source can afford' when married to men who drink, gamble or commit adultery.[40] Whereas Helen Huntingdon uses her strength to leave her profligate husband in Brontë's more radical text, Wood's heroines (with the obvious exception of Isabel Carlyle) rarely contemplate escape from their marriages, despite increasing public knowledge about divorce and separations. Contemporary reviewers picked up on the fact that the novel did not sufficiently punish men behaving badly; the *Athenaeum* voiced the opinion that 'Mrs Wood has dealt too leniently with the gay and gallant George Godolphin, whose sins bring so much woe upon innocent people'.[41] Maria's bearing of her husband's shame can then be read either in terms of her ignorance or her innocence, depending on the reader's views on the demands of domestic economy.

Wood dramatizes the differences between alternative models of femininity as her heroine's weaknesses may divert the reader's attention towards stronger female characters, more able to cope with domestic difficulties and public opinion. Maria is compared unfavourably with Charlotte, the powerful independent woman, at the same time as being distanced from the implied reader. Although she is initially seen as 'everything that was desirable as a wife' (p. 146) in comparison to the more transgressive, independent Charlotte, the other woman is attractive to the reader in her flamboyance, her sexual power and control over men and her ability to speak her mind and ignore the

---

[39]   Langland, p. 12.
[40]   Daniel Duffy, 'Fiends instead of Men: Sarah Ellis, Anne Brontë and the Eclipse of the Early Victorian Masculine ideal' in *Signs of Masculinity: Men in Literature 1700 to the Present* ed. Antony Rowland, Emma Liggins and Eriks Uskalis (Amsterdam: Rodopi, 1998), pp. 93, 94.
[41]   Review of *Shadow of Ashlydyat, Athenaeum*, 23 January 1864, p. 119.

opinions of others. Rather than being mistress of a house, Charlotte is 'mistress of her own actions', agreeing to marry Rodolph only on the condition that 'I have my own way in everything' (p. 156). As Maria embraces her disgrace, we are informed that 'had [Charlotte] enjoyed the honour of being George Godolphin's wife, she would not have shed a tear' (p. 314), even that 'other women, like Charlotte, might have been *renovated* by what happened' (p. 316). Indeed, we are told that Charlotte's husband has died, when in actuality his gambling has obliged him to fake his own death, allowing Charlotte even greater liberty. The reader is pushed away from the heroine's emotional state: 'Can you picture the sensations of Maria Godolphin during that night? No: not unless it has been your lot to pass through such' (p. 315). Contemporary reviews of the novel highlighted the plurality of positions of identification and sympathy for readers. The *Athenaeum* claimed that 'even the female reader is inclined to forgive [Charlotte]' whilst the heroine's angelic nature might both endear her to and distance her from less virtuous readers: she 'is sure of the reader's sympathy [as] she is a sweet and perfect wife. Too perfect'.[42] Another review referred to Charlotte as a 'pleasant, unprincipled flirt' and complained that 'None of [Wood's] characters are realized vividly enough to engage sympathy or excite aversion'.[43] Wives who are too perfect and forgivable flirts then offered readers contradictory models of femininity, suggesting that Wood's punishment of her heroine was meant to activate a variety of interpretations of the domestic woman, rather than simply making an example of a bad manager.

Her novels also raised questions about women's sexual and emotional needs and how they might be accommodated into prescriptive versions of the domestic woman. Davidoff and Hall have argued that domestic ideology of the 1840s, particularly the writing of John Loudon, helped to strengthen an image of woman as 'sexually controlled', where the woman's body was 'the body of the contained and domesticated woman'.[44] In her reading of *East Lynne*, E. Ann Kaplan notes how the text articulates 'the lack of any place in the system for female desire'.[45] By the 1860s some popular novels were

---

[42] Review of *The Shadow of Ashlydyat, Athenauem*, 23 January 1864, p. 119.

[43] Review of *The Shadow of Ashlydyat*, *Saturday Review*, 16 January 1864, p. 82. The reviewer also commented on her 'heedless slipshod writing' and compared her unfavourably with novelists of 'true psychological power' like George Eliot, whose work was often set against that of more popular writers in order to demonstrate their inferiority.

[44] Davidoff and Hall, p. 192. They argue that woman's physical presence 'was only legitimated when it expressed a proper sense of belonging to a delicate, refined and gentle domestic world'.

[45] E. Ann Kaplan, *Motherhood and Representation: The Mother in Popular Culture and Melodrama* (London and New York: Routledge, 1992), p. 86.

challenging received views, stressing the need for women to express their sexualities. As the daily realities of domestic economy and the ideology of gendered spheres continued to separate husband and wife, Wood's fiction dwells on husbands who significantly avoid their wives' bedrooms for more exciting forms of homosocial entertainment, directing the reader's attention towards her own dissatisfactions with her partner. Katherine in *Danesbury House* complains that her husband does not visit her 'to say goodnight' when he returns from the gin-palace, whilst Maria's illness and her husband's gambling result in his absence from the marital bed, even on their honeymoon. Wood's exploration of women's feelings of sexual rejection and frustration, combined with her emphasis on the problem of men's 'absent presence' from the home, contributes to her deconstruction of the ideal of domestic woman, diverging from Ellis' views that women who fail to make themselves desirable to their husbands have only themselves to blame. Maria's fears that George is having an affair with Charlotte precipitate emotional scenes, which invite the reader's sympathy. Cvetkovich has discussed Wood's foregrounding of women's emotional excesses in *East Lynne*, suggesting that 'nineteenth-century culture *invented* the suffering woman [who] serves political purposes beyond the need to tell her story'. Women's inability to control their emotions is manifested as a form of suffering to which the reader has privileged access.[46] What Kaplan has referred to as woman's 'incompleteness'[47] in the domestic space is then indicated in scenes of female suffering which work on the reader's sympathies.

Women's experiences of sexual rejection are inclined to bring on symptoms of illness, an area in which Wood could draw upon her own experience of invalidism. This proves one of the tell-tale signs of women's inability to live up to prescriptive images of domestic superwomen in both Ellis' and Beeton's work. Beeton admits that the naturalness of the maternal instinct may be checked by a mother being 'physically or socially incapacitated'.[48] For Ellis the suffering wife is unable to minister to her husband's needs, being indulged herself 'as a favour, rather than ... as a right'.[49] She offers a stern reminder of the wife's responsibilities: 'There is a vast difference between being as ill as you can be, and as well as you can be. To aim at the latter, rather than the former, is the duty of everyone, but especially of the married woman'.[50] Giving into or, it is implied, fabricating

    [46]   Cvetkovich, pp. 98, 100. She suggests that the suffering of Isabel Vane seems 'to exceed any moral or didactic requirement that the heroine be punished for her sins' (p. 99).
    [47]   Kaplan, p. 80.
    [48]   Beeton, p. 1025.
    [49]   Ellis, *The Wives of England*, p. 92.
    [50]   Ibid., p. 159.

illness, is figured as a defiance of wifely duties, as the passage goes on to apologise to those who are 'really afflicted' whilst in the same breath urging the suffering reader to try to 'bear ... pain with cheerfulness and resignation' and forget her illness 'in the intensity of her desire to make others happy'. In the case of Katherine Danesbury, who marries one of the drunken younger sons, a direct link is forged between men's neglect and female incapacity: 'My husband is going all wrong. It is that which makes me ill' (p. 260). Once it is revealed to Maria that her husband is a compulsive gambler and has stolen money from the Bank where he works, her retreat into illness is exacerbated and she declines steadily until her death, unable to rise above the shame he brings upon her. Medical readings of her ailments confirm that there is no organic complaint, suggesting that the physical symptoms are produced by her mental state. However we are told that she has 'a tendency to keep ill, which might have arisen without any mental trouble at all' (p. 395). Women's tendency to embrace illness can be interpreted as either a reaction against the domestic role or linked to the frequent pregnancies women often endured during the early years of marriage; Maria loses four children in the course of the narrative.[51] Despite the advice of her doctor and the pleading of her daughter, she makes little attempt to fight her illness. In another of the symbolic arguments she has with George over the packing of a heavy box, his lack of patience with her behaviour is illustrated, suggesting that her illness represents a withdrawal from her wifely responsibilities:

> [She is crying] 'If you show this temper, this childish sorrow before me, I shall run away' he chafed – he knew how unjustly – at Maria. Very, very unjustly. She had not annoyed him with reproaches, with complaints, as some wives would have done; she had not, to him, shown symptoms of the grief that was wearing out her heart . . . Even now, as she dried away her rebellious tears, she would not let him think they were being shed for the lost happiness of the past, but murmured some feeble excuse about a headache. (p. 385)

---

[51] Judith Rowbotham has discussed the significances of 'the retreat into invalidism' in her examination of the changing feminine stereotype in girls' fiction of the later Victorian period. She claims that 'Authors indicated that an "early Victorian invalidishness" was neither attractive nor desirable nor even Christian in women. Any girl with a tendency to it should work hard to overcome it'. See *Good Girls Make Good Wives: Guidance for Girls in Victorian Fiction* (Oxford: Basil Blackwell, 1989), pp. 36–7. See also Jane Lewis (ed.), *Labour and Love: Women's Experience of Home and Family, 1880–1940* (Oxford: Basil Blackwell, 1987) for an analysis of frequent pregnancies as a cause of women's ill-health and incapacity in the home.

Bearing his shame has meant that she has repressed her own feelings and silenced the 'complaints' she has against him, though the authorial addition that 'some wives' would have reproached him severely suggests that once again she has not perfected her role. The passage ends with her attributing her emotion to a headache, a woman's 'feeble excuse' to cover up her dissatisfaction and recognition of the lack of romance in their relationship, 'the lost happiness of the past'. The suffering woman is then held up as an example of one who cannot achieve the selflessness required to diffuse household tensions, as the male threat to economic security appears less important than woman's inability to control her emotions.

Far from indulging in the 'luxury of obscuring' the bourgeois household manager, Wood's early fiction then spotlights the difficulties involved in modern marriage in the face of contradictory advice about marital roles and domestic duties. Unable to juggle her desires and needs for a well-managed home, a fulfilling sexual and romantic relationship and control over her emotions, the heroine is increasingly criticized for her failures to keep her house and husband in order. The image of the 'perfect' wife is questioned and readers encouraged to adopt the strategies of stronger, more transgressive women in addition to the qualities of the domestic angel. Even as popular fiction then promoted a conservative view of domestic femininity, it also highlighted the inadequacies of the icon of domestic woman and registered women's debilitating experiences of married life, inadvertently urging readers to reject the role of perfect housewife advocated by Ellis and Beeton.

Chapter 5

After Lady Audley: M.E. Braddon, the Actress and the Act of Writing in *Hostages to Fortune*

Kate Mattacks

The recent publication of *Beyond Sensation: Mary Elizabeth Braddon in Context* [1] is timely evidence of Braddon's rising status as a critical subject. As the first collection dedicated to Braddon, it illustrates a continuing concern with the issues first raised by Tillotson, Sadleir and Wolff,[2] namely the historical discourses that her texts utilise and inform. Consequently, the volume includes essays on Braddon's treatment of the legal, medical, and social positioning of women, ranging from Katherine Montweiler's discussion of subtextual consumer demands for beauty products that enabled the reader to mimic Lady Audley's class mobility, to an attempt by Lillian Nayder to connect images of female rebellion with the contemporaneous Indian Mutiny of 1857.[3] Despite ground-breaking research by Toni Johnson-Woods and the collaboration between Jennifer Carnell and Graham Law, the collection relies heavily upon Braddon's pair of bigamy novels *Lady Audley's Secret* (1862) and *Aurora Floyd* (1863) to the detriment of the rest of her works, many of which go literally beyond sensation and into the generic realms of realism, historical romance, drama and essays. However, what the volume does show is the critical trend towards popular fiction, particularly that written by women, the

---

[1]   Marlene Tromp, Pamela K.Gilbert and Aeron Haynie (eds), *Beyond Sensation: Mary Elizabeth Braddon in Context* (Albany: State University of NewYork Press, 2000).

[2]   See Kathleen Tillotson, 'The Lighter Reading of the Eighteen-Sixties', introduction to Wilkie Collins, *The Woman In White* (Boston: Houghton Mifflin, 1969), Michael Sadleir, *Things Past* (London: Constable, 1944) and Robert Lee Wolff, *Sensational Victorian: The Life and Fiction of Mary Elizabeth Braddon* (New York: Garland, 1979).

[3]   See Katherine Montweiler, 'Marketing Sensation: *Lady Audley's Secret* and Consumer Culture', and Lillian Nayder, 'Rebellious Sepoys and Bigamous Wives: The Indian Mutiny and Marriage Law Reform in *Lady Audley's Secret*', in Tromp, Gilbert and Haynie.

difficulties of assessing a vast literary output and most crucially, Braddon's contradictory nature.

Developments in criticism have mobilised a shift from 'resisting' popular texts outside the canon to an exploration of how popular fiction itself contains emblems of resistance and subversion.[4] *Lady Audley's Secret* has proved the most attractive to the critics due to its availability and particular use of visual tactics in order to sustain the reader's interest after the early revelation of its eponymous heroine's secrets in the proposal and portrait scenes.[5] Throughout the text, Lady Audley is represented as a series of images, clarifying that the only stable aspect of this central character is her fluidity. Her image is constructed through her use of melodramatic gestures which employ the body in an attempt to counter the verbal/written evidence against her, undermining the authenticity of the written text as a single mode of interpretation. The search for meaning becomes a complex negotiation between the visual and the verbal, the combination of which forms the sensation narrative. In this light, the text could be argued as being a subversive illustration of Victorian anxieties surrounding the reading of the body, or as a conservative display of the methods by which the body can be managed or contained.[6]

What is clear is that Braddon's enduring popularity with her contemporaries and the critics alike is sourced in her contradictory representations of the spectacular female body. Her heroine's recourse to bodily tactics aligns her with the figure of the actress, for as Lyn Pykett notes, Lady Audley:

> is staged as spectacle, just as written in the narrative the character is staging herself. This latter kind of performance is central to Braddon's novels, since, like Lucy Graham, virtually all of her heroines have something to hide, and are to that extent actresses.[7]

Indeed, all of Braddon's novels contain representations of the actress, from the appropriation of social roles by Lady Audley, Aurora Floyd's inheritance of the

---

[4]   See Bob Ashley, *The Study of Popular Fiction: A Source Book* (London: Pinter, 1989).

[5]   M.E. Braddon, *Lady Audley's Secret* (1862; Oxford: Oxford University Press, 1987), vol.1, Ch. 1 and Ch. 8.

[6]   See Katherine Mattacks, *Acting & Theatricality in the Novels of M.E. Braddon* (PhD thesis, Keele University, 2000).

[7]   Lyn Pykett, *The Improper Feminine: The Women's Sensation Novel and the New Woman Writing* (London: Routledge, 1992), p. 89.

taint of 'play-acting' from her mother,[8] through the domestic histrionics of Eleanor Vane to the professional actresses Flora Sandford and Kate Lurgan of *A Lost Eden* (1904) and *Our Adversary* (1909) respectively. The fluid and enigmatic figure of the actress is paradoxically the one element that remains consistently visible throughout Braddon's writing career. In an output that embraced the growth of realism, the emergence of the New Woman and the outbreak of the First World War, the repetition of a particular image or character denotes more than a subversion of social issues. What concerns me here is not so much the how the visual tactics of gesture, costume and illustration combine to construct the image of the actress, but rather why her figure proved so central to Braddon's literary imagination.

This chapter argues that Braddon's continued interest in bodily spectacle acts not only as an illustration of the heroine as the distressed product of patriarchal culture,[9] but more crucially as a metaphor for literary creativity. My introductory section will explore the direct connections between Braddon and the actress, outlining how the theatre and images of theatricality infiltrated both her professional and personal life. I will briefly explore her early career as an actress on the Provincial stage, how theatrical images of performance permeated popular cartoon images of Braddon as an early sensation writer and that her domestic arrangements with Maxwell encouraged a masquerade of respectability that destabilised the boundaries between the theatrical and social spheres. The main section will address the question of why the actress remains crucial to any reading of Braddon's fiction by analysing the literary representation of the actress Myra Brandreth in the little known novel *Hostages to Fortune* (1875) which was serialised in monthly instalments in Braddon's *Belgravia Magazine* from November 1874 to November 1875. It represents an ideal text with which to evaluate the notion of Braddon as a performer of sensational tactics, for it contains Braddon's first successful professional actress and appears at a pivotal time in her literary career.

Written at the height of her productivity, *Hostages to Fortune* reflects on Braddon's status as 'the Author of *Lady Audley's Secret*', allowing a retrospective look at the histrionic strategies that both made her a household name and structured the formulaic narrative her readers expected. The re-enactment of melodramatic codes established by *Lady Audley's Secret* that underpin her subsequent novels was artistically restrictive yet financially

---

[8]   M.E. Braddon, *Aurora Floyd* (1863; Oxford: Oxford University Press, 1996), p. 20.

[9]   Ann Cvetkovich, *Mixed Feelings: Feminism, Mass Culture, and Victorian Sensationalism* (New Brunswick: Rutgers University Press, 1992).

empowering. For as Jennifer Carnell and Graham Law admirably document, by 1875 Braddon and Maxwell, her publisher husband, were syndicating her novels to provincial newspapers world-wide. Braddon's astute business sense counters her representation as a mere victim of consumer demands, rather she emerges as a novelist whose works subvert the structures that govern them, 'using popular fictional paradigms in order to challenge specific social and sexual prejudices'.[10] In the case of *Hostages to Fortune*, Braddon challenges the strictures of genre governed by the readers' desires for another Lady Audley. By describing Myra Brandreth's descent into increasingly scandalous and melodramatic roles, the text illustrates the role that Braddon's actresses play in providing a pleasurable spectacle of a heroine's search for a mode of expression whilst dramatising the author's negotiation between popular demands and artistic integrity. Braddon's increasing use of the actress figure therefore functions as a site for the re-evaluation of methods of engaging and communicating with an audience, the success of which ensures financial security and iconographic status. However, unlike the majority of her fictional actresses and the narratives which frame them, Braddon's theatrical career was a failure.

Until the publication of Jennifer Carnell's book *The Literary Lives of Mary Elizabeth Braddon*,[11] relatively little was known of Braddon's stage career. This new research attaches a greater importance to Braddon's early time in the theatre, having revealed that she was on the stage from 1852 to 1860 and not the mere two years that Wolff cited.[12] To avoid bringing the family name into disrepute, Braddon adopted the stage name 'Mary Seyton',[13] although her

---

[10]   Jennifer Carnell and Graham Law, '"Our Author": Braddon in the Provincial Weeklies', in Tromp, Gilbert and Haynie, p. 158.

[11]   Jennifer Carnell, *The Literary Lives of Mary Elizabeth Braddon* (Hastings: Sensation Press, 2000). This work should prove to be a key text in Braddon studies as its detailed and original research throws new light upon Braddon's life and fiction. I am therefore heavily indebted to the contribution it makes to our knowledge of Braddon as a literary figure and actress. Carnell is also responsible for the current availability of rare Braddon texts such as *The Black Band: or, the Mysteries of Midnight* (Hastings: Sensation Press, 1998).

[12]   Wolff used obituaries and odd playbills to source Braddon's career as an actress, however these articles, written long after the fact were misleading as Carnell argues. Compare Wolff, p. 53 to ibid., p. 16.

[13]   No source for Braddon's stage name has been found, although it is interesting that Virginia Woolf uses the name as one of a list of possibles for the narrator of *A Room Of One's Own* (1929; London: Hogarth Press, 1935), p. 8. I am grateful to John Drew for this point and his comments on this chapter in general.

choice of profession was sanctioned by her mother who acted as her companion and chaperone. Like many of her heroines, including Lady Audley and Lucy St Albans, Braddon became an actress out of financial necessity following her family's separation from her dissolute father. Evidence of her entry into the profession remains obscure, however the descriptions of her fictional actresses record a slow process from participating in crowd scenes to speaking parts. Flora Sandford of *A Lost Eden*, generally taken as Braddon's most autobiographical novel in terms of its theatrical content at least, gains her training through watching her co-workers at The Phoenix Theatre on the Strand. After changing direction from art to theatre, Flora is aided by a keen sense of the pictorial and the knowledge that theatrical gestures were legible somatic signs that constituted the 'ABC of her art'.[14] Set back in the 1850s Flora's self-tuition via surveillance and experience is contemporaneous with Braddon's time in the theatre, indicating that her fictional creations were derived in part from real experience.

Braddon's actual stage career began in the Theatre Royal, Southampton and its varied repertoire provided an ideal introduction to the spectrum of plays Braddon was to perform and re-enact in her novels. The range included pantomimes, burlesques, melodramas and Shakespeare, typically three of which were performed each evening. The arduous task of learning new parts in such a number was moderated by the repetition of Shakespearean plays, accounting for Braddon's detailed references to the legitimate drama in her later fiction. After touring in Stamford, Glasgow and Aberdeen, Braddon returned to Southampton and made her London debut in March 1856 at the Surrey Theatre. Acting in Johnstone's *The Sailor of France* and *How We Live in the World of London*, Braddon played the female leads, achieving some critical acclaim as 'a debutante from the provinces, with a most attractive stage figure and a thorough command of all those airs and graces that make up the artless beauty of melodrama'.[15] Despite her naturalistic affect of somatic display, Braddon's career in London was short-lived, prompting a return to the provincial circuit, this time in the north of England.

Appearing with the Hull company at the Beverley Assembly Rooms, Braddon's career adopted a pattern that plagued her later years as an actress. For on 1 May Braddon as Seyton played Mrs Sternhold in Tom Taylor's *Still Waters Run Deep* (1855), a part that required a much older woman. Apart from brief appearances in pantomimes that befitted her young age, Braddon's

---

14   M.E. Braddon, *A Lost Eden* (1904; London: Hutchinson, [nd]), p. 95.
15   See Carnell, p. 38.

list of accomplishments seems dominated by older characters such as Gertrude
in *Hamlet* in September 1857, Widow Melnotte of *The Lady of Lyons* in
Brighton in January 1858, often appearing as the 'mother' to actresses who
were actually her contemporaries. Perhaps what the *Brighton Gazette* termed
as her 'pleasing and natural manner' and the 'statuesque dignity' noted by H.C.
Porter lead to Braddon being given more sedate parts that required less
pictorial gestures and acting.[16]   When given the option of bodily display,
Braddon appears to have enjoyed playing male characters more, having shown
a 'rather too evident inclination to appear in male habiliments' as Paris in
Romeo and Juliet and Francois in Bulwer-Lytton's *Richelieu* in 1858.[17]

Her later years as an actress were marked by a diversity of roles which saw
the emergence of a melodramatic style and tendency to repeat characters that
became the formulae for her sensation fiction. The Brighton Company's return
to their home town in mid-July of 1858 saw Braddon repeat the role of the
Widow Melnotte and appear in the lead of *Lallah Rookh* by Robert Brough.
Lallah Rookh was essentially a musical burlesque, a lower form of drama that
diverted the actor's style in the direction of histrionic expression. Braddon's
own style was gauged 'inanimate' by the *Brighton Guardian*, hinting at the
reasons for her failure as an actress, but the review also reveals attitudes to the
burlesque as a corrupting genre. In a similar vein to the criticism levelled at the
sensation novel, the reviewers saw the burlesque as a contaminating threat to
the legitimate modes of expression through its tendency to 'lure the actor from
the "legitimate" school and to corrupt his style'.[18]   Despite the article's bias
against the genre, its comment upon Braddon's shift from high to low cultural
iconography was to echo throughout her final years as an actress and into her
career as a writer.

Before leaving the stage in February of 1860, Braddon's acting portfolio
mainly comprised secondary female leads in both the legitimate drama of
Shakespeare and popular contemporary plays. Her proficiency was illustrated
by her repetition of the role of Mrs Sternhold at only an hour's notice, playing
to an audience at Brighton's Theatre Royal on 24 October, and her
appropriation of the Nurse's role in *Romeo and Juliet* in December of the same
year at equally short notice. However, despite the diversity of roles she
undertook and her ability to recall them if the need arose, Braddon's acting
career was inconsequential enough for her to be able to conceal it from the

---

[16]   Ibid., pp. 46–7.
[17]   *Era*, 2 May 1858, p. 11. Quoted in ibid., pp. 52–3.
[18]   Ibid., p. 56.

majority of her family and critics alike. The reasons for her failure cannot be discerned due to the subjective nature of the critics' comments on her performances, many of which hugely differ from each other even when reviewing the same play.[19] However, one contemporary account of Braddon's acting seems particularly relevant. Playing Nan in Charles Reade's *It's Never Too Late to Mend* in May 1859, Braddon's style appears to have shifted from naturalistic to histrionic, as *The Doncaster Chronicle* records:

> Her style is polished and only the result of considerable study, and with a tall and elegant figure her appearance is imposing. She, however, assumes a little too much of the majestic and 'Tragedy Queen' in her acting, which in comedy mars the effect extremely. By throwing off this and making her figure a little more flexible, she would place herself beyond criticism.[20]

An image of an actress well-versed in the study of the somatic sign and its melodramatic potential pervades this review. The disposition towards the scale of tragedy rather than that which the situation requires hints at a style that is carefully rehearsed for effect and one that is not based upon an intuitive response to situation. The lack of flexibility alludes to a rigid approach to performance designed to gain the maximum effect from the viewer, adding to the sense of role-play that belies any naturalism. Such an analysis of Braddon's acting style indicates the distinguishing features of her early sensation fiction, with melodramatic display, calculated effect and theatricality all deriving from her career as an actress. These stylistic elements can not only be sourced in her time in the theatrical profession, thematically linking Braddon the actress and Braddon the writer, but more crucially, seem to have constructed Braddon as a literary performer in the public consciousness.

The first issue of *The Mask*, (June 1868), contained a short article upon Braddon's novels to date, and defended her use of sensational effects as necessary for the 'sustaining of interest'. It positions Braddon alongside Victor Hugo and Dickens in terms of dramatic style and narratives of criminal deeds, arguing that her brand of sensation is not designed to glorify immorality unlike her French counterparts. The article also aligns Braddon's technique with a 'male power', the characteristics of which were a 'great penetration and

---

[19]   See for example the contrasting reviews of Braddon in *Still Waters Run Deep* of October 1859, quoted in ibid., p. 67.

[20]   Ibid., p. 64.

judgement of character in all the details she introduces' and a 'power of description' that communicates her thoughts directly to the reader.[21]

Given the article's attempt to defeminise the reputation of Braddon, the accompanying cartoon seems an unlikely choice. For it depicts Braddon as a scantily-clad circus girl leaping through hoops which are labelled with the titles of her novels. She has just competed the act of jumping through the *Birds of Prey* and *Charlotte's Inheritance* hoop, with the image of Maxwell on the right of the picture, holding another marked *Dead Sea Fruit*.[22] Maxwell retains the position of a ring-master, surveying Braddon's performance of sensation novels at a distance, leaving another figure to hold the hoops for her to jump through. Interestingly, this figure on the left, whilst remaining anonymous, refers to Braddon's less legitimate works written under the pseudonym of Babington White. On its clown costume are written the titles of *Circe* and the as yet undiscovered *Nobody's Child*, indicating her sideline as a less salubrious writer and plagiarist of French drama.[23] To add to the image of Braddon's versatility as an artist, she is pictured performing upon horseback with the horse bearing the banner of the *Belgravia Magazine*.

The cartoon depicts the analogy between Braddon and the performer, alluding to her oeuvre as a repetitive act of display for the benefit of an eager audience and the financial reward gained by Maxwell. Its visualisation of the phrase 'jumping through hoops to please' also alludes to a sense of artistic restraint involved in her performance of the texts, a feeling borne out by the fixed, expressionless gaze of Braddon's figure, transferring the attention from the imaginative elements of literary creativity to the demands placed upon the writer keen on poplar success. The analogy between Braddon's sensation fiction and other lower forms of entertainment, here the circus, enables the cartoonist to comment upon the genre's perceived low origins, the class of audience it attracted and its centralization of images of female performance.

---

[21]   See *The Mask* 1 (1868), p. 138.

[22]   The cartoon mistakes the order of Braddon's latest three novels, *Birds of Prey* did come first running from vol. I–III (November 1866–October 1867) of the *Belgravia Magazine*, but *Dead Sea Fruit* appeared next, from vols III–VI (August 1867–September 1868), appearing between *Birds of Prey* and its sequel *Charlotte's Inheritance* (vol. V–VII, April 1868–February 1869). Given the time of this cartoon, June 1868, *Dead Sea Fruit* was far nearer completion than *Charlotte's Inheritance*.

[23]   *Circe* appeared under Braddon's pseudonym Babington White in the *Belgravia Magazine* from vol. II–III (April 1867– September 1867). The text of *Nobody's Child* is, as far as I am aware, an undiscovered work.

Here the body on display is not that of a fictional sensation heroine but the literary sensation that was M.E. Braddon.

The display of the creator of *Lady Audley's Secret* continued to be of interest to the Victorian reading public over a decade later in the 1880s. In 1881, *Punch* printed a caricature of Braddon entitled 'Just as I am!'. Taking its title from Braddon's latest fictional offering to the public, the cartoon pictures Braddon as a stout, comical woman holding a mask labelled 'sensation' in her left hand.[24] The mask is similar to those used in ancient Greek tragedies, where the audience were given visible signs of a character's function and emotion via large masks which had exaggerated features. Here the mask features a female face in an expression of extreme terror, mid-scream and framed by long, luxurious hair. It is in direct contrast to the placid, almost smirking face of Braddon next to it, depicting Braddon's assumption of a different persona when writing under the guise of a sensation novelist. The juxtaposition of writer and subject matter again links Braddon to the performer, with *Punch's* cartoonist emphasising the distance between Braddon and her immoral subjects that early critics were so keen to connect. This disparity between the real Braddon and her fictional genre is underlined by the signifiers of creativity on the right of the picture, namely the pen Braddon holds in her other hand and the skull inkwell nearby. The black skull, potentially signifying Braddon's darker nature and the criminal deeds located in her novels, contrasts with her full, healthy face although they are both grinning. Potentially the skull also represents the metaphorical death of Braddon's creative freedom as she became increasingly confined to the sensational tactics of role-play, gesture and melodrama by an audience who envisaged her in the role of 'the author of *Lady Audley's Secret*', although it appears to have been a role that Braddon capitalised upon in the second half of her career.

Images of Braddon as an actress were not confined to her stage career or popular cartoons of her as both a sensation and a sensation writer. This sense of performance also extended to Braddon's personal life, as revelations surrounding her assumed marriage to Maxwell appeared just two months before the serialisation of *Hostages to Fortune* began. In the September of 1874, Richard Brinsley Knowles publicly exposed the domestic affairs of Maxwell on the occasion of the first Mrs Maxwell's death. As her brother-in-law, Knowles had previously defended the family through his public reminders that Braddon was fashioning herself as Mrs Mary Maxwell in the 1860s despite

---

[24]   See 'Punch's Fancy Portraits – No.21', *Punch, or the London Charivari*, 5 March 1881. Quoted in Wolff, in between pp. 402–403.

the fact the 'real' Mary Maxwell was still alive and separated from her husband. The first Mary Maxwell's death on 5 September 1874 was duly advertised in the major newspapers, causing acute embarrassment to Braddon and Maxwell who had been pretending to be husband and wife since the last scandal died down. Maxwell's attempts to privately refute what he termed as a 'maliciously-intended announcement' resulted in a response from Knowles that both undermined Braddon as 'Mrs Maxwell' and heavily critiqued Maxwell's treatment of the funeral arrangements.

Knowles' letter to the press reminded the public that Braddon had been acting a part she was not legally entitled to, and that Maxwell had tried in vain to cover up the reminders of his first wife to the extent of sending terse telegrams to her grieving family requesting a 'strictly private' funeral with no publicity.[25] Braddon's masquerade as Maxwell's wife links her with the social actresses in her fiction, providing her readership with a visible parallel between author and text that replicates the plot of her infamous sensation novels. For the author is implicitly connected to the image of the actress, accompanied, here quite literally, by the 'mad double' that Gilbert and Gubar famously argue haunts the margins of the female text as an externalisation of the guilt encountered on transgressing into the phallocentric world of literary creativity.[26]

This interplay between the actress, the madwoman and the writer is at its most effective in Braddon's novel *Hostages to Fortune* (1875), with the central figure of Myra Brandreth providing a problematic spectacle of pleasurable display as an actress and unnerving self-destruction during the assumption of melodramatic roles that precipitate a mental breakdown. Myra's search for an effective mode of expression provides the sensational spectacle of artifice that typified Braddon's style, however Myra's position as an actress-manager allows a close connection between writer and creation to develop. Here Braddon fictionalises not only her first successful professional actress, but more importantly one that mirrors her own contradictory situation. For Myra retains a level of artistic freedom in her control over which plays and characters are to be performed yet she is also limited by the audience's demands which dictate popular and financial success, echoing Braddon's own complaints that the 'mercantile sense' needed to market her novels often seemed irreconcilable

---

[25]   A printed copy of Knowles' letter is located in the Braddon Archive at Richmond Public Library, London.

[26]   Sandra M. Gilbert and Susan Gubar, *The Madwoman in the Attic: The Woman Writer & the Nineteenth-Century Literary Imagination* (New Haven and London: Yale University Press, 1984).

with the artistic demands of her mentor Bulwer-Lytton: 'I want to serve two masters. I want to be artistic & to please you. I want to be sensational, & to please Mudie's subscribers'.[27] Yet finances were no longer a driving concern for Braddon after 1863, as she declares to Bulwer-Lytton that upon the completion of *Eleanor's Victory* and *John Marchmont's Legacy* 'I shall have earned enough money to keep me & my mother for the rest of our lives'.[28] She makes no mention of Maxwell's ailing finances, a problem that might have motivated her to continue writing until their control of the syndication of her novels after 1873. However, even after she left the stage Braddon enjoyed the relative security of a sponsor, problematising the importance she places upon financial constraints.

The figure of Myra Brandreth seems to articulate these concerns from the outset of the novel. She runs the Frivolity Theatre which has been built specifically for her by the married Lord Earlswood. Despite Myra's introduction to the novel as a 'woman with a history' (p. 11),[29] she manages both the theatre and Lord Earlswood in a respectable fashion, avoiding his advances whilst retaining his patronage. Her attentions are directed elsewhere, mirroring Braddon's own dubious position at the beginning of her writing career. Braddon's stage departure had been facilitated by a wealthy patron, John Gilby whose support was withdrawn upon learning that she was living with Maxwell. Braddon's fictional counterpart retains her integrity by presenting Earlswood with a monthly rent cheque to avoid becoming part of his speculation whereas Braddon resisted Gilby only to live with a married man. However, despite Myra's comparative virtue, her figure comes to represent Braddon's duplicitous reaction to female empowerment through creative expression. For Myra represents an actress who has the rare ability to translate the playwright's meaning to the audience through the use of voice and gesture, whilst retaining ownership of the sphere in which she becomes the object of desire. Her ownership of the Frivolity Theatre presents the reader with a gynocentric world where the female leads and ballet girls master the art of expression, but this fragile world collapses with Myra's punitive breakdown at the end of the novel.

---

[27] Letter to Bulwer-Lytton, May 1863, quoted in Robert L. Wolff, 'Devoted Disciple: The Letters of Mary Elizabeth Braddon to Sir Edward Bulwer-Lytton, 1862–1873', *Harvard Library Bulletin* 12 (1974), pp. 5–35 and 129–61, (p. 14).

[28] Letter dated 13 April 1863, quoted in ibid., p. 12.

[29] All quotations are taken from M.E. Braddon, *Hostages to Fortune* (1875; London: Maxwell, stereotyped edition, [nd]).

Before restoring conventional moral codes through the nervous collapse of the socially transgressive Myra, Braddon's text focuses upon the nature and validity of dramatic training. Like Henry James' *The Tragic Muse* (1890), the novel uses the figure of the actress as a medium through which the author questions the creative process and its reception. Myra and her more famous counterpart Miriam Rooth both negotiate between the dramatic techniques of gesture that the audience expects and their own innovative modes of expression. Interestingly, both Braddon and James use the actress as part of a dual discourse on the arts, with James' artist Nick Dormer paralleling Braddon's writer Herman Westray. However it is the centralisation of the actress and the legitimate artist's rejection of what she represents that I wish to focus on here.

Unlike James' detailed narrative description of Miriam's technical training and evolution, Braddon's text introduces Myra as a professional actress/manager. She progressively embodies each of the technical requisites, those of costume/posture, voice and gesture, echoing Victorian reading discourses that relied upon the primacy of the bodily image. Her first appearance in Westray's adaptation of Augier's *La Cigue*, entitled *Hemlock*, casts her as the captured slave Helena, objectifying her in a submissive role. Myra's power of expression increases with her next performance, in Westray's comedy *Kismet*. Her translation of his written word into a visual reality is conveyed through a rehearsal scene in which she is able to negotiate her interpretation of the character with that of its creator. As an actress Myra translates the text into a bodily text which ensures its success with an audience trained in the reading of legible somatic signs. However, the symbiotic relationship between actress and writer sours when Myra hears of Westray's marriage to the devout Editha Morcombe.

The marriage signals a rejection of the actress and Westray's career fails without her theatrical inspiration, mirroring Braddon's failure to enlist popular acclaim with the more realistic novels of the 1870s. Westray falls into ruin and deserts Editha for a job as a war reporter on the continent, whilst Myra's suffering finds its outlet in private re-enactments of Shakespearean and melodramatic heroines. At this point in the narrative, Myra's medium shifts from the public to the private sphere, infiltrating the home with theatricality. She constructs two sensational scenes to discredit Editha, taking on the guise of the archetypal schemer Lady Macbeth. She stages a meeting between Editha and an infamous villain in order to make the returning Westray believe her infidelity. This first social scene relies upon Editha's belief that an extract from Westray's play manuscript is a love letter, and the sudden death of the villain at her feet in the second meeting highlights the novel's descent into sensational tactics. The truth is unveiled in an ironic role reversal, for Myra is symbolically unable to deny her part in the scene as she suffers a seizure similar to that of Lady Audley's inability to carry through her declaration of Robert Audley's monomania. This leaves Editha to express her innocence through the use of melodramatic gestures that signify virtue in distress, and although she and Westray are reunited her performance of despair signifies an infiltration of theatricality into the home. Myra's punishment, like Editha's reward, is mediated through theatrical signifiers.

Her transgression against Editha is problematised by the nature of the evidence against her. Westray produces her handkerchief, found in the telegram office from which the false message was sent to Editha to join Westray in Belgium, but the use of a handkerchief as evidence of guilt is reminiscent of Othello's assumption of Desdemona's infidelity via the same means.[30] However complicit in the scene, Myra's transgression is completed via theatrical means. Her final performance fuses the use of costume, voice and gesture in her re-enactment of a scandalous French play, the aptly titled *L'Ange Dechu* (*The Fallen Angel*). Containing melodramatic scenes and immoral subject matter that Myra had concealed from the censors, the play proves her ultimate artistic success. Her public, dramatic 'other' becomes fused with her private 'self' when she collapses on stage during the final suicide scene. Reduced to a liminal world of insensibility to parallel Lady Macbeth's sleeping scene, Myra ends the novel as a paralysed wreck incapable of expression. The demands of repeatedly performing a demanding, sensational role reduce her to a shadow that haunts the final pages of the narrative, just as Lady Audley's image rests in the reader's mind long after her burial in the private institution.

Myra's career is emblematic of Braddon's continued negotiation between high artistic ideals and popular sensation, with her repetition of sensational tactics synonymous with Lady Audley proving to be artistic autophagy. Like her creator, Myra's performative spectrum encompasses the roles of custom-written comedies and adaptations of French tragedy, indeed Braddon's appropriation of plots based upon French plays and novels infiltrated much of her fiction, from her version of *Madame Bovary* as *The Doctor's Wife* (1864) or the more direct plagiarism of Octave Feuillet's *Dahlia* in the novel 'by' Babington White entitled *Circe* (1867). Myra's career, like the early sensation novels, begins in the home with her introduction of charades to her father's household. Here, and indeed throughout the novel Myra is distinguished by her vocal prowess, with her 'elocutionary displays' (p. 77) signifying her alterity

---

[30]   See the final act of Shakespeare's *Othello* (1622)[1604], Act 5, Sc.2.

and potential for impropriety. After learning the impassioned speeches of Juliet, Queen Katherine, Constance, Lady Macbeth, Cordelia, Rosalind and Beatrice, her father informs her dramatic powers with the inflections and histrionic touches of her forerunners:

> He teaches Myra how the O'Neill used to pause here, or linger fondly there, or rise at such point to indignant passion. He remembers Sarah Siddons' awful whisper as that noble form brooded over the pit, appalling in its majestic beauty, while those dark intense eyes of hers seemed to pierce the gloom of the theatre, seeking the spirits of evil her solemn whisper invoked. (pp. 76–7)

It is the presence of these great actresses that legitimise Myra's decision to enter the dramatic sphere, undermining the assumed immorality of the theatrical profession. The 'awful whisper' of Siddons echoes throughout the text as Myra is not only surrounded by images of the great actresses decorating the walls of the Frivolity Theatre, but more crucially she re-enacts Siddons' most famous role of Lady Macbeth in the social sphere. Myra paradoxically utilises the histrionic gestures of Lady Macbeth to express her private anxieties, blurring the boundaries between theatrical and domestic spheres.

The conflation of theatre and home is sustained in the narrative of *Hostages to Fortune*, with the descriptions of the frivolity theatre resembling a large country house rather than a theatre: 'The straw-coloured quilted satin; the amethyst velvet cushions, chair covers, curtains; the medallion portraits' construct an image of domestic Victorian interior on a luxurious scale. Myra's dressing-room is significantly devoid of any velvet or gilding, the trademarks of theatrical decor, presenting a verisimilar reproduction of a boudoir with 'walls upholstered in sky-blue satin embroidered with butterflies and birds – birds and butterflies so artistic that they seemed living creatures' (p. 65). Indeed, Myra's management of the Frivolity is compared to Madame Vestris in terms of her propensity for realistic costume and scenery, with Myra's verisimilar style extending to her acting lessons, as she:

> had a knack of training her ballet ladies to look like real flesh and blood, and even patrician flesh and blood. She shows them how to group themselves, how to fall into natural attitudes…in all small details Madame Vestris herself could not have been more exacting. (pp. 174–5)

Madame Vestris' management of the Olympic Theatre in the 1830s was noted for her use of realistic properties, historically accurate costumes and the introduction of a box-set with a ceiling that framed the stage within the context of a domestic setting and the comparison with Myra both legitimises her control over the theatrical medium and aligns her taste with refinement rather than the extravagance of Earlswood's speculation. Myra's attention to detail even influences Herman Westray's choice of decor for his new home, arranging his hall and dining-room in the image and Pompeian style of the scenery in his first dramatic success *Hemlock* (p. 139). Here, theatricality is not just sourced in the home through Myra's initiation of private theatricals, but is actively replicating new stage innovations. This conflation of home and theatre was also a key feature of sensation fiction with its domestic setting for somatic displays contributing to the affective nature of the genre.

For the sensation novelists Braddon and Wilkie Collins the home itself was the source of artificiality that pervaded public life, an idea that directly countered the mid-Victorian ideology that envisioned the home as the refuge from the contaminating ills of public life. Ruskinian notions of the domestic sphere as the region in which woman is 'the centre of order, the balm of distress' are subverted,[31] replacing the composed image of femininity with one that typically displays signs of distress. This conflation of drama and narrative in order to contest definitions of psychological persona and narratology has been admirably documented by Jenny Bourne Taylor, who explores the notion of the performative self that creates both a sensation within Wilkie Collins' fiction and without in its readers.[32] This is the main function of Myra Brandreth's character, as she displays distress and enervates the reader through her transferral of stage management to the domestic sphere, creating another image of affliction in the form of Editha.

Myra's command of visual presentation is dissected into the three component parts of costume, voice and gesture, each represented by her stage performances of *Hemlock, Kismet* and *L'Ange Dechu* respectively. The progression from customised comedies to scandalous sensationalism ironically reverses the literary pattern Braddon's novels were to follow. However, Myra's display illustrates dramatically the dangers of imitation, particularly as the choice is one that offends English propriety in the same way that sensation

---

31   John Ruskin, *Sesames and Lilies* (London, 1865), quoted in J.M. Golby (ed.), *Culture and Society In Britain 1850–1890* (Oxford: Open University Press, 1986), p. 119.
32   Jenny Bourne Taylor, *In the Secret Theatre of Home: Wilkie Collins, Sensation Narrative and Nineteenth-Century Psychology* (London: Routledge, 1988).

fiction did. Both author and actress share not only initials but a popularity based upon performances of transgression.

The narrative display of Myra's artistic power begins with her representation of a captured slave Helena in the comedy *Hemlock*, suggested (or rather plagiarised) from Augier. Here the reader is repeatedly subjected to visual stimulus, ranging from detailed descriptions of the theatre's decor to Myra's penchant for realistic scenery and period costume. As the manageress she occupies the singular position of commissioning the dramatic text she is to embody, however her gestural method is ignored in favour of the visual spectacle of her demonised sexuality signified by her costume:

> Myra Brandreth stands before the cheval-glass, dressed for her part. The long, straight robe of white cashmere, like Vivien's sea-green samite, rather expresses than hides her slender figure; each round, slim arm is clasped with a golden serpent, and a golden serpent binds her chestnut hair. These are her sole ornaments. (p. 65)

Cast as Tennyson's Vivien from *Idylls of the King* (1859–72) who bewitches men through her display of female sexuality, Myra's costume, although expensive, retains a simplicity that contrasts with the splendour of a theatre resembling a 'parrot cage' with its 'perforated Moorish dome' (p. 71). The potential for impropriety is finely balanced between suggestion and actual representation, with Myra's objectification being undercut by her appearance after the play in a plain dark-green dress. This costume, 'made as neatly and as plainly as a riding habit' (p. 70) is the uniform of respectability and signals her underlying alterity from the traditional views of the actress and indeed her position as Lord Earlswood's supposed mistress.

Having depicted the fragility of assessing personality through dress alone, rather like the notion that a book cannot be judged by its cover, Braddon assesses the issue of authorial control through Myra's next performance. In an exchange between the actress and the writer, Myra encourages Westray to capitalise upon the success of his last play by repeating the same formula: 'Don't you think that having succeeded in one line it is hazardous to attempt another?' (p. 88). His answer forms the other creative impulse of the author, for 'remuneration is not the ultimate aim of art' (p. 89). The dual concerns of Braddon are reflected in their dialogue, where financial gain and artistic imagination are ultimately envisaged as irreconcilable, for Westray's next play *Kismet* is their last collaboration. Myra follows the demands of the audience in order to gain economic stability, whilst Herman eventually claims a place in the literary world. Both retain a sense of individuality, for even Myra's histrionic abilities are separated from standard portrayals of mimicry. Her modes of expression are juxtaposed with the hackneyed mimic Miss Belormond whom she befriends to throw her alterity into the spotlight. Miss Belormond's imitative qualities are the result of study, introducing Braddon's discourse upon the difficult incorporation of originality within the standard framework an audience expects:

> So she is handed over to one of the dramatic grinders, and is taught the same tones, and turns of the head and arm, and inflections and tremulosos, that have been ground into Miss Wilson and Miss Milson, Miss Stokes and Miss Noakes and due course turned out of hand a finished Juliet. (pp. 124–5)

This repetition of the ideal representation of archetypal character echoes Braddon's own restricted formulae for the sensation novel that simultaneously defines and constricts the writer. During the rehearsals for *Kismet*, Myra negotiates between the need for a legible somatic text and the desire for artistic licence. The play offers her scope for verisimilar emotions, as it centres upon the reunion of two lovers who portray the notion that first love is the strongest, finding its parallel in the narrative in her repressed desires for Westray, a mirroring that aids Editha's suspicions of his infidelity. Her performance blends the naturalistic and the histrionic to great effect:

> Every movement of the graceful form, every turn of the small, classic head, has been studied with deliberation. Yet at the last moment hidden fires flame out, and she electrifies her fellow-actors by some unpremeditated look or action which nothing less than genius could inspire. (p. 172)

Her paradoxical display of hidden emotions and desires resembles the sensation heroine's attraction for Braddon's readers, providing a dramatic externalisation of secrecy passions to excite the viewer of the somatic text. Myra's expression enables a mediated individuality to emerge from Westray's version of her character, balancing formulae with creativity to form the ideal text, which is simultaneously sensational and realistic.

However, after the performance of *Kismet* the melodramatic and the verisimilar diverge into the respective careers of Myra and Westray. The actress becomes increasingly aligned with the sensational and illustrates prophetically the dangers of dramatic repetition in both personal and professional terms. For Myra embodies the aims and contradictory status of the sensation writer as popular yet notorious. She transforms the third volume of the novel into an archetypal sensation novel and pictures the destructive result of a formulaic repetition her author was accused of. Myra popularises the text by transferring the site of histrionic gestures from theatre to home. Indeed, her first melodramatic expression occurs in the domestic sphere when she learns of Westray's marriage to Editha. Her rage and inner turmoil are projected onto the archetypal gesture for virtue in distress as:

> she falls on her knees and raises her clasped hands, and takes an awful oath – not to the God of Christians assuredly, who can hardly be supposed to receive such vows to Nemesis, or the three fatal spinsters who deal calamity to man. (p. 160)

But, although her somatic text reads as one in despair, the written text aligns Myra with the play *Macbeth*, re-casting her as Siddons' Lady Macbeth. This new role has been foreshadowed by her rendition of Lady Macbeth's sleeping scene in successful private theatricals and the combination of written and visual text re-casts Myra in the guise of the an archetypal schemer who enlists male help to further her ambition. She constructs a scene between Hamilton Lyndhurst, a gambler and profligate, and Editha, staging a drama of infidelity with Westray as the intended audience.

Theatre infiltrates the domestic sphere to create the spectacle expected from a novel by 'the author of *Lady Audley's Secret*', displaying sensational scenes to disrupt the realism represented by Westray. The disruptive influence of the dramatic text has already been foregrounded with Lyndhurst producing a fragment of a play manuscript under the guise of a love letter to test Editha's faith in Westray. When this fails, Myra stages an entire act in a domestic setting to precipitate divorce proceedings, constructing the oppositional images of femininity in her improper behaviour of framing the innocent Editha. The resulting drama however, explores the connection between the two versions of the female image through their common use of melodramatic gesture. For when Editha discerns Lyndhurst's intentions she attempts to commit suicide, depicting the proper image of distress to parallel Myra's promise of retribution:

> 'Then God help and pardon me in my extremity!' she cries, with clasped hands and eyes uplifted, and with one wild rush flies to the window which stands ajar, the long casement window opening on a frail balcony. (p. 288)

Here the gestural texts are similar, and the proper or improper codes of conduct are distinguished through religious terms, with Editha's Christian beliefs acting as the indicator of morality to counter Myra's secular homage to literary figures. Whereas Editha is brought back within the confines of the house by Lyndhurst who subsequently dies of a heart attack at her feet to provide a lasting image of domestic drama, Myra shifts the site of her melodramatic gestures back into the theatrical sphere. This re-instates the boundaries between home and theatre necessary to resolve the plot, but Braddon's narrative resists any complete containment of theatricality or naturalism in her presentation of Myra's final professional performance, just as her fiction remained poised upon the boundary between social realism and melodramatic excess.

Myra's appropriation of the histrionic leads her to a French drama *L'Ange Dechu*, though she merely translates the text rather than adapting it for English sensibilities as Westray did with his version of Augier's *La Cigue*. In fact, Myra deliberately aims to create a sensation, to 'make such an effect as Rachel in *Adrienne Lecouvreur*' (p. 348). Her insistence upon translation rather than adaptation reveals an insight into Braddon's own problems with rewriting French texts, for propriety dilutes emotion, forcing the action to supplant character:

> A purely English style of construction, in which probability is sacrificed to propriety. In order to escape the charge of immorality, we make our plots more improbable than the wildest fairy tale. Now your French dramatist starts with a motive strong enough to overturn a family or an empire, and builds his dramatic edifice upon a substantial foundation. (p. 349)

Here Braddon attempts to paradoxically source the sensational events that brought her genre into ridicule in the need for restraint and propriety. The restrictions upon the popular writer that create its contradictory nature are not generic but social. By using Myra to re-enact her social situation on stage Braddon fuses the real and the dramatic in an ideal play. Acting as an angel of corruption who poisons herself after failing to despatch her rival in love, she is able to blend public verisimilitude with private theatricality. She repeats 'every look, every tone, every phase of agony in the great poisoning scene at the end' (p. 348) to the delight of her audience who seek to imitate her costumes by wearing the 'Fallen Angel bonnet'. Her constant repetition of the character in public and on stage twice every Saturday and every week day reflects the consumer demand: 'That serpent-like grace, that poetic despair, that agonising death in the last scene – these things have thrilled to the heart of society, always ready for sensation' (p. 350). Like her creator, Myra becomes a popular success through the use of somatic tactics and images of improper behaviour; she learns that modes of excess bring fame, but it is of a transient nature.

The constant pressure of re-enactment proves disastrous to author and creation alike, as Myra suffers a real breakdown during a performance of the final suicide scene, symbolically committing suicide through repetition of the histrionic. Her mental collapse is marked by a failure to express herself, paralleling Braddon's own destruction of her creative impulses through the performance of the sensation text. Myra's finale provides the expected and proper ending for the demonised sensation heroine's descent into madness and clearly has implications for the author also. For it shows Braddon's increasing self-awareness of her own problematic status as a popular writer. In the figure of the actress Braddon depicts her history as professional player, her present as a social impersonator, and her future as a literary entertainer. The actress Myra Brandreth dramatises her creator's subjugation of high ideals in favour of melodramatic modes. Doomed to re-enact the formula of *Lady Audley's Secret*, Braddon performs the sensational displays that secured her financial status at the price of artistic integrity. Behind the histrionic figures that now marginalise her works lies an implicit critique of the readership which made it such a transient success.

Chapter 6

See What a Big Wide Bed it is!:
Mrs Henry Wood and the
Philistine Imagination

Deborah Wynne

In 1874 an anonymous reviewer in the *Spectator* contrasted the different styles of the two leading female sensation novelists, Mrs Henry Wood (the pen-name of Ellen Price Wood) and Mary Elizabeth Braddon. Both writers had gained success in the early 1860s, Wood with *East Lynne* (1860–61), a melodramatic tale of adultery and murder, and Braddon with *Lady Audley's Secret* (1861–62), based on the criminal career of the 'angelic' Lady Audley. Looking back over more than a decade of the regular appearance of their sensation novels, the reviewer argued that each had her own particular strengths. Braddon's speciality lay in her 'blue-eyed murderess manner', mixing 'golden-haired ghouls' with the risqué world of Bohemia. Wood's speciality, on the other hand, centred on an ability to transform the domestic into a 'gorgeous commonplace'. Chastising Braddon for recent attempts to encroach upon Wood's territory, the reviewer insists that:

> she cannot touch her veteran rival in gorgeous common-place, the nice adjustment of murder-and-morality, servants'-hall episodes, the romance of the apothecary and the greengrocer, funeral etiquette and expenses, the gossip of the back-shop, and pulpit eloquence. Miss Braddon lacks the direct, bold, entirely confident Philistinism of Mrs Henry Wood ... She resorts to no garnishes for her plain English fare, but serves up murders and mutton, suicides and rice-pudding, stolen cheques and thick bread-and-butter.[1]

Other reviewers drew attention to the 'commonplace' qualities of Wood's work. Eliza Lynn Linton in the *Saturday Review* argued that 'the heart of Mrs Wood's shortcomings [is] her pettiness. This is the secret of her vulgarity'.[2] Wood's

---

[1]   Review of *Lost for Love*, *Spectator*, 17 October 1874, p. 1303.
[2]   [Eliza Lynn Linton], Review of *Elster's Folly*, *Saturday Review*, 28 July 1866, p.

popularity was incomprehensible to Linton, who remarked, 'who can find pleasure or profit in her writings is to us a puzzle not to be easily solved'.[3] Yet thousands of readers enjoyed Wood's vulgar gorgeous commonplace and Linton's inability to understand its appeal indicates a rift within British middle-class culture between an educated minority and the less securely positioned bourgeoisie.

Wood's apparent 'pettiness' functioned as a crucial element of her philistine imagination; her novels promoted the trivial, offering spectacular accounts of clothes, trinkets, and furniture, catering to the fantasies of readers who dreamed of participating in the burgeoning consumer culture of mid-Victorian Britain. By bringing together the trivial and ordinary with the splendid and showy, Wood created a popular literary subgenre, part sensation novel, part domestic novel (a 'hybrid work', as one reviewer noted in 1866),[4] which offered middle-class readers a materialist alternative to the morally didactic novels of such writers as George Eliot, Anthony Trollope, and Elizabeth Gaskell. Despite frequent accusations of vulgarity and philistinism, Wood was seen by reviewers as the most wholesome of the female sensation writers, as the *Spectator*'s reference to her ordinary 'plain English fare' indicates. Although she lacked the flamboyant Bohemianism of Braddon, Wood's 'plain' literary ingredients are always seasoned with piquant dashes of crime and transgression, infusing the commonplace of domestic realism with an incongruous gorgeousness. Her domesticated sensationalism was inoffensive in the sense that it lacked the more obvious socially and sexually subversive qualities of the sensation novels of Braddon, Collins, and Reade. Yet her 'respectability' was balanced with a 'vulgarity' which foregrounded what many reviewers considered to be the less 'tasteful' aspects of domestic life: the best cure for a bad chest, the correct way to make a stew, the complexities of mourning etiquette, the detailing of diseased and dying bodies, and an unashamed delight in commodities. Her championship of this type of detail, a trait which G.H. Lewes condemned as 'detailism',[5] rendered her work ludicrous and distasteful to intellectual contemporaries, yet satisfied a large audience of 'philistine' readers.

I need to emphasize here that I do not use the term 'philistine' in a derogatory sense. Indeed, the Victorian female philistine, her writing practices and reading

---

117.

[3] Ibid., p. 117.

[4] Review of *St Martin's Eve*, *Saturday Review*, 31 March 1866, p. 387.

[5] G.H. Lewes, *The Principles of Success in Literature* (1891), quoted in Vineta Colby, *Yesterday's Woman: Domestic Realism in the English Novel* (Princeton: Princeton University Press, 1974), p. 22. See also Lyn Pykett, *The Improper Feminine: The Woman's Sensation Novel and the New Woman Writing* (London: Routledge, 1992), p. 119, for a discussion of Wood's preoccupation with the trivial.

habits, along with her enjoyment of the 'gorgeous commonplace', indicates a fascinating and relatively uncharted area of women's experience. The purpose of this chapter is to consider Wood's philistine imagination in the light of gender and class insecurities of the mid-Victorian period in order to show the ways in which Wood designed her fiction to console female readers trapped within the vagaries of capitalism and patriarchy. Wood never advocates rebellion or political agitation in her novels: her advice to female readers is to seek security through the acquisition of as much portable property as possible because (as her work quietly implies) men and the financial markets can be unreliable.

Women, Property and Philistinism

Wood's gorgeous and vulgar commonplace is most evident in her preoccupation with property. Inheritance and disinheritance form the basis of virtually all of her plots. Although the ownership of land features prominently in her work (as it does in many domestic novels of the period), the more portable property associated with women and domestic life, such as furniture, jewellery, and clothing, is especially important. Like Jane Austen before her, Wood is interested in plotting women's exclusion from landed property entailed along the male line. In her 1866 novel, *St. Martin's Eve*, Mrs Norris marries a wealthy man to become mistress of the imposing Norris Court; however, her enjoyment of the property is brief:

> almost ere her baby was born, Mr Norris died, and the whole thing seemed to pass from her as a dream. Had the child proved a boy, she had been well off, and Norris Court still been hers as a residence; proving a girl, it lapsed from her to the next male heir in the entail.[6]

Emphasizing, but not making any outright complaint against, the intangibility of landed property for women, Wood encourages her female readers to pursue more realizable ambitions in the area of portable property. Like the lower-middle-class Wemmick in Dickens' *Great Expectations*, portable property functions as a form of security in a society designed to protect and privilege property owners. Wood's fiction stresses the value of property for women. Borrowing from the language of advertising, she fosters fantasies of possession with lavish descriptions: carpets are 'rich and soft as moss', furniture is 'dainty', 'tasty', or 'good and handsome', clothes are made from gorgeous fabrics to extravagant designs, while bedrooms

---

[6]   Mrs Henry Wood, *St Martin's Eve* (1866; London: Macmillan, 1907), p. 24.

are rarely private spaces, but elaborate showcases of wealth and signifiers of reproductive status. The domestic world of Wood's fiction is always tinged with the gorgeousness of spectacle.

Writing in the wake of the Great Exhibition of 1851, 'the largest display of commodities that had ever been brought together under one roof',[7] Wood and her philistine values belong to the spirit of the Crystal Palace as a commodity display. An example of this tendency to isolate commodities and promote their desirability occurs in *Verner's Pride* (1863), a novel based on suspicions of bigamy with a subplot detailing polygamous Mormon marriages. When the bankrupt Lionel Verner returns to live with his mother, bringing with him his spendthrift wife, Sybilla, he finds the bedrooms have been reorganized. The married couple survey their room:

> Lionel's chief attention was riveted on the bed, an Arabian, handsomely carved, mahogany bed, with white muslin hangings, lined with pink, matching with the window-curtains. The hangings were new; but he felt certain that the bed was one hitherto used by his mother. (p. 491)[8]

Alongside this foregrounding of the bed's value as a desired commodity and piece of portable property, Wood makes the bed work in other ways. The rearrangement of the bedrooms reinforces Lionel and Sybilla's position as the 'legitimate and procreative couple', identified by Michel Foucault in his *History of Sexuality* as the focus of Victorian sexual discourses. Foucault argues that, 'A single locus of sexuality was acknowledged in social space as well as at the heart of every household, but it was a utilitarian and fertile one: the parents' bedroom'.[9] The younger married couple displace the elderly widow from her bed, as the new procreative centre of the home. Yet, the exoticism of Wood's handsome Arabian bed, with its carvings and hangings, and suggestive undertones of Eastern polygamous practices, indicates that the social space of Victorian sexuality was (in imagination at least) not necessarily a 'utilitarian' one. Indeed, Queen Victoria, a model of bourgeois respectability, shares Wood's philistine fascination with glamorous beds. In her journal entry of 15 April 1855, she describes the bedroom in which she has placed the visiting Empress of France, 'all crimson satin, with

---

[7]   Thomas Richards, *The Commodity Culture of Victorian England: Advertising and Spectacle, 1851–1914* (Stanford: Stanford University Press, 1990), p. 17.

[8]   All quotations are taken from Mrs Henry Wood, *Verner's Pride* (1863; London: Collins, [nd]).

[9]   Michel Foucault, *The History of Sexuality: An Introduction Volume 1*, trans. Richard Hurley (London: Penguin, 1978), p. 3.

very fine old pictures and very handsome furniture, and a really beautiful bed. The top, with feathers, is the same which used to be in the state bedroom ... with curtains of violet satin'.[10] The fact that the Queen shared the female philistine's fascination with furniture indicates that for many women (whatever their class position) arrangement of domestic space was crucial to their sense of well being.

Many women were unable to satisfy longings for elaborate furnishings, and Wood's descriptions of the gorgeous interiors of her characters' homes were designed to appeal to the fantasies of her female readers. Wood's 'bold, entirely confident Philistinism' points towards her discovery and exploitation of a niche in the market for popular middle-class fiction. Her best-sellers spoke to a largely (but not exclusively) female readership who had been recently initiated into the new consumer culture. Shopping (and window-shopping) became an increasingly important part of Victorian middle-class women's experience, as Rachel Bowlby has argued:

> The second half of the nineteenth century witnessed a radical shift in the concerns of industry from production to selling and from the satisfaction of stable needs to the invention of new desires ... From now on, it is not so much the object in itself – what function it serves – which matters, as its novelty or attractiveness, how it stands out from other objects on sale.[11]

Wood's championship of materialism offered an aid to newly unleashed fantasies of consumption. Her exciting mystery plots provided additional thrills in the form of 'peeping into wealthy homes and bedrooms',[12] fuelling fantasies of possession in a society where property ownership for women was atypical.

Wood's obsession with women's property needs to be read in the light of the agitation for reform of the marriage laws during the 1850s and 60s, culminating in the Married Women's Property Acts of 1870 and 1882. These allowed married women to possess their own property and to make a will. As Mary Lyndon Shanley has argued, the new laws were responses to the needs of the rising middle-class who owned portable property and could not afford the legal costs of

---

[10]   Queen Victoria, *Leaves from a Journal*, ed. Raymond Mortimer (London: White Publishing, 1977), p. 26.

[11]   Rachel Bowlby, *Just Looking: Consumer Culture in Dreiser, Gissing and Zola* (New York and London: Methuen, 1985), p. 2.

[12]   Sally Mitchell, Introduction to *East Lynne* (New Brunswick: Rutgers University Press, 1984), p. xii.

arranging a 'separate estate' for daughters who were about to marry.[13] The Act of 1882 allowed middle-class women to retain some independence.[14] Wood makes no attempt to plead for married women's rights to own property, avoiding controversy by making her fictional female property owners widows and spinsters. However, her focus upon the rise of the middle classes, the importance of moveable property, and the necessity for unmarried women to work rather than be dependent, highlights her awareness of the importance of women's property as a signifier of social identity and domestic power.

An interest in property and drives to possess consumer items have long been associated with the dreams of the bourgeoisie. Friedrich Engels, in his *The Origin of the Family, Private Property and the State* (1884), argued that the bourgeoisie of Protestant countries were 'Philistines', their culture focused upon monogamous marriage which manifests itself in the establishment of a home and the 'leaden boredom, known as domestic bliss'.[15] Wood is a representative of the desiring middle-class philistine, placing an inordinately high value on property and genteel domestic appearances. By the mid-nineteenth century an overt preoccupation with property and money was, as Engels makes clear, specifically associated with philistinism, and it is worth pausing here to consider the meanings which had accrued around this term during the Victorian period.

In the late 1860s the figure of the Philistine was put on the cultural map by Matthew Arnold in his *Culture and Anarchy* (1867–69). According to the OED, the term, originally associated with the warlike enemies of the Israelites, eventually came to signify any enemy, often those who were persistent in pursuit, such as bailiffs and literary critics. (Indeed, Wood uses the term in this sense in her 1876 novel *Edina*, when a stranger, presumed to be a bailiff, is described as a 'Philistine'.)[16] It was also applied to the drunken and debauched. In the early nineteenth-century, it referred to those who were not students at a university and thus became associated with lack of culture and education. Arnold extends this meaning when he labels the British middle class 'Philistines' because of their belief that 'our greatness and welfare are proved by our being very rich, and who most give their lives and thoughts to becoming rich'.[17] Their spiritual darkness is

---

[13]   Mary Lyndon Shanley, *Feminism, Marriage and the Law in Victorian England, 1850–1895* (London: I.B.Tauris, 1989), p. 16.

[14]   Ibid., p. 68.

[15]   Friedrich Engels, *The Origins of the Family, Private Property and the State* (1884; London: Lawrence and Wishart, 1972), p. 134.

[16]   Mrs Henry Wood, *Edina* (1876; London: Bentley and Son, 1896), p. 278.

[17]   Matthew Arnold, *Culture and Anarchy and other Writings* ed. Stefan Collini (Cambridge: Cambridge University Press, 1993), p. 167.

signalled by the fact they prefer 'business, chapels, tea-meetings' to the pursuit of 'sweetness and light'.[18] Once Arnold's definition gained currency, defenders of Philistinism were prominent in the periodical press. In 1883, *Good Words* complained, 'There are some among us, nowadays, who sneer at all common-sense as philistinic',[19] while the *Quarterly Review* at the end of the century argued that 'Philistinism, after all, stands for two great habits, decency and order'.[20]

Arnold's definition is too general to be useful as he lumps together the whole of the British middle class into the Philistine category. Yet a middle-class barrister or schoolteacher did not necessarily live by the same values as a clerk or shopkeeper. The *Spectator* reviewer, however, writing five years after the publication of *Culture and Anarchy*, narrowed down Arnold's broad definition of the philistine to mean someone interested in 'the romance of the apothecary and the greengrocer ... the gossip of the back-shop', in other words the most insecure and inadequately educated members of the bourgeoisie: the lower-middle class. Applying the term 'Philistine' to Wood in the wake of the debates surrounding Arnold's book, the reviewer singles her out as a representative philistine. Arnold identified industrialists as 'forming, for the most part, the stout main body of Philistinism',[21] and in this respect Wood was well qualified as the daughter of a successful glove manufacturer to champion in her fiction the tradesman and entrepreneur. She was also a representative philistine in her determination to make a decent income from her writing rather than entertain pretensions to artistic integrity, thus falling into Arnold's category of one who gave 'her life and thought to becoming rich'. The *Spectator* reviewer accurately measured her philistinism as bold and confident, a defiant stance against the enemies of 'business, chapels and tea-meetings'.

Arnold's perception of the philistine was of an enemy working within, the new middle class who had risen to affluence and political power during the early and mid-Victorian period. The fluidity of class identities was not only alarming to thinkers such as Arnold, who saw his cultural ideals under attack; there was also considerable anxiety experienced by the new middle classes themselves, particularly in relation to 'proper' social behaviour, and to reversals of fortune. Their identity crises were often represented in the popular periodical press as a comic feature of modern life. *Punch*, for example, satirized lower-middle-class

---

18   Ibid., p. 104.
19   *Good Words* (1883), p. 493. Cited in OED.
20   *Quarterly Review* (1899), p. 438. Cited in OED.
21   Arnold, p. 72.

insecurities about genteel appearances, on the one hand, and attempts to put a distance between themselves and the working class on the other. Discussing *Punch*'s comic representations of this class group, Roger B. Henkle has argued that it was within the home that 'the efforts for self-definition were taking place'.[22] Indeed, the social and cultural anxieties generated by new-found wealth and leisure among the middle classes were largely managed by women within the domestic field. As Nancy Armstrong has demonstrated, fiction played a crucial role in shaping new subjectivities, as the domestic novel aimed at the woman reader 'mapped out a new domain or discourse as it invested common forms of social behaviour with the emotional values of women'.[23]

Victorian women, however, cannot be categorized as a homogeneous group sharing a single domain or discourse. Apart from the more obvious differences between women of the three classes identified by Arnold,[24] middle-class women themselves formed part of a highly stratified group. Wood positioned herself as the friend and counsellor of those women who had recently risen or fallen in the social scale, inhabiting the marginal, insecure areas of bourgeois experience. While she was unsubtle in spiritual matters (Charlotte Riddell once wrote that Wood 'is simply a brute; she throws in bits of religion to slip her fodder down the public throat'),[25] she did cater for readers' emotional needs, social and domestic ambitions, and in some cases, a sense of nostalgia for lost status. Drawing upon the tradition of domestic fiction and the new sensationalism, Wood adapted the genres to the special needs of the petit-bourgeoisie, focusing on the central themes of the family and class transition. Her characters are always moving, in the sense that their class positions are unstable: an unexpected legacy moves families into a more genteel suburb and comfortable house, while an unexpected loss on the financial markets plunges families into shabby lodgings in cramped city streets, forcing wives and daughters out to work. Wood's concern is with the ways in which domestic arrangements are adjusted to changing circumstances. A full range of domestic detail is included: furniture styles, housework practices, the cost of living, the proper role of the mistress of the house, the necessity for women to earn money while still retaining their domestic identities, the upbringing of

---

[22]   Roger B. Henkle, *Comedy and Culture: England, 1820–1900* (Princeton: Princeton University Press, 1980), p. 221.

[23]   Nancy Armstrong, *Desire and Domestic Fiction: A Political History of the Novel* (Oxford: Oxford University Press, 1987), p. 29.

[24]   Arnold divides the British people into Barbarians (aristocrats), Philistines (middle classes) and the Populace (working class).

[25]   Quoted in Malcolm Elwin, *Victorian Wallflowers* (London: Jonathan Cape, 1934), p. 241.

children, and the limits and pleasures of status display. To avoid producing novels which read like advice manuals, Wood adds plenty of gossip, innuendo and mild vulgarity, comic episodes, sentiment, pathetic deathbed scenes, mysterious events, and her standard criminal plots. In labelling Wood a 'bold confident Philistine' (who, by implication, was writing for philistines), the reviewer was positioning her as a popular novelist who attempted to reassure readers caught up in the matrix of shifting class identities.

Wood's fiction was successful on a number of different levels. While readers valued entertaining fiction (and Wood's compelling mystery plots and comic scenes catered to this taste), they also desired certain (usually private) areas of domestic life to be revealed and openly discussed. Fiction offered an easy way of understanding the complex codes surrounding the different conventions of genteel life. Wood offered valuable information in her fiction on the suitable arrangement of domestic space, the genteel codes of bedroom etiquette, receiving visitors, and the correct costumes and proper display of jewellery for various social occasions.

Wood's philistine imagination also had the advantage of boldly taking the reader into those private domestic spaces (often the bedroom, the laundry, and the back kitchen) where other novelists feared to tread. She precisely measures the cost of living in various circumstances, and advises her readers to be stoical when faced with reversals of fortune. In *The Master of Greylands* (1873), when the wealthy banker's daughter, Mary Ursula Castlemaine, is faced with a reduction in her fortune she says, 'My hundred and fifty pounds a-year will seem a sufficient income to me when I have brought my mind down from its heights'.[26] This advocacy of flexibility is a characteristic of Wood's approach to her career as a writer. During her apprentice years in the 1850s, she adopted a flexible approach to genre and style, always willing to adapt to the demands of the market.

Wood and the Literary Marketplace

Wood developed her generic and narrative specialisms after an apprenticeship of nearly a decade as an unpaid contributor to W. Harrison Ainsworth's *The New Monthly Magazine*. Between 1851 and 1860 (when *East Lynne* began serialization), her numerous short stories and sketches appeared regularly in the magazine. After *East Lynne*'s phenomenal success she published thirty-five more novels, along with hundreds of short stories and numerous non-fiction magazine

---

[26]   Mrs Henry Wood, *The Master of Greylands* (1873; London: Bentley and Son, 1890), p. 119.

features. From 1867 to her death in 1887, she also owned and edited *The Argosy*, a popular magazine aimed at the 'Philistine', 'genteel, middle-class lady public of low to fair educational standard'.[27] According to Sally Mitchell, Wood has been identified as 'the most truly representative woman novelist of the mid-Victorian era'.[28] This needs to be qualified, however, for although she was prompted to write because of the failure of her husband's income, (the reason for most middle-class women's entry into a professional writing career), Wood's financial success was unusual. As Nigel Cross has shown in his discussion of the nineteenth-century literary 'female drudge', many women who became professional writers frequently failed to make an adequate income, as their petitions to the Literary Fund signify.[29] While Wood's enormously successful career as a popular author does not accurately reflect the conditions of literary production for most women writers, it does, however, reveal how an enterprising female author could work the system.

Wood disregarded the attacks upon her qualities as a writer as she unashamedly provided a large audience with 'philistine' fiction.[30] While she lacked the talent and cleverness of her rival Braddon (who felt uneasy at her inability to enter into respectable literary culture),[31] Wood possessed a quality which helped her in a competitive marketplace, the ability to adapt genres to meet market demands. Wood makes the bold move of putting the rice pudding with the suicide (to borrow the *Spectator*'s terminology), the domestic details with forgery and imposture. This strategy was carefully thought out, for she pursued her career as cannily as any of the entrepreneurs depicted as the heroes of her novels. During her apprentice years she experimented with various voices and styles, sorting through and sifting many of the popular genres of the day into the brand of sensational/sentimental/comic/melodramatic/domestic literature, which later became her trademark 'gorgeous commonplace'.

Her ability to adjust her style to the changing demands of the literary marketplace owed something to the training she received in preparation for proper genteel wifehood, which largely focused on learning the skills needed to attract a suitable husband. As Gill Frith has suggested in a discussion of femininity as a

---

[27]   Alvar Ellegard, *The Readership of the Victorian Periodical Press in Mid-Victorian Britain* (Gothenburg: Goteborg Universitets Arsskrift, 1957), p. 32.

[28]   Mitchell, p. viii. See also Elwin, p .232.

[29]   Nigel Cross, *The Common Writer: Life in Nineteenth-Century Grub Street* (Cambridge: Cambridge University Press, 1985), pp. 164–203.

[30]   See Elwin, p. 244.

[31]   See Robert Lee Wolff, 'Devoted Disciple: The Letters of M.E. Braddon to Sir Edward Bulwer-Lytton, 1862–73', *Harvard Library Bulletin* 22 (1974), pp. 5–35 and pp. 129–61.

'chameleon' quality, Victorian women were guided by means of conduct books and magazines to be always 'flexible' and adaptable, to develop a 'capacity to alternate roles, shift subject positions and identifications'.[32] This education aided Wood's ability to please different audiences. Without compromising her feminine respectability, she entered into and succeeded within the literary marketplace as a highly paid professional writer. Altering her writing styles to suit other people's tastes, flowing from one literary fashion to the next, trying out another style if the previous one did not suit, Wood found the feminine training in flexibility could work to her advantage. Similarly, her 'philistine' upbringing taught her to despise waste, and once she had made a name with *East Lynne*, she thriftily stitched her short stories together (for which she had never been paid) into full length novels, so that they would not be wasted.[33] It did not matter if some of the stitches showed in places, and that the threads of the plots were occasionally entangled: the important point was that she was not wasting her labour and was pleasing her reader.

Wood's anonymous entry into the literary marketplace was in the male-orientated pages of the *New Monthly Magazine*, where fiction played only a minor role. Apart from occasional serial novels and short stories, the main focus was politics and social comment which were presented in substantial articles intended to be informative rather than entertaining. After finding her sentimental tales marginalized in the magazine, Wood decided to advance her career by writing as a man, borrowing the journal's jaunty masculine bias. In 1854, during the Crimean War, she adopted the persona of Ensign Thomas Pepper, a young soldier sent out with his regiment to the front. His letters home appeared in three instalments under the title, 'Stray Letters from the East' in July, September, and December 1854. According to Wood's biographer, the Ensign Pepper letters were taken by many readers to be authentic.[34] Reading this series, it is hard to find traces of the future author of *East Lynne* as she convincingly captures the comic bravado of the young man away from home. The most significant feature of the series is the way it encapsulates in miniature Wood's flexible writing practices in terms of awareness of the demands of different audiences.

Pepper's letters to his doting aunt, his guardian, his girlfriend, and his best friend have unaccountably come into the hands of the hostile dissenting minister, the Rev Jonadab Straithorn, who asks the editor to publish them as a warning to

---

[32]   Gill Frith, 'Transforming Features: Double Vision and the Female Reader', *New Formations* 15 (1991), pp. 67–81 (p. 67).

[33]   Novels developed from short stories include *Mildred Arkell* (1865), *Elster's Folly* (1866) and *Red Court Farm* (1868).

[34]   Charles Wood, *Memorials of Mrs Henry Wood* (London: Bentley, 1894), p. 166.

the young against the evils of hypocrisy. To his aunt, Ensign Pepper adopts a
virtuous tone, pleading for a hamper full of jam and sweets, explaining he needs
the latter because 'as you forbid me to learn smoking ... I must suck something
instead, so please let me have plenty'.[35] The next letter to Gus Sparkinson, his
friend, outlines the extravagance in Malta which leaves him penniless, 'smoking
and drinking took away a lot, and billiards and other things a lot more ... and the
drink's so cheap a fellow may get sewn up for threepence'.[36] To his guardian,
Pepper adopts an adult sobriety, outlining government mismanagement and the
worsening political situation, ending with a reassurance that he is 'very steady, as
you enjoined'.[37] To his girlfriend, Fanny, Pepper adopts the literary language of
heroic endeavour: 'We are in the midst of gore and glory, and it is uncertain
whether I may ever see you again'.[38] He claims he has been singled out (along
with 'our other bravest officers') for a secret mission.[39] The final letter from
Scutari is addressed to his guardian and presents a dramatic account of the
'horrors of the battlefield' and the criminal mismanagement of the Admiralty in
allowing wounded troops to die because of chronic shortages of equipment and
medical personnel.[40]

With the 'Ensign Pepper' series, Wood imitates the male discourse of the *New
Monthly Magazine* of the 1850s at a time when the issues of masculinity and the
moral and managerial imperatives of the British Army were foregrounded by the
Crimean War. In the late 1850s, however, Wood sensed a change emerging in the
literary culture, and her new stories returned to a focus on female experience in
the middle-class home. When Wilkie Collins' *The Woman in White* began
serialization in Dickens' magazine, *All The Year Round* in 1859, Wood swiftly
adapted her style along the lines of the emerging sensation genre. The publication
of the sensational *East Lynne* (originally serialized in the *New Monthly Magazine*)
identified Wood as a new sensation novelist.[41]

Wood is today remembered for *East Lynne*, yet this is not typical of her
subsequent novels. The foregrounding of aristocrats, such as Lady Isabel Vane
(the repentant adulteress) and Sir Francis Levison (the dandified villain), was

---

35   'Stray Letters from the East', *New Monthly Magazine* 101 (1854), p. 345.
36   Ibid., p. 348.
37   Ibid., p. 354.
38   'Stray Letters from the East', *New Monthly Magazine* 102 (1854), p. 50.
39   Ibid., p. 52.
40   Ibid., p. 467.
41   A valuable introduction to the sensation novel can be found in Winifred Hughes,
The Maniac in the Cellar: Sensation Novels of the 1860s (Princeton: Princeton University Press,
1980).

dropped by Wood in later novels in favour of an exclusively middle-class focus. This use of titled protagonists was borrowed from Collins' novel, with its sensational plot centred on Lady Glyde, Sir Percival, and Count Fosco. *East Lynne*'s bourgeois characters, Archibald Carlyle and Barbara Hare, were Wood's real concern, and her later fiction details the trials and triumphs of the 'working' (as opposed to leisured) middle classes. Wood realized that in order to succeed in the new genre, she needed to offer her own particular product. While Ouida (whose early novels were serialized alongside Wood's in the *New Monthly*) offered extravagant pictures of high society, and Braddon presented sensational events in Bohemia, Wood desired her own niche and found it in representing (in all senses of the word) the bourgeoisie, transforming images of their domestic world into a sensational and gorgeous commonplace. Once she had experimented with various literary genres and voices, Wood's novels from the mid-1860s onwards were all written to this formula.

Class, Femininity and Furniture in Wood's fiction

Wood's literary formula depends upon the interplay between property ownership and crime. Forgery, murder, imposture, smuggling, and bigamy are all roads towards gaining property, offering characters temptations, which Wood understands but does not openly condone. Her sympathies are exclusively directed towards the middle classes, particularly those whose social position is in decline. In *Mrs Halliburton's Troubles* (1862), the heroine, left penniless when her husband dies, is forced to work as a glove-maker in order to support herself and her children. Wood engages the reader's sympathy by deflecting attention away from the more publicized evils of working-class poverty to focus on the plight of the insecure bourgeoisie, 'Can you realise these troubles of Mrs Halliburton's? Not, I think, as she realised them. We pity the trials of the poor; but, believe me, they are as nothing compared to the bitter lot of reduced gentlepeople' (p. 129).[42] Wood endorses the desire on the part of the middle classes to rise in the world, but condemns working-class ambitions for advancement. In her novels class mobility had its 'proper' limits: while she condemned those who put obstacles in the way of tradespeople and manufacturers rising socially, she is contemptuous of working-class people who entertain social ambitions. Wood sympathized with her audience of 'philistine' middle-class

---

[42]   All quotations are taken from Mrs Henry Wood, *Mrs Halliburton's Troubles* (1862; London: Walter Scott Publishing, [nd]).

readers, representing their anxieties to distance themselves from the working class, along with their desires for alignment with the more secure propertied classes.

Property, in Wood's novels, is significant for its way of precisely pinpointing a character's respectability and social status. For her female characters furniture in particular functions as a major indicator of class position: owning furniture bestows power and influence, while its loss can plunge women into the abyss of lost caste. Unsurprisingly, furniture and other domestic property are fetishized as powerful objects able to transform lives. Mrs Halliburton, unable to pay her rent, begs her landlord not to take her furniture: 'We have no resource, no home; we shall have to lie in the streets, or die. Oh, sir, do not take it' (p. 96). As the sale will cover the arrears of rent, Mrs Halliburton will not be evicted from the house, yet without her furniture she has no 'home', and *its* loss (rather than eviction) is the equivalent to her of destitution. In *Edina* the worst punishment Wood can inflict upon an improvident and idle family is the destruction of their (uninsured) furniture in a fire, a loss which finally brings the family to its senses. The same novel also shows how the possession of furniture has considerable powers of consolation. When the genteel Daisy, wife of an impoverished doctor, faces the daunting prospect of life in a working-class back street, 'It seemed to her that in coming to dwell here, she must lose caste for ever'. Yet when she enters her new drawing-room she cheers up on seeing 'furniture that was good and handsome'.[43] The possession of 'good' furniture reassures its owner that she belongs to the genteel classes, offering consolation during periods of instability. Shopping for furniture is for Wood one of the main pleasures anticipated by engaged couples. In *The Master of Greylands*, when a couple contemplate buying the furniture for their new home, they experience the transcendence of a 'bliss unutterable'.[44] Owning property not only gives a woman a sense of social empowerment, but also allows her to indulge in the pleasures of showing off, as Lady Verner does with her carriage, 'the most fascinating carriage in all Deerham, with its blue and silver appointments, [and] its fine horses' (p. 273).

Yet, despite the pleasures of property ownership, the responsibility of such possession is not to be taken lightly. Although many women, particularly married women, were excluded from property ownership, the laws surrounding paraphernalia, such as clothes, ornaments, and personal gifts of furniture or household objects, allowed married women some rights of possession.[45] Wood

---

[43]   *Edina*, p. 324.

[44]   *Master of Greylands*, p. 50.

[45]   See Lee Holcombe, *Wives and Property: Reform of the Married Women's Property Law in Nineteenth-Century England* (Toronto: University of Toronto Press, 1983), pp. 23, 41. See also Anthony Trollope's fictional account of these laws in *The Eustace Diamonds* (1873).

states that the difficulties of distributing fairly even a small amount of property are awesome, and that all women should think carefully before bequeathing their paraphernalia. In *Mrs Halliburton's Troubles,* when the impoverished widow, Mrs Tait, tries to give her furniture to a daughter who has offered her a home, her son-in-law is reproachful and insists on buying it from her. Wood solemnly adds, 'Mr Halliburton in this was firm. And he was right. Had Mrs Tait made him a deed of gift of it, her younger children might have risen up later, and reproached Mr Halliburton with taking their property' (p. 28). Women, in Wood's novels, are forced into awareness of their duties as property owners and the agonizing problems of making a scrupulously fair will.

Along with the duties and anxieties of furniture ownership, Wood can sometimes use furniture for sensational purposes. The handsome Arabian bed, which 'rivets' Lionel's attention in *Verner's Pride* plays a significant role in the bigamy plot. When Lionel asks the servant, Catherine, if he and his wife, Sybilla, are to have his mother's bed, Catherine replies:

> 'To think that you should have found it out, Mr Lionel!' echoed Catherine, with a broad smile. 'Well, sir, it is, and that's the truth. We have been making all sorts of changes. Miss Lucy's bed has gone in for my lady, and my lady's has been brought in here. See what a big wide bed it is!'she exclaimed, putting her arm on the counterpane. 'Miss Lucy's was a good-sized bed, but my lady thought it would be hardly big enough for two; so she said hers should come in here.' (p. 492)

The size of the Arabian bed ('big enough for two') signifies Lionel and Sybilla's status as the 'legitimate and procreative couple', yet the reader knows that their marriage is an unhappy one, and that Lionel and Lucy love each other. Wood carefully states that the married couple now have the big wide bed, but this juggling of beds also serves to remind readers that Lionel and Lucy now live under one roof, and the confusion of beds allows Wood to offer hints of illicit passion. Wood also foregrounds sleeping arrangements elsewhere in *Verner's Pride* when Lionel 'feels a pricking of conscience' when he realizes that some families living on his estate all sleep in one room:

> He could not help comparing the contrast: Verner's Pride, with its spacious bedrooms, one of which was not deemed sufficient for the purposes of retirement, where two people slept together, but a dressing-closet must be attached; and those poor Hooks, with their growing-up sons and daughters, and but one room, save the kitchen, in their whole dwelling! (pp.322–3)

When the Hooks' eldest daughter becomes pregnant, Wood blames this upon her family's sleeping arrangements, where nine people sleep in one room with 'no curtains, no screen, no anything' (p. 382). Wood darkly hints here that incest may result from a lack of beds and bedrooms, reminding readers of the horrors of poverty which many feared as a real possibility.

In Wood's novels beds function as the centre of the genteel home: they can be objects of 'state', luxurious commodities and valuable property, an arena for procreation, where women give birth, or the focal point of illness and death. This multiplicity of functions is emphasised in *Lord Oakburn's Daughters* (1864), a novel in which the elderly Lord Oakburn marries a young governess, prompting his eldest daughter Jane (who has hitherto acted the role of devoted surrogate wife) to leave home. When she visits her dying father, she expects to find him centre stage in the majestic bed she had presented him with. However, the bed's symbolic function as emblem of her father's power within the home is undermined when Lady Oakburn takes possession of it as the theatre for the birth of a son and heir. On seeing 'Miss Lethwaite' in her father's bed (Jane persists in using her step-mother's maiden name), she considers this the ultimate rejection, 'On the state bed which Jane Chesney had lovingly chosen for her father ... lay Eliza, Countess of Oakburn, an infant cradled at her side', Wood adding 'Jane resented the news in her heart'.[46] The bed is a daughter's gift, a scene of a father's death and a step-mother's triumph, an object of 'state, and a focus for the family's power battles. Wood's novels indicate that furniture and other domestic objects are not always trivial or commonplace features of women's lives.

Other Victorian novelists refer to furniture in their fiction. Dickens frequently transforms ordinary household objects into grotesque extensions of his characters, or makes them a source of comedy, as in *Martin Chuzzlewit* when Charity Pecksniff longingly contemplates a 'full-sized four-post bed' in anticipation of her marriage to Mr Moddle. When Moddle jilts her he hopes 'the Furniture [may] make some amends'.[47] The reader, however, is meant to find humorous Charity left with the big bed and no husband to put into it. In George Eliot's work, furniture is usually bound up with a moral lesson as she represents an overt preoccupation with it as either the result of ignorant narrowness or self-centred materialism. In *Middlemarch*, for example, Rosamond Vincy's overriding desire for a handsome establishment and Lydgate's fatal 'spots of commonness' in

---

[46]   Mrs Henry Wood, *Lord Oakburn's Daughters* (1864; London: Bentley and Son, 1897), pp. 271, 276.

[47]   Charles Dickens, *Martin Chuzzlewit* ed. P.N. Furbank (1843–4; London: Penguin, 1968), pp. 773, 915.

relation to 'ugly crockery' offer warnings against placing too high a value on material goods and splendid appearances.[48]

Surprisingly, Wood's rival in sensation fiction, Mary Braddon, shares Eliot's view of furniture-love as a sign of moral degeneracy. In *Lady Audley's Secret*, when Lady Audley's criminal career is brought to a close, her 'mercenary soul hankered greedily after the costly and beautiful things of which she had been mistress', Braddon reminding us 'how much she had perilled for a fine house and gorgeous furniture'. Lady Audley's punishment for materialism is incarceration in a madhouse furnished with 'the faded splendour of shabby velvet, and tarnished gilding' with 'a bed so wonderously made, as to appear to have no opening whatever in its coverings, unless the counterpane had been split asunder with a penknife'.[49] Her uninviting room and bed appear a suitable punishment for a murderess and impostor whose motives have been purely mercenary.

In Wood's *East Lynne*, Lady Isabel's punishment for adultery also takes the form of furniture deprivation, although readers are encouraged to feel sympathy for her heroine's loss. When she returns to East Lynne disguised as the governess, Isabel is shown upstairs and passing the bedroom she formerly inhabited as Mr Carlyle's wife, she experiences a 'yearning' for lost furniture and ornaments:

> The doors of her old bed and dressing-rooms stood open, and she glanced in with a yearning look. No, never more, never more could they be hers ...The fire threw its blaze on the furniture: there were the little ornaments on the large dressing-table, as they used to be in her time, and the cut glass of the crystal essence bottles glittered in the firelight ... No: these rooms were not for her now.[50]

Although mercenary motives are occasionally punished in Wood's fiction, a suitable appreciation of good furniture is usually a sign of worth in a character. Wood's inability to equate a desire for furniture with a moral flaw is the result of her belief in the possession of furniture as a guarantor of self-respect for women. To her critics, educated and intellectual, Wood's values appeared crassly philistine. Yet she offered reassurance to those women who struggled to attain (or retain) a social identity within the uncertainties of a capitalist economy, where

---

[48]   George Eliot, *Middlemarch* ed. W.J. Harvey (1871–2; London: Penguin, 1988), p. 387.

[49]   Mary Elizabeth Braddon, *Lady Audley's Secret* ed. David Skilton (1861–2; Oxford: Oxford University Press, 1991), pp. 383, 374, 388–9.

[50]   Mrs Henry Wood, *East Lynne* ed. Stevie Davies (1870–71; London: Dent, 1984), p. 409.

men held most of the property and virtually all of the power. Her readers were acutely aware of how easily money and security could be swept away by fluctuations in the markets, marriage, unemployment, accidents, or deaths. The solidity and visible worth of furniture offered women a sense of reassurance, a symbol of one's social existence in an alienating world.

Wood's championship of the 'philistine' value of materialism forms an important component of her fiction. Her preoccupation with the gorgeous commonplace tapped into the dreams and aspirations which industrial capitalism had created around commodities. Middle-class consumers were being taught to abandon their traditional culture of thrift in order to find new ambitions in the ownership of consumer items. Wood, aligned with manufacturers by birth and inclination, draws upon the glamour of advertising to furnish her fictional world with desirable commodities. Her novels appeared at a time when middle-class women gained greater spending power and increased opportunities to control the appearance of the domestic environment. Shopping for the home became an important activity for the middle-class married women, an indicator of her taste and her husband's status. As Adrian Forty has argued in *Objects of Desire*, before the 1860s men tended to be responsible for selecting household furnishings, while later in the century women were expected to choose and manage all aspects of interior decor.[51] The 1860s was also a period when increasing numbers of books on home furnishing were published indicating a growing interest on the part of middle-class consumers to create homes as showcases for the desirable commodities they possessed. Wood caters to this interest on the part of bourgeois women, newly empowered as purchasers of household commodities, to be informed about domestic taste. While a preoccupation with domestic details characterizes her commonplaceness, the ability to render the ordinary gorgeous aligns her with the advertising industry, which fed the idea that the home was 'a place of unreality, a place where illusions flourished'.[52]

While Victorian reviewers of Wood's novels recognized her tendency to make the domestic spectacular (one remarked that the 'really wonderful thing' about Wood's fiction 'is the extraordinary superfluity of minute and entirely unimportant detail'),[53] they failed to account for its significance in terms of her popularity with readers. Yet in a society where the lower middle classes were experiencing increasing prosperity and women were finding new powers within the home,

---

[51]   Adrian Forty, *Objects of Desire: Design and Society since 1750* (1986; London: Thames and Hudson, 1992), p. 105.

[52]   Ibid., p. 101.

[53]   Review of *Mildred Arkell*, *Saturday Review*, 17 June 1865, p. 734.

Wood's language of the gorgeous commonplace was finely attuned to the needs of the female philistine. She promoted the sense of security and self-respect, which came from the ownership of property, while her writing transformed the most ordinary pieces of household furniture into gorgeous objects. Thomas Richards has argued that during the mid-Victorian period, 'material culture became a drama that played to packed houses' as a new emphasis on shopping brought the excitement of the commodity into the shops of provincial cities.[54] Wood harnessed this 'drama' for her own purposes, bringing into her novels displays of objects which allowed the female readers of her sensational mystery plots the additional pleasures of window-shopping.

---

[54]   Richards, p. 55.

Chapter 7

'Weird Fascination': The Response to Victorian Women's Ghost Stories

Clare Stewart

Whether instinctive or conscious, awareness of a certain bond drew Victorian women to the supernatural genre at a time when all women's writing was suspect: 'both ghosts and women were subject to the same kind of criticism and liable to be met with the same dismissive hostility in their attempts to gain recognition'.[1] The way in which nineteenth-century ghost stories were written, and received by critics and a wider reading public, was intimately bound up with perceptions of womanhood and delineations of femininity. As one contemporary character lamented: 'Because a women has *mind*, she is supposed to have no *heart*'.[2] Such a prospect supports the Victorian ideal of the purely passive wife, invalid, or mother, quite innocent (and glad to be) of all worldly matters, existing only as someone relative to her husband or father. It was the standard propounded by the proliferation of conduct books, such as those by the popular Sarah Stickney Ellis in her *Women of England* series. Intellectual pursuits, such as writing, were held to be incompatible with domestic happiness.[3] As a society which placed great emphasis on regulations and etiquette, it cannot be denied that a male-imposed definition of 'normal' female behaviour was in place, but it would be a mistake to accept that this was adhered to unquestioningly by all Victorian women, as ghost stories written by them clearly illustrate. On the other hand, society's rules were difficult to overturn, particularly as no one coherent feminism emerged in the developing interest of women in their circumstances and rights. What becomes apparent, is that an enormous amount of tension existed around women's attitudes to traditional duties and expressions of independence, individuality and creativity.

---

[1]   Diana Basham, *The Trial of Woman: Feminism and the Occult Sciences in Victorian Literature and Society* (London: Macmillan, 1992), p. 152.

[2]   Grace Aguiler, 'The Authoress', in Kate Flint (ed.), *Victorian Love Stories: An Oxford Anthology* (Oxford: Oxford University Press, 1997), pp. 1–17 (p. 6).

[3]   See, for example, 'A literary woman is the very antipodes to domestic happiness', in Aguiler, p. 2.

Specifically, this struggle is reflected in women's reading and writing, a situation which has bearing on the popularity amongst women writers of the ghost story, and the ambiguity with which the form was received amongst readers and critics.

Within this hugely successful, but frequently trivialized form, most celebrated women writers of the time have at least one, and sometimes many, stories of the supernatural to their names. Jenny Uglow regards the ghost story as a means of exorcising 'unnamed tensions within'.[4] Diana Basham makes the important point that: 'Victorian women, even as late as the 1890s, tended not to use the ghost story form for overtly feminist purposes. Instead, their attraction to the form seems to have been directed by its potential for covert meanings and excluded presences'.[5] Women in journalism may have been happier to write more openly about their situation and risk the consequences, but in supernatural fiction they seem to have appreciated the subversive possibilities. Basham identifies this specifically as 'the narrative of female absence', and in particular cites Amelia B. Edwards and Margaret Oliphant as practitioners of this technique.[6] Significantly, these two women differed widely in their overt political sentiments. The former openly acknowledged her feminism, whilst Oliphant, – although her views altered over time – avoided any such overt disclosure. It is Oliphant (1828–97), however, who gained a significant reputation over the course of her career as a writer of supernatural tales,[7] who is selected by Basham to illustrate this point, using her story, 'The Open Door' (1882): 'In all its aspects, the story itself is an open door, a two-way mirror, and as such it brilliantly realises the feminist potential of the ghost story mysteriously to reflect the exclusion of women and their inadequate representation'.[8] By this interpretation, the story comes from the pen of a writer who has all along had the reputation of being an anti-feminist, but who eventually, nonetheless, did not see why, as a tax-paying householder and head

---

[4]   Jenny Uglow, 'Introduction', in Richard Dalby (ed.), *The Virago Book of Victorian Ghost Stories* (London: Virago, 1992), pp. ix–xvii, (p. x).

[5]   Basham, p. 158.

[6]   Ibid., p. 159.

[7]   Oliphant's ghost stories were published mainly individually in magazines, but recent collections are: Margaret Oliphant, *Selected Short Stories of the Supernatural*, ed. Margaret K. Gray (Edinburgh: Scottish Academic Press, 1985), and Margaret Oliphant, *A Beleaguered City, and Other Stories*, ed. Merryn Williams, (Oxford: Oxford University Press, 1988).

[8]   Basham, p. 171.

of the family, she should not have a vote if she so wished.[9] She did, for part of her life at least, believe in the doctrine of 'separate spheres', but at no point agreed it followed that women were inferior to men: 'if anyone will tell us that the nursery is less important than the Exchange, or that it is a more dignified business to vote for a county member than to regulate a Christian household, we will grant that the woman has an inferior range of duty'.[10] She was very clear on this position, and when, earlier in her career, J.S. Mill appealed for her support in extending the suffrage to women, she responded to what she felt to be his patronizing attitude to women with: 'We are not men spoiled in the making, but women',[11] a vision of distinctness she always retained. Clarke has argued that, 'her views were changing from year to year and she came to share most of the less extreme views of nineteenth-century feminists'.[12] Merryn Williams regards her as an 'Old Feminist', placing her within her own time.[13] In other words, perhaps Oliphant, though feeling inadequate – or objecting to – challenging the entire machinery of patriarchy openly, did subvert the system covertly through her supernatural fiction.

If it is true that women writers of supernatural fiction wanted to subvert gendered norms, what was it about the genre which allowed them to immediately throw a critical male readership off guard? One possible answer is that, with its roots deep in the past, the ghost story was very much an oral tradition. Perhaps men, jealous of their profession as a serious one, would instinctively feel less threatened by the image of women – metaphorically speaking – sitting round a fire, telling each other spooky stories. This is borne out by the Victorian tradition of the ghost story forming a crucial part of the Christmas annual, to be read to the whole family, once again round the fire. In the stories themselves, however, the oral tradition rapidly emerges as a specifically female one, with the authoritative voice being that of a matriarchal figure. Anna Maria Hall's 'La Femme Noir' (c.1850) illustrates a chain of female narrative voices; Elizabeth Gaskell's 'The Old Nurse's Story' (1852)

---

[9]   Merryn Williams, 'Feminist or Antifeminist? Oliphant and the Woman Question', in D.J. Trela (ed.), *Margaret Oliphant: Critical Essays on a Gentle Subversive* (London: Associated University Presses, 1995), p. 172.

[10]   Margaret Oliphant, 'The Laws Concerning Women', *Blackwood's Edinburgh Magazine* 79 (1856), pp. 379–87, (p. 381).

[11]   Margaret Oliphant, 'The Great Unrepresented', *Blackwood's Edinburgh Magazine* 100 (1866), pp. 367–79, (p. 376).

[12]   John Stock Clarke, *Margaret Oliphant (1828–1897): A Bibliography* (Queensland: University of Queensland, 1986), p. 6.

[13]   Williams, p. 179.

and Dinah M. Mulock's 'The Last House in C- Street' (1856) are similar examples.[14] As will be seen later in this chapter, it is not that men completely failed to notice the subject matter of such stories, but it would seem that the popular form in which they were presented allowed them into print initially, whilst the supernatural element and the social comment, were, cleverly, so indistinguishable as to make vague misgivings difficult to identify and vocalize. Within these female narratives, as Basham argues, 'the challenge of the supernatural is made directly to notions of masculinity itself'.[15] This can take differing forms: a male character being worsted or humbled by a supernatural force more powerful than himself is one, and appears in numerous stories, such as Margaret Oliphant's 'The Open Door', and Rhoda Broughton's 'The Truth, the Whole Truth, and Nothing but the Truth' (1868).[16] It could involve a depiction of communities of women – spanning the living and the dead – such as Elizabeth Gaskell's 'The Old Nurse's Story', or, as in one of her more unusual stories, 'The Grey Woman (1861), boundaries between gender and sexuality could be completely blurred. We must think of the minister's wife, mother of four children, and anxious to remain a dutiful member of both her family and society, when we consider a remarkable tale that involves bigamy, cross-dressing, and a possible lesbian relationship. Even given the bravery in her choice of subject and withstanding of criticism for *Ruth* (1853) would Gaskell (1810–65) have felt able to write such a narrative except under the guise of a 'harmless' ghost story? The woman who was plagued by the great number of 'Mes' she felt divided her,[17] revealed through her ghost stories the extent to which the conflict between the demanded role, and what must be repressed, ruled the lives of so many women. In other words, not only did the genre allow for the expression of subversively feminist ideas, but it also made

---

[14]   The first of these stories can be found in Jessica Amanda Salmonson (ed.), *What Did Miss Darrington See? An Anthology of Feminist Supernatural Fiction* (New York: Feminist Press, 1989), and the latter two in Richard Dalby (ed.), *The Virago Book of Victorian Ghost Stories*, (London: Virago, 1992). Elizabeth Gaskell's supernatural stories are also collected in Elizabeth Gaskell, *Curious, If True* (London: Virago, 1995), and Elizabeth Gaskell, *Mrs Gaskell's Tales of Mystery and Horror*, ed. Michael Ashley, (London: Victor Gollancz, 1978).

[15]   Basham, p. 158.

[16]   This particular story can be found in *The Virago Book of Victorian Ghost Stories*, and also in the collection of Rhoda Broughton's ghost stories: Rhoda Broughton, *Ghost Stories and Other Tales of Mystery and Suspense* (Lincolnshire: Paul Watkins, 1995).

[17]   Letter 69 to Eliza Fox (1850) in Elizabeth Gaskell, *The Letters of Mrs Gaskell*, ed. J.A.V. Chapple and Arthur Pollard (Manchester: Mandolin, 1997), p. 108.

possible the exploration of dangerous territory which would have been closed off completely in any other context.

Victorian women's supernatural fiction, therefore, is multi-layered; beneath the acceptability of a traditional form of entertainment lies the distinct purpose of voicing assertive beliefs and views which frequently challenge contemporary patriarchal ideology. The time-span is a large one, and historical changes do have to be taken into consideration. Margaret Oliphant's opinions regarding women's position in society can be seen to become more liberal over the course of her lengthy career; this is apparent in her non-fiction, but also emerges in her characters and plots. Elizabeth Gaskell clearly manifests, and is aware of, a troubling pull between traditional and more progressive attitudes with regard to a woman's role. Rhoda Broughton's reputation at the hands of critics and a reading public, and her delineation of female behaviour, shifts dramatically over the years. However, the work of women writing ghost stories in many ways exhibits similar concerns about women's lives, and allows them, in common, to depict strong, capable, determined, and independent notions of womanhood normally denied them.

In the course of the Victorian period, the style of the ghost story shows a move away from the more narrative-based tales of Oliphant and Gaskell towards the psychological hauntings of, for example, Vernon Lee (1856-1935), whose first supernatural collection, *Hauntings* was published in 1890. A change in emphasis had already been witnessed from the gothic stories of the early part of the nineteenth century and end of the eighteenth, in that ultimate responsibility for events was placed, not on unstoppable fate, but on the human characters and their choice of actions. Neither were the supernatural circumstances negated by physical explanations at the end. This lack of answers could perhaps be viewed as surprising given the technological and scientific advances of the period, but the writers seem to suggest that increased knowledge serves only to generate more questions. To some extent, most supernatural tales written by Victorian women retain certain elements of the traditional ghost story, ensuring its recognition as such by readers, and demonstrating a constancy in human anxieties surrounding the vexed issues of death, bereavement and a possible afterlife. Yet at the same time they manipulate and extend the boundaries of what may be expected within a ghost story. There may be the traditional apparition, although this in itself can be subject to experimentation, as when in Oliphant's 'Old Lady Mary' (1884) the perspective is partly that of the ghost. There may not even be a ghost, as in Gaskell's 'The Grey Woman', the title signifying instead the death-in-life of the eponymous heroine. Owing to the emphasis on the haunted rather than the haunters, doubt is frequently cast over whether the ghost is a product of a character's imagination or 'real'. In addition, most of the writers feature other supernatural phenomena, such as witchcraft, curses, premonitions and dreams, and so it is necessary to extend any strict definition of the ghost story during this period.

I would argue that the supernatural fiction of Victorian women is distinct from that of their male counterparts. One logical reason for this is that, as there was not the same policing of men's opinions, there was not the same need to express them subversively. Although there were limits and definitions placed on what any author could expect to have allowed into print, such rules were constructed by men, who were also responsible for deciding what was appropriate in respect of women writers and readers. Male writers, then, were more inclined to utilize the genre (and they expected women to do likewise) as entertainment, and thus concentrated more exclusively on the element of fear as the ultimate point of the tale. Examples of this would be Lord Lytton's 'The Haunted and the Haunters, or The House and the Brain' (1859), Bram Stoker's 'The Judge's House' (1891), W.W. Jacob's 'The Monkey's Paw' (1902), and Algernon Blackwood's 'The Kit-Bag' (1908).[18] In all of these stories there is a steady accent towards a horrifying climax. They (the first in particular) also illustrate the theme of a struggle between supernatural forces and a masculine assumption of dominance. Such a tendency would be frequently challenged and examined in women's stories, such as Oliphant's 'The Open Door', where a military father, used to assuming control and solving every problem brought to him, finds himself completely at a loss when he is called to first believe in, and then put an end to, a haunting which is literally frightening his cherished son to death. One could also offer one of the most famous ghost story writers, M.R. James, and the closed, masculine world of academics he delineates, which almost completely excludes women, as another example of gender differences in supernatural writing.

Perhaps the closest affiliation between men and women's ghost stories may be observed in Henry James' *The Turn of the Screw* (1898).[19] James uses a

---

[18] See Edward Bulwer-Lytton, 'The Haunted and the Haunters, or, The House and the Brain', in V.H. Collins (ed.), *Ghosts and Marvels: A Selection of Uncanny Tales from Daniel Defoe to Algernon Blackwood* (London: Oxford University Press, 1924), pp. 71–125; Bram Stoker, 'The Judge's House', in Richard Dalby and others (eds), *Best Ghost and Horror Stories* (New York: Dover, 1997), pp. 113–31; W.W. Jacobs, 'The Monkey's Paw', in John Grafton (ed), *Great Ghost Stories* (New York: Dover, 1992), pp. 61–70; Algernon Blackwood, 'The Kit-Bag', in Michael Cox and R.A. Gilbert (eds), *Victorian Ghost Stories: An Oxford Anthology* (Oxford: Oxford University Press, 1992), pp. 480–89.

[19] Henry James, *The Turn of the Screw* (London: Penguin, 1994).

similar psychological approach to that of Vernon Lee – whom he knew – and adopts a female protagonist and narrator. Yet there are still differences, primarily in that James' assumption of a female voice could be regarded as a means to an end. Punter reads this tale as one of 'psychological doubt' in which the author illustrates the difficulties of accessing the past, and where James' themes symbolize 'the locked room of the unconscious'.[20] Thus, his governess and her gender are picked for the vulnerability they immediately infer. That she is a woman in her particular circumstances allows James to develop the characteristics of guilt, sexual anxiety, repression and religious mania which could believably be construed to have arisen from her gender and resultant upbringing. Ultimately it will allow for an examination into an unbalanced state of mind. In other words, a male author, in this instance, is using a female protagonist for literary purposes, whereas for a woman writer, her female character would often have been the point of the story, representing all of her social concerns.

The Victorian ghost story, therefore, gains particular significance when applied to the general sociology of women's writing and reading of the time. Within the mainstream patriarchal society, the ideal held out to women was to become perfect wives and mothers, and nothing else. Writing, especially as a profession, and even more particularly as an outlet for feminist feelings and beliefs, did not fit into this ideal. This created tension for women who wanted to write, for whatever reasons, between their traditional domestic duties and their individual wish to assert their independence and creativity. Many writers rejected open radicalism for two reasons, the first being that they felt a genuine pull towards the duties they had been brought up to, and the second being that radicalism would have been noticed and objected to. The ghost story proved an ideal discourse for hidden agendas and deeper textual levels, as well as representing, on the wider level, women's own marginalization, like the supernatural, to the realms of the irrational/Other. The more the subject is examined, the more it seems that Victorian society, women's reading and writing, and the ghost story are irrevocably intertwined.

It seems that reviewers did not quite know what to make of Victorian women's ghost stories. Normally confident in discussing the authors' more mainstream work, they struggled to impose reason and meaning on this particular genre, not even quite sure if it met with their approbation or not. Today, the genre is frequently dismissed as less important than other facets of a

---

[20]   David Punter, *The Literature of Terror: A History of Gothic Fictions from 1765 to the Present Day*, 2nd ed, 2 vols (London: Longman, 1996), ii, p. 48.

writer's work. It has been declared, for example, of a reprint of a collection of Elizabeth Gaskell's supernatural fiction that, 'Excepting "The Old Nurse's Story" and "Lois the Witch," none of these tales is likely to enhance Mrs Gaskell's literary standing'.[21] The critic does admit of the former that 'the constituents are subtly blended by means of the old narrator's keen gauge of her listeners' emotional receptivity. The impressive tale, after all these years, continues to grip readers',[22] and his criticism is as much about the editor's arrangement as the tales themselves. However, the fact remains that the criticism avoids discussing the collection in terms of its supernatural content. When the body of supernatural fiction is considered for its own sake, the contributions of women writers to the genre is now at least being recognized, with writers such as Vernon Lee belonging 'to a ghostly sisterhood which, from the 1880s onwards, was to be responsible for much of the most interesting terror fiction'.[23] It has been argued recently that one aspect of the ghost story which makes it attractive is that 'the past will often be seen as superior to the present, with its dreary rationalism and materialism'.[24] It could be viewed as escapist, therefore, but could also be regarded as taking a more serious aim: 'Some have chosen the supernatural tale as a vehicle for conveying their beliefs about the natural and the spiritual worlds and their inter-relations'.[25] The reviews of contemporary critics reveal a confusion of attitudes towards what, indeed, a ghost story should, and did, encompass.

One memorial of Margaret Oliphant concentrated exclusively on her work in the supernatural field, as an extract shows:

> SEER, who beyond the untrodden bourne
>   Where meet the Viewless and the Seen,
> In dreams that voyage and return
>   With doubtful news, hast pilgrim been;
> Romancer of the lands that lie
> More unexplored than faëry.[26]

[21]   Benjamin Franklin Fisher, '*Mrs Gaskell's Tales of Mystery and Horror*, ed. Michael Ashley', *Studies in Short Fiction* 18 (1981), p. 111.

[22]   Ibid., p. 110.

[23]   Karl Miller, '*Supernatural Tales*, by Vernon Lee', *London Review of Books* 9 (1987), p. 14.

[24]   Ibid.

[25]   Review of *Victorian Ghost Stories*, ed. Montague Summers, *The Times Literary Supplement*, 23 November 1933, p. 817.

[26]   John Huntley Skrine, 'In Memoriam: Margaret Oliphant', *Macmillan's Magazine* 76 (1897), p. 241.

Considering the range of her work, this is significant, and demonstrates the kind of impact the genre could have. One of her obituaries praised her ghost stories for their 'well-selected detail',[27] and another rated 'A Beleaguered City' (1880) with the supernatural tales of Scott and Lord Lytton.[28] Possibly they could strike a chord, and arouse universal emotions and questions. A contemporary reviewer felt that, 'Mrs Oliphant's work approached greatness when she was inspired to write as a mother who had lost children' because of the added depth, believing the stories of the Unseen to be her best work.[29] Thus the main concern is not the element of fear, but their profundity.

In Vernon Lee's case, her exploration of the supernatural genre continued, on the whole, to elicit the appreciation with which she had begun her career.[30] She first came to public notice, and critical acclaim, in 1880, when, at the age of only twenty-four, she published the innovative *Studies of the Eighteenth Century in Italy* (the country in which she spent most of her life). It was an area which had received little previous attention, and the precocious and highly intelligent Lee (or, to use her real name, Violet Paget) had been deep in research for her subject since her early teens. Critics were amazed by the young woman, 'Who has made such good use of uncommon powers and opportunities that she has been able, at an age when most girls have barely realized the emancipation from the school-room, to shed light on the annals of a comparatively neglected period'.[31] The same reviewer declared, 'The great days of the Academy live again under this vivacious pen'.[32] Lee had first been inspired as an adolescent, when, with her life-long friend, the painter John Singer Sargent, she would roam the remains of ancient buildings, and wander galleries and museums for hours at a time. She became completely immersed in the period, and in particular its music, the influence of which is clearly apparent in her supernatural fiction. Significantly, she herself was a woman of two

---

[27]　　　Obituary of Margaret Oliphant, *Morning Post*, 28 June 1897, National Library of Scotland, MSS 23211, fol. 84.

[28]　　　Obituary of Margaret Oliphant, *The Times*, 28 June 1897, NLS, MSS 23211, fol. 88.

[29]　　　Gaye Tuchman, with Nina E. Fortin, *Edging Women Out: Victorian Novelists, Publishers, and Social Change* (London: Routledge, 1989), p. 192.

[30]　　　Vernon Lee's supernatural stories were collected in three volumes: *Hauntings: Fantastic Stories* (1890), *Pope Jacynth, and Other Fantastic Tales* (1904), and *For Maurice: Five Unlikely Stories* (1927). A recent collection is Vernon Lee, *Supernatural Tales: Excursions Into Fantasy* (London: Peter Owen, 1987).

[31]　　　Harriet Waters Preston, 'Vernon Lee', *Atlantic Monthly* 55 (1885), pp. 219–27, (p. 220).

[32]　　　Ibid.

centuries, writing in both the nineteenth and the twentieth. According to her biographer, Peter Gunn, 'She said of herself that she had been born before her time, that she had spent her life struggling against Victorianism; but Victorian she was by birth and upbringing, cosmopolitan Victorian in her actions and reactions'.[33] This speaks of her complex and personal involvement with the past, present, and future, and illustrates perhaps where her fictional concerns arose. The themes of love, cruelty, and the continuity of the past haunt the pages of her tales as much as any ghost, providing the motivation, and all-too frequently the downfall, of most of the characters she creates. Her favoured device is a Victorian setting, characterized by the ordinary, everyday lives of the upper classes at that time. Using this as her frame, she then creates within this a world of the past: a story within a story. This is sometimes medieval, frequently seventeenth or eighteenth century, and they usually rely greatly on the legends of the continent of the period. Of *Hauntings*, one verdict was that, 'These four curiously interesting stories have a weird fascination quite unlike any other of their order'.[34] Again, a certain perplexity can be seen in that 'curiously', and the idea of unexplained fascination. The general consensus towards her ghostly fiction was, rightly, that 'it may not be Vernon Lee's real business to freeze the blood',[35] and, doubtless due to her factual writing about art, the reviewers chose to concentrate on the aesthetics of her work. Judged at 'the centre of her magic: a poetry of impressions that is also a kind of poetry of time',[36] and that 'the treatment has always poetic grace and romantic flavor'.[37] Apart from their content, it was enough that, 'for those who care more for exquisite form than solid substance these airy creations of a rich and lively imagination are excellent reading'.[38] *The Times Literary Supplement* lighted on the theme of the past which ran through so much of Lee's work: 'As though by instinct she interweaves the past and present, so that old things come to life at a personal touch and a new scene, with all its bloom of freshness, is mellowed by some associated light of memory'.[39] Another aspect of her work was highlighted: 'the attraction of the artist to perfect beauty is shown with

---

[33]   Peter Gunn, *Vernon Lee: Violet Paget, 1856–1935* (London: Oxford University Press, 1964), p. 4.

[34]   Review of *Hauntings*, *Academy* 70 (1906), p. 358.

[35]   Review of *For Maurice: Five Unlikely Stories*, *The Times Literary Supplement*, 15 December 1927, p. 956.

[36]   Ibid.

[37]   Review of *Pope Jacynth, and Other Fantastic Tales*, *Dial* 43 (1907), p. 124.

[38]   Ibid.

[39]   Review of *For Maurice*, p. 956.

terrible force'.[40]   Again there is the contrast between modern living and the sense of escape offered by such stories: 'Vernon Lee has a dream-world of her own; it is a tragic world, but we may envy her ability to live apart from the sordid and unromantic world of today'.[41] Evocations of the past are always viewed romantically, and here is no exception; Vernon Lee's ghost stories are valued for their beauty and complexity rather for any fear they inspire, and in this appraisal a modern-day interpretation would doubtless concur.

Lanoe Falconer's novella, *Cecilia de Noël* (1891), was dubbed by the *New Review*, with a seemingly unintentional pun, as 'welling over with the best spirit of the age',[42] and the *Catholic World*, in a substantial review, felt it 'revives and intensifies the impression of original power and something uncommonly like genius which was produced by *Mademoiselle Ixe*. Both the plan and the treatment of the new tale are strikingly clever'.[43] As a ghost story, *Cecilia de Noël* is remarkable. It captures the dilemmas of an age, seething with the conflict of both society and individuals bewildered by a world which has rejected anything but the latest uncompromising scientific advances, yet which can seemingly unleash terrifying supernatural influence. The plot centres on the experiences of a group of guests staying at Weald Manor, the haunted country home of Lord and Lady Atherley. The appearance of the ghost to most of them shakes the foundations of their own personal creeds, and in different ways makes them reassess their life views. That these creeds are strongly held (however misguided) is emphasized by each guest being designated a chapter called a 'gospel'. This device also functions in an ironic way, as most of the guests' opinions are shown to be dogmatic, silly, or harsh, even though their status (members of the clergy, for example), could establish expectations to the contrary. Throughout the traumatic experiences of the tale, the eponymous Cecilia de Noël, though absent until the final chapter, is mentioned constantly, not as some brilliant intellectual, who will arrive bearing answers, but as someone who will be able to inexplicably ease their personal situations of fear and self-doubt brought on by their encounters with the apparition. Falconer keeps her chief character as mysterious near-legend for the greater part of the story, the build-up making the revelation of the real woman all the more surprising. As such, the narrator, Lyndsay, himself struggling with near-suicidal depression after a hunting accident leaves him crippled, forms an

---

40   Review of *Hauntings*, p. 358.
41   Ibid.
42   Evelyn March-Phillipps, 'Lanoe Falconer', *Cornhill Magazine* 3 (1912), pp. 231–44, (p. 234).
43   Review of *Cecilia de Noël*, *Catholic World* (1891–2), p. 451.

intense interest in her by the time she makes an appearance, due to his own desperate need. It is Lyndsay's own personal journey to a new 'gospel' of life, which Cecilia's revelation brings, that forms the central strand of the story.

Lanoe Falconer (1848–1908) is largely unheard of today, exemplifying the comment that 'the works of women writers tend to lack a survival kit'.[44] This intensely private woman lived quietly with her family in a Hampshire village, choosing, when it came to seeking publication, to shade her identity with a pseudonym. Born Mary Elizabeth Hawker, she adopted her father's first name coupled with a synonym of Hawker. Her first novel, *Mademoiselle Ixe* (1890), is the story of a female Russian spy bent on a mission of assassination, and was an instant success. In fact Falconer had already written *Cecilia de Noël*, the ghost story which was to be published second, and had been trying to place it for some time, only to have it rejected by publishers who believed it would not be appreciated by a sensation-loving public.[45] However, she persevered with the story she felt to be 'her own child',[46] and eventually Macmillan's accepted it, with the result, ironically, of instant sensation. The editor of the *New Review* regarded it as an 'almost flawless gem',[47] Gladstone was an admirer, 40,000 copies were sold initially in English, and it was translated into French, German, Dutch and Italian.[48] The publisher Mr Fisher Unwin wrote to Falconer to give his impressions: 'To me your strong point is your vivid photographic pictures of society and characters'.[49] In a very short space of time, Falconer found herself in the somewhat uncomfortable position of having her work discussed throughout society, from dinner tables to church pulpits. However, almost as rapidly as fame had overtaken Lanoe Falconer, it faded. Though *Cecilia de Noël* has been reprinted in *The Virago Book of Victorian Ghost Stories*, Falconer – and her other work – has now sunk from public view. Her disappearance from the literary scene was initially due to the frustrating reason of illness. From shortly after the publication of *Cecilia de Noël* until her death, Falconer was plagued by ill-health, and though she did maintain a small output, it led to her turning down most of the numerous requests, often from prestigious publishers, for more material. The way in which women writers

---

[44]   Anna Walters, 'When Women's Reputations are in Male Hands: Elizabeth Gaskell and the Critics', *Women's Studies International Quarterly* 3 (1980), pp. 405–13, (p. 405).

[45]   Evelyn March-Phillipps, *Lanoe Falconer* (London: Nisbet, 1915), p. 128.

[46]   Ibid.

[47]   Ibid., p. 136.

[48]   'Lanoe Falconer', *Dictionary of National Biography* [on CD-ROM].

[49]   March-Phillipps, *Lanoe Falconer*, p. 150.

were categorized by contemporary reviewers, and the subsequent early twentieth-century revolt against the bulk of Victorian fiction, which effectively buried so many women writers, leaving only the most famous unscathed, were the final pronouncements of doom for a writer who provided such an original contribution to the supernatural genre.

The Times asserted that 'The author of *Mademoiselle Ixe* must always write brilliantly', and that she 'has never written anything more powerful than when she makes Cecilia describe what passed in the haunted room in the silent watches of that terrible night'.[50]   Sir Arthur Quiller-Couch concluded that, 'Here ... we have a new writer filled with love of her fellow-beings'.[51]   The issue of the story's supposed moral purpose triggered a great deal of debate; Falconer herself commented that it contained her own gospel, and the message she had to give to the world.[52]   It was even appropriated by the clergy: 'Principal Tulloch wrote to tell her that he had embodied her beautiful story in a sermon which he preached to a large congregation in Glasgow'.[53]   The very fact that it was reviewed in the *Catholic World* is suggestive; its approach, unsurprisingly, concentrated almost exclusively on the religious aspect, rather than the supernatural, and concluded that 'Cecilia's gospel is a very beautiful one. It is good to have it preached in a form so attractive as is here given it.'[54] Falconer regarded it as 'an attempt to express my conviction that in the goodness of human beings, especially of some exquisite characters, we possess a revelation which scientific criticism cannot account for or explain away'.[55] Some did adopt it on this very personal level, one friend writing to say, 'it is quite impossible to read such a book as *Cecilia de Noël* without thanking you for it from my heart ... a veritable oasis in the desert, a fountain of refreshment and healing'.[56] Falconer's non-dogmatic approach to Christianity also raised criticism. Charlotte Yonge acidly remarked that it was 'a pity that so fine a book as *Cecilia de Noël* should be injured by the entire absence of Christianity', and though she later asked Falconer to contribute a story to the *Monthly Packet*, she added a footnote on publication disclaiming responsibility for any of its opinions.[57]   One Canon Alfred Ainger also expressed anxiety

50   Review of *Cecilia de Noël*, *The Times*, 11 November 1891, p. 14.
51   March-Phillipps, 'Lanoe Falconer', p. 236.
52   March-Phillipps, *Lanoe Falconer*, p. 136.
53   Ibid., p. 139.
54   Review of *Cecilia de Noël*, *Catholic World*, p. 453.
55   March-Phillipps, *Lanoe Falconer*, p. 137.
56   Ibid., p. 157.
57   March-Phillipps, 'Lanoe Falconer', pp. 236–7.

about what he saw as her willingness to replace Christianity with individuals like Cecilia, reading in it a 'vein of cynicism that seems to me to endanger the good you might otherwise do'.[58] Whilst he was quick to flatter that, 'I so truly admire your books for the fine and rare quality they show – their humour (as delicate as it is rare), their style and their character-drawing', he perhaps took secret affront at the portrayal of Canon Vernade, worrying about her preaching 'that we are all bad together', which 'leaves a certain bad taste in the mouth'.[59] The *Spectator* provided 'a review which gratified Marie extremely', but it believed she 'does not sufficiently realize that the highest and purest kind of love is potent to repel as well as to attract, and that those whom it repels may harden themselves, till the attitude of defiance constitutes an impassable gulf'.[60] It was the religious aspects which preoccupied the reviewer of *The Times* also, who thought that it bordered on 'a many-sided speculative discussion over a treatise on theology' and a 'somewhat sombre and abstruse narrative'.[61] Cecilia they found 'an angel far too good for this earth and quite unfitted to inhabit it'.[62] Andrew Lang agreed that 'I read *Cecilia* with much interest, but I am not sure she was not better before she got lost in theological discussion'.[63] (In a footnote, March-Phillipps adds that it was Lang who, as a reader for Arrowsmith, refused *Mademoiselle Ixe* because she was 'too violent a lady'.[64]) These seem odd criticisms to make, given the strong sense of humour – compared to that of Austen[65] – which pervades the story, in spite of the narrator's melancholy. There seems to be a resistance to the threatened crossover between religion and the ghost story, again as if the latter is expected to be for entertainment only. Anything of a weighty nature is criticized, whereas, for example, the 'two most delightful children' are spoken of highly.[66] Modern readers, if finding anything objectionable, would probably point to the children, who provide the only instances of Falconer verging on Victorian sentimentality. There is also a letter from a friend, who found 'much of the talk very clever and good except perhaps the servants', as she believed there not to be much difference of pronunciation between the latter's talk and that of the

---

58   March-Phillipps, *Lanoe Falconer*, pp. 155–6.
59   Ibid., p. 153.
60   Ibid., pp. 138–9.
61   Review of *Cecilia de Noël*, *The Times*, p. 14.
62   Ibid.
63   March-Phillipps, *Lanoe Falconer*, p. 159.
64   Ibid., p. 158.
65   Ibid., p. 144, review of *Cecilia de Noël*, *Catholic World*, p. 452.
66   Review of *Cecilia de Noël*, *The Times*, p. 14.

masters in reality, which led her to preferring *Mademoiselle Ixe*.[67] Thus the
general tone of the reviews is mixed. There are many definite admirers of
Falconer, and a welcome for her work, but unlike her first, less problematic,
spy novel, there is an apparent discomfort with the subject matter of *Cecilia de
Noël*. Much debate concentrated around the religious complications, and
although some of this was positive, there were also many ill-defined
accusations that the author – especially as a woman – was impertinently
entering realms upon which she was not qualified to comment.

   Lanoe Falconer encountered the dichotomy of critics versus public;
whatever the latter thought, it was the reviewers who dictated what was
worthy of lasting attention. This in itself was gendered: 'Most library readers
were probably women. Most publishers' readers were men'.[68] More
frustrating is the fact that, as in Falconer's case, the reviews did not necessarily
have to be completely, or even mostly, negative, for a woman's work to be
edited out of history and the canon. Women's writing could be denigrated
two-fold, the result of both being that women writers were relegated to
'second rank'.[69] Firstly, as in the reviews above, there was the question of
whether the woman writer remained within the accepted ideology: 'literary
reputations were formed less by the author's sexual identity than by the way
their works conformed to or transgressed from the gendered framework of
reviewers' expectations'.[70] Falconer, in approaching the male bastions of
theology and science, clearly, in the eyes of her critics, fell into the latter
division. Favourable reviews were easier to come by if the stereotype was
adhered to: 'For the most part, literary critics admired and endorsed writing by
women that formed an extension of their domestic role'.[71] Secondly, the natural
result of such relegation was that the subject matter of women was
automatically considered less important than that which occupied the minds of
male writers and readers: 'Victorian attitudes about genre shaped and continue
to shape the canon today. One obvious result, of course, was to exclude
authors like M.E. Braddon or Rhoda Broughton from consideration as
canonical, thus allowing them to go out of print and be forgotten'.[72] Critics

---

[67]   March-Phillipps, *Lanoe Falconer*, p. 148.

[68]   Tuchman, p. 66.

[69]   Nicola Diane Thompson, *Reviewing Sex: Gender and the Reception of
Victorian Novels* (London: Macmillan, 1996), p. 19.

[70]   Ibid., p. 108.

[71]   Ibid., p. 16.

[72]   Pamela K. Gilbert, *Disease, Desire, and the Body in Victorian Women's
Popular Novels* (Cambridge: Cambridge University Press, 1997), p. 182.

worked 'on the assumption that, having discovered any writer to be a woman, we may expect to find a profound exploration of feeling but a singular lack of coherence on the level of ideas'.[73]   Thus writers like Lanoe Falconer were caught in a double bind: if they wrote what was expected of them, they were congratulated and then forgotten; if they daringly explored wider subjects, they were castigated and then ignored. Happily for today's reader and historian, many women writers chose to risk the censure of the latter, and their trust has not been entirely misplaced. The fact that such ghost stories were usually well-received by the general reading public at the time, combined with continuing efforts of modern scholars to uncover unjustly neglected women writers and their work, as well as the determined, if somewhat marginalized, enthusiasm for the supernatural genre, ensure that not only did the authors gain public approval whilst living, but they can also be critically re-evaluated now.

Another collection which illustrates the dilemma of the uncertainty surrounding the woman's ghost story and how to interpret it, whether to look to it for instruction or entertainment, and indecision as to which is preferable, is Mary Louisa Molesworth's *Four Ghost Stories* (1888), several of the reviews for which survive. They depict the now-familiar confusion as to meaning and aim, whether favourable or not. Molesworth (1839–1921) was held in high esteem as a children's writer; the critic Edward Salmon, writing in the *Nineteenth Century* in October, 1887, declared, 'I have left till last any mention of the lady who, by right of merit, should stand first', adding that, 'Mrs Molesworth's charm is her realism'.[74]   It was perhaps this quality which perplexed the critics of her supernatural stories, as this was what they were continually searching for.   One reviewer mentioned 'true', 'fact', and 'reality/realism' eight times in twenty-seven short lines, and whilst affirming that 'the art and mastery with which they are told is remarkable' he or she concluded 'that we part from them with a puzzled and unsatisfied mind - as to their reality, in the first place, and, as might be expected, as to the import and meaning, if they are matter of fact'.[75] Although the overall tone is positive, there is a keen sense of frustration that the mysteries of the afterlife and the purpose of humanity have not been solved neatly and conclusively. Another review concentrated on their power to convince, which it rated highly, owing to the plainness of the narrative. This time there is a firm emphasis on the need

---

[73]   Walters, p. 407.
[74]   'By the Same Author', Mrs Molesworth, *Four Ghost Stories* (London: Macmillan, 1888), [np].
[75]   Review of *Four Ghost Stories, London Quarterly Review* 10 (1888), p. 186.

for ghost stories to have a purpose, namely that of a responsibility for providing answers and 'proof'.[76] The *Academy* judged that:

> Everything that Mrs Molesworth writes is worth reading; but it might be almost a question whether she was altogether well advised in her latest attempt. It is superfluous to say that these ghost stories are well told; but, unless we are to understand that the author vouches for the actual truth of them, it seems almost a pity to make a little child, as in 'Unexplained', the ghost-seer, the poor thing would be so frightened.[77]

Given her position of writer of children's stories, this was rather a pointed remark, and it also underlines attitudes to the issue of fear. The *London Quarterly Review* decided, 'They will not terrify their readers, though they are weird',[78] although this trait was not judged negatively. The *Literary World*, however, was of a different opinion: 'Our own taste, we confess, is for apparitions of a more practically terrifying kind',[79] and therefore conflated contemptuously her supernatural fiction with that meant for children. This was one review which was generally negative: 'Mrs Molesworth's ghosts are of an unremarkable sort. They do nothing, say nothing, prove nothing; they simply appear and disappear, leaving a disagreeable impression on the minds of the observers, but in no wise serving to clear perplexities from the paths of the living or in any way to instruct them'.[80] This approach demands a combination of the didactic and the diverting; whilst wanting to be pleasurably thrilled, they too wanted their ghost stories to 'instruct'. The complexity of the reader response engendered like confusion in the authors. Tuchman notes that 'Aspiring women novelists wrote to the society [of authors] to learn where to place "ghost stories" '.[81] She argues that by the time Molesworth published her collection, such stories had lost much of their appeal, despite still managing favourable reviews: 'Women who wrote 1860s-style ghost stories in the 1890s were out of tune with the times'.[82]

Yet tales of the supernatural have always retained their 'weird fascination', never wholly going out of fashion, and frequently enjoying renewed periods of

---

[76]   Review of *Four Ghost Stories*, *Cambridge Review* 9 (1888), p. 207.

[77]   Review of *Four Ghost Stories*, *Academy*, 33 (1888), p. 167.

[78]   Review of *Four Ghost Stories*, *London Quarterly Review*, p. 186.

[79]   Review of *Four Ghost Stories*, *Literary World*, 19 (1888), p. 170.

[80]   Ibid.

[81]   Tuchman, p. 188.

[82]   Ibid.

intense popularity. Their appeal is complex, and even more so when penned by Victorian women writers, for whom authorship was complicated enough in any genre. These women gained a freedom both in this particular form, and the prolific periodical press and growing publication opportunities which made their work more available to ever greater numbers. For women writers, supernatural tales enabled exploration of dangerous subjects and an entrance into the kind of theological arenas normally only accessible to men. Readers, although not necessarily able to identify or vocalize this specifically as a problem, were aware that there were differences between supernatural fiction and more mainstream literature that they struggled to contend with. It is this attempt to label, to recognize the cause of a vague feeling of discomfiture, to deal with the unfamiliar, which is often at the root of any unfavourable reviews. Vitally, for women writers, the delineation between the opinions of critics and public – although the voice of the former group was crucial in establishing official reputation – did not ultimately control their fate. Even at the time, critical opinion found much to admire, whilst not always being fully decided on what may, in the stories, have been worrying them. Equally, although literary critics wielded great power, some books could be runaway successes on the strength of public opinion. Over the intervening years, the gap has closed, and, although some digging is usually required, it is now possible to take a fresh look at women's ghost stories and the debate that surrounded them. Alternatively, the very fact that ghost stories cannot be tidily compartmentalized and dismissed could well form part of their enduring attraction. Whilst there are those who express dissatisfaction that they fail to provide conclusive answers, most of their appeal would instantly vanish if it were otherwise. Victorian women's ghost stories may have been regarded at times by their contemporaries as being variously mystifying, complicated, frustrating and infuriating, but it is for all these reasons that they retained their popularity, and also why they hold such magnetism for a modern reader. Their hidden agendas and multifarious layers ensure that they will enjoy life eternal.

Chapter 8

Feminist Discourse in Popular Drama of the Early- and Mid-Victorian Era

Daniel Duffy

While representations of the women's movement of the late-Victorian era in a range of plays from the 1880s and 1890s have been much discussed, the dramatization of feminist ideas and agencies on the early- and mid-Victorian stage has gone largely unrecognized. As a number of important recent works indicate, the prevailing feminist view of Victorian drama still seems to accord with Gail Finney's belief that it featured 'individualized and memorable female characters' only from the 1880s.[1] For Kerry Powell and Gail Marshall, for instance, the earlier period's largely male-generated and commercial dramatic material was unrelentingly sexist and conservative, condemning the actress simply to 'ancillary' playing or to a 'superficial spectacle of femininity'.[2] I do not want to suggest that Powell and Marshall are wrong to insist that sexism was an integral part of this material; rather, the following chapter aims to demonstrate that sometimes contemporary feminist discourse could *also* be found in it, resulting in focal heroines who are highly complex in terms of sexual politics. Thus I will be portraying the plays discussed here much as feminist critics have portrayed certain New Woman dramas – as plays in which, to appropriate Jill Davis' words on the

---

[1] Gail Finney, *Women in Modern Drama: Freud, Feminism, and European Theater at the Turn of the Century* (Ithaca and London: Cornell University Press, 1989), p. 1.

[2] Kerry Powell, *Women and Victorian Theatre* (Cambridge: Cambridge University Press, 1997), p. 125; Gail Marshall, 'Ibsen and Actresses on the English Stage', in Inga-Stina Ewbank, Olav Lausund and Bjørn Tysdahl (eds), *Anglo-Scandinavian Cross-Currents* (Norwich: Norvik Press, 1999), p. 181. See also Marshall's *Actresses on the Victorian Stage: Feminine Performance and the Galatea Myth* (Cambridge: Cambridge University Press, 1998). As Michael Booth points out in his *Theatre in the Victorian Age* (Cambridge: Cambridge University Press, 1991), p.141, in Allardyce Nicoll's handlist of plays for the nineteenth century, '427 authors of plays either printed or produced, or both . . . are clearly identified as women, out of a total of 3,486'; most of these authors were writing between 1800 and 1825 or between 1880 and 1900. For a persuasive account of the scarcity of women playwrights in the period see Powell, ch. 4. Powell is less persuasive when claiming that the Victorian actress could be subversive in contemporary plays only when they were penned by women dramatists, all of whom, he declares, 'wrote against the masculinist grain' (ibid., p. 125). Marshall sees the actress's liberation as coming with the advent of Ibsen.

New Woman in Shavian drama, 'progressive ideas and patriarchal reaction combined to produce ambiguous representations' of feminist forces.[3]

The existence of this ambiguity in commercial drama is helpfully illuminated by Christine Gledhill's essay on the 1977 film *Coma*. Gledhill demonstrates that the gender project of *Coma* is profoundly contradictory, since it positively invokes the American women's movement of the day in a courageous and independent heroine while simultaneously upholding male supremacy in an antifeminist hero who is eventually required to save the girl and defeat the villain. Gledhill argues that this fissure is due to the film's status as popular culture in a capitalist economy; precisely in order to be popular, products like *Coma* must accommodate 'a range of determinations, potentially resistant or contradictory, arising from the differential social and cultural constitution of readers or viewers – by class, gender, race, age, personal history, and so on'.[4] Thus their 'cultural "work" ... concerns the generation of different readings; readings which challenge each other'.[5] What *Coma* does, then, is ensure that both feminist (or 'not necessarily feminist') and sexist spectators 'have a route through' it; this, I believe, is exactly what the two plays I will be examining here do too.[6]

Like *Coma*, the melodrama *Isabelle; or, Woman's Life* (1834) and the comedy *A Woman of Business* (1864), penned by the prolific hack dramatists J.B. Buckstone and Benjamin Webster respectively, were produced to be commercially successful during periods of feminist insurgence and patriarchal domination. Both plays were first staged at the Adelphi Theatre, which stood in the fashionable West Strand and which came as a result to cater for a predominantly middle-class audience.[7] The social level of the feminisms that the plays dramatize, and the prominence of those feminisms in the plays, suggest that Buckstone, Webster, and their theatrical teams were soliciting a portion of this audience, acting on the knowledge that the period's feminists, as Christine Bolt reminds us, were 'articulat[ing] the dismay of middle-class women especially at their lack of

---

[3]   Jill Davis, 'The New Woman and the New Life', in Viv Gardner and Susan Rutherford (eds), *The New Woman and Her Sisters: Feminism and Theatre 1850–1914* (Hemel Hempstead: Harvester Wheatsheaf, 1992), p. 22. See also the discussion of New Woman drama in Viv Gardner's 'Introduction' to *The New Woman and Her Sisters*. The New Woman was the controversial symbol of 1890s feminism.

[4]   Christine Gledhill, 'Pleasurable Negotiations', in E. Deirdre Pribram (ed.), *Female Spectators: Looking At Film and Television* (London and New York: Verso, 1988), p. 70.

[5]   Ibid., p. 74.

[6]   Ibid., p. 87.

[7]   See, for instance, Maurice Willson Disher, *Blood and Thunder: Mid-Victorian Melodrama and Its Origins* (London: Frederick Muller, 1949), pp. 215–18.

independence, individuality, opportunities and legal rights'.[8] It should be noted that the plays' simultaneous – and climactic, in narrative terms at any rate – endorsement of the middle-class sexism against which these feminisms formed and fought would not have been directed only at the rest of the audience, since all playscripts were subject to the scrutiny of the Lord Chamberlain's office. This was an institution which aimed, in John Russell Stephens' words, 'to exclude from the stage ... anything which might be said to encourage disaffection with or disturbance of the existing political and social structure'.[9] It should also be noted that, aside from the tantalizing fragments of critical opinion and of audience reaction that are offered in the largely narrative-orientated reviews of them, the plays appear to be all that remain to tell us of their original spectators' demands and interpretive pathways. Spectatorial readings in this field have to be evoked, to borrow Judith Mayne's phrase, as 'horizons of possibility', although it is worth observing that these possibilities do accord with the reception practices of modern cinema-goers, which have been documented in the ethnographic work of film critics like Jacqueline Bobo.[10] In this chapter I will be articulating routes through *Isabelle* and *A Woman of Business* that suggest, to use Bobo's terms for spectatorial behaviour, that some spectators responded to the plays dominantly, valuing their sexist meanings, while others responded to them oppositionally, seizing upon their feminist ones. And although I do not attempt to imagine ambivalent reactions to the plays, I do believe that still other spectators would have accepted and rejected elements from both sets of meanings.[11]

---

[8]   Christine Bolt, *The Women's Movements in the United States and Britain from the 1790s to the 1920s* (Amherst: University of Massachusetts Press, 1993), p. 92. Other plays containing feminist subject matter were also first produced at theatres with entirely or significantly middle-class audiences. For example, the melodramas *Still Waters Run Deep* (1855) by Tom Taylor and *Broken Ties* (1872) by Palgrave Simpson were staged at the Olympic, and the comedies *The Rights of Woman* (1840) by Joseph Lunn and *MP* (1870) by T.W. Robertson were staged at the Strand and at the Prince of Wales respectively. Limited space prevents me from discussing these and other plays, but *MP* is helpfully referred to in Anthony Jenkins, *The Making of Victorian Drama* (Cambridge: Cambridge University Press, 1991), ch 3. For a discussion of the feminism that was espoused by proletarian women during the socialist agitation of the early nineteenth century, and of the ways in which that feminism was represented in popular drama of the era, see Daniel Duffy, 'Heroic Mothers and Militant Lovers: Representations of Lower-Class Women in Melodrama of the 1830s and 1840s', *Nineteenth-Century Theatre* 27 (1999), 41–65.

[9]   John Russell Stephens, *The Censorship of English Drama 1824–1900* (Cambridge: Cambridge University Press, 1980), p. 52.

[10]   Judith Mayne, *Cinema and Spectatorship* (London and New York: Routledge, 1993), p. 92; Jacqueline Bobo, '*The Color Purple*: Black Women as Cultural Readers', in Pribram, pp. 90–109.

[11]   Obviously I assume that each of the spectatorial positions I have alluded to were

As I have indicated, the venue at which *Isabelle* and *A Woman of Business* were first performed played an important part in determining the feminisms that they incorporated. Generic laws were also crucial in this, since they dictated the modes of middle-class feminism that could be incorporated. In the most substantial study to date of feminism on the pre-New Woman stage, Leona Fisher has shown that the fantastic and topsy-turvy universe of farce enabled it to carry feminist visions of female domination – of a *Petticoat Parliament*, to cite the title of a farce from 1867.[12] Melodrama and comedy were not able to portray such visions, since from the 1830s their dramatic worlds were predominantly 'domestic', a term which was used to denote an everyday verisimilitude.[13] Further, the two forms could not carry whatever feminist visions remained; their heroine stereotypes mandated the dramatization of quite different ones. In what follows I will endeavour to demonstrate that the heroine of melodrama, being serious, moralized, and frequently anguished due to her symbolic role as persecuted virtue, could constitute an effective vehicle for the feminist exposure of the frustration and unhappiness of the period's ideal middle-class woman, the so-called 'angel in the house'.[14] I will

---

occupied by both men and women. The period saw male feminists just as it saw women who were devoted to maintaining female subordination.

[12] Leona W. Fisher, 'Mark Lemon's Farces on the "Woman Question"', *Studies in English Literature 1500–1900* 28 (1988), pp. 648–70. Fisher sees a degree of ambiguity in the sexual politics of her farces, noting that while they 'predictably make the same point: clubs and Parliament properly "belong" to men', women being '[s]illy, irrational, argumentative, and competitive', they also '[present] the weakened moral condition of the bourgeois gentleman and the possibility of female solidarity and control' (pp. 652, 655, 658).

[13] The rise of domestic drama, which usurped the popularity of exotic gothic drama, was explained by the theatre critic George Daniel in his preface to a published version of a Buckstone play from 1826. In the 'Remarks' on *Luke the Labourer* (London: Cumberland's Minor Theatre, [nd]), p. 5, Daniel writes, 'A subject, to come home to the business and bosoms of men, must needs be of a domestic nature. The truest sympathy is excited by characters and events that come under the general observation of mankind ... It is scenes of everyday life, as approximating nearer to *our own* condition, that affect us most'. For critical discussions of domestic drama see Gilbert Cross, *Next Week – 'East Lynne': Domestic Drama in Performance 1820–1874* (London: Associated University Presses, 1977), and Martha Vicinus, '"Helpless and Unfriended": Nineteenth-Century Domestic Melodrama' (1981) in Judith Fisher and Stephen Watt (eds), *When They Weren't Doing Shakespeare: Nineteenth-Century British and American Theatre* (Athens and London: University of Georgia Press, 1989), pp. 174–86.

[14] For discussions of the melodrama heroine's function in the form's definitive manichaean conflict between virtue and vice, and for descriptions of her suffering, see Booth, *English Melodrama* (London: Herbert Jenkins, 1965), pp. 26–30, James L. Smith, *Melodrama* (London: Methuen, 1973), pp. 19–23, and Cross, p. 58 and p. 151, where it is noted that '[f]requent mention and emphasis is found throughout "heroine-in-distress"

then attempt to show that, conversely, the heroine of comedy, being a descendant of the spirited and enterprizing heroine of earlier comedy, could capture the feminist movement's dynamic agency.[15]

'The Trials Of Woman': Feminist Discourse in *Isabelle*

Middle-class feminism has often been seen as 'quiescent or nonexistent' during the first half of the nineteenth century.[16] However, the late Georgian and early Victorian eras did see a stream of books, pamphlets, and articles that attacked middle-class marriage as an institution that women entered, as Harriet Taylor put it in 1831, only to 'cease to exist as to anything worth calling life or any useful purpose'.[17] A striking example of this far from quiescent feminist writing is Anne Richelieu Lamb's *Can Woman Regenerate Society?* (1834). The title of this book questions the period's ubiquitous discourse of 'woman's influence', which strove to mask the inequality and injustice of the middle-class wife's domestic immurement by proclaiming that, in Lamb's words, 'in her hands is placed that mighty engine "the morals of society"' – a responsibility that was devolved upon her precisely because of her isolation from the corrupting competitive public world and that was to be realized through her guidance and education of her less fortunate civic husband.[18] The book itself exposes this discourse as illusory, as a notion that 'would be gratifying ... did the words convey aught to us but sound'.[19] Lamb argues that in reality the wife is little more than a servant and a toy to her husband,

---

speeches of "helplessness", "loneliness", "wretchedness", "friendlessness", and other terms of deprivation'. The nineteenth-century middle-class ideal of womanhood has, of course, come to be called the 'angel in the house' after the title of Coventry Patmore's sequence of poems (1854–63), which feature a heroine who is a domestic paragon of selflessness and virtue.

[15]   Beatrice, Harriet Woodvil, and Kate Hardcastle are, of course, classic examples of the earlier comedy heroine. There is very little material on her early- and mid-nineteenth-century counterpart, but see Jacky Bratton, 'Irrational Dress', in Gardner and Rutherford, pp. 83–4, for a tantalizing reference to the stereotype's potential for gender subversion.

[16]   Leonore Davidoff and Catherine Hall, *Family Fortunes: Men and Women of the English Middle Class 1780–1850* (London: Routledge, 1992), p. 454.

[17]   Harriet Taylor, 'Marriage and Divorce' (1831), in Alice S. Rossi (ed.), *John Stuart Mill and Harriet Taylor Mill: Essays on Sex Equality* (Chicago and London: University of Chicago Press, 1970), p. 85. For a helpful discussion of this feminism and of the feminist text referred to below see Barbara Caine, *English Feminism 1780–1980* (Oxford: Oxford University Press, 1997), ch 2.

[18]   Anne Richelieu Lamb, *Can Woman Regenerate Society?* (London: John W. Parker, 1834), p. 31.

[19]   Ibid.

a fact that engenders a sneering misogyny on his part which not only prevents her from having any moral influence over him and thus society, but which also destroys the possibility of significant conjugal togetherness. When a woman 'leads the way to pleasure or amusement', Lamb asserts,

> she is followed for a day, a short-lived day, and is admired; when she points to stern duties, and speaks of man as the being of immortality, rather than the mere pleasure-hunter, or lover of the world; when she reasons of self-government, or the principle of self-regulation; what is the result? She is tolerated, perhaps, but laughed at for her pains; she may dance, sing, and be a child as long as she pleases, write pretty stories, string rosy words in rhyme, – but to help in devising or practising such schemes, as may be for the real benefit of mankind, becomes in her a matter for ridicule, a subject of merriment, impertinence not to be endured![20]

Lamb describes woman's true sphere as 'a prison within which she is doomed to dwell', and paints an arresting picture of her misery, 'chained and fettered' and so powerless, in spite of her best efforts, to prevent man from ignoring her and doing 'as he pleases' with no consideration of his immortality.[21]

This female misery was exposed in 1834 in a melodrama as well as in Lamb's book. Indeed, Buckstone's *Isabelle*, which opened at the Adelphi on 27 January, was advertised as a feminist drama. The author's preface to the 1835 edition of the text asserted that 'its object is to illustrate some of the "Trials of Woman"' and a playbill for an 1837 provincial production promised a portrayal of 'the Life of Woman as Maid, Wife, and Mother' and of 'The arduous duties of each station'.[22] We do not in fact see all of the 'arduous duties' implied here, but the playbill is accurate in its communication of a sense of the melodrama's concern with the pain that is involved in being an ideal woman in a sexist society. It should be emphasized that we are meant to see the 'trials' of the eponymous heroine as those of all house angels; this is clearly indicated by the lack of an individualizing 'a' or 'one' before 'woman' in Buckstone's description and in the play's subtitle, *Woman's Life*.

The first actress to essay the part of Isabelle was Elizabeth Yates, for a long time the Adelphi's leading lady. Yates was celebrated for what Mrs Baron-Wilson called her 'chaste and ladylike' style of playing; Edward Fitzball, for instance, rather

---

[20] Ibid., p. 32.

[21] Ibid., pp. 8, 125.

[22] J.B. Buckstone, 'Advertisement' for *Isabelle*, in *Popular Dramas by John Baldwin Buckstone* 3 vols (London: William Strange, 1835), II, [np]; playbill in the William Salt Library, Stafford.

pompously declared that she was '[i]n her acting, a little reserved perhaps; but in her that was a beauty, like the faint blush, on what is called the maiden rose; she was so feminine'.[23] Yates's 'ladylike' demureness was exactly what was needed to realize the feminist dimension of *Isabelle*. The heroine is a perfect angel, 'born to bestow happiness on all around her' (1 p. 4).[24] She is, however, prevented from doing so by her tyrannical and dissipated husband, whose view of women is the prevailing one as described by Lamb and her ilk. Isabelle's conventional femininity is feminist, then, not only in that her dignity and benevolence render her superior to her husband, but also in that her efforts to assist him and her sorrow at the scorn she meets with constitute a powerful and tragic impression of the lost potential of circumscribed angelhood. Thus the fact that Yates apparently gave 'the highest possible effect to the graceful melancholy tenderness of domestic unhappiness' was entirely appropriate.[25]

To point up, for its feminist spectators, its later exposure of the despondent realities of wifehood and motherhood in a society where these states are meant to be revered but are actually trivialized, and to imply that 'domestic unhappiness' comes only with a woman's assumption of these more male-centred roles, the heroine is shown to be happy and vibrant as 'The Girl' in Act One (Acts Two and Three are entitled 'The Wife' and 'The Mother' respectively). She laughs with the comic woman Sophie over her fiancé Eugene Le Marc's latest love letter and shows her how she will dance at the balls he has promised to take her to (she is at this point a Savoyard girl; he is a high-born army man) (1 p. 4). She is also shown to be devoted to Eugene and to the house angel role she will take up fully as his wife, a role they both profess to believe in here:

> *Eugene.* [M]an is a strange and variable being. Yet, at this moment, as I gaze upon your dear face, I think, should I ever forget the love I now feel for you, that one glance from your eyes, one tone of tenderness from your lips, will always recall me to my heart's first and dearest affection.
> *Isabelle.* Bless you for those words of hope! They give a promise of happiness in which I will trust with confidence. (1 p. 5)

What the first act leads the audience to expect, then, is an official vision of patriarchal marriage, a picture of a happy wife keeping her adoring husband,

---

[23]   Mrs C. Baron-Wilson, *Our Actresses; or, Glances at Stage Favourites, Past and Present* 2 vols (London: Smith, Elder & Co, 1844), II, p. 183; Edward Fitzball, *Thirty-Five Years of a Dramatic Author's Life* 2 vols (London: T.C. Newby, 1859), II, p. 194.

[24]   All quotations are taken from Buckstone, *Isabelle; or, Woman's Life* (1834; London: John Dicks, [nd]).

[25]   Review of *Isabelle*, *Examiner*, 2 February 1834, p. 70.

however 'strange and variable', to the path of virtue. What the audience actually gets in the rest of the play, though, is a marriage that Lamb would have endorsed as closer to the real thing. Indeed, Act One is not devoid of hints of what is to come. In a very odd song for a wedding celebration, Sophie sings of how an angelic maiden entered the married state only 'To kill her hopes and wreck her mind' (her husband abandons her):

> She trusted, and she liv'd to rue,
> She e'er put trust in man – weak Louise!
> ...
> Then soon was heard her mournful knell .
> Oh, fair ones, ere you love too well,
> Think on the tale I've sigh'd to tell,
> Or you the fate may know – of poor Louise! (1 p.7)

As well as encapsulating the ensuing radical message of the play by warning single women, both directly and symbolically, of the joyless, deathly nature of wifehood, Sophie's song serves a related dramatic function. Just before she sings we see the hero Eugene and the villian Scipio (who has established himself as such by accosting Sophie) colluding to maintain an obviously dark secret of the former's. Sophie's allusion to the untrustworthiness of all men ('trust in man – weak Louise!') is thus a timely clarification of what seems to be a blurring of hero and villain. This blurring augurs particularly ill for the coming marriage, for Scipio has confided to us the following: 'What a fool any man is, that loves liberty, to marry! To think of being tied by the leg to a log of a woman for life! No change, no variety!' (1 p. 6)

In their analysis of the comic action of *Isabelle* Simon Shepherd and Peter Womack argue that the play's two clowns, Sophie's husband Andrew and his friend Apollo, are ambiguous figures as they riot in Sophie's pantry and parlour in Act Three. 'Masculine drunkenness, frivolity, wastefulness and destruction are placed alongside woman's housekeeping and propriety', Shepherd and Womack aver, '[but] [t]here remains an attractiveness, something even joyously mucky, about the comical sweep and his theatrical friend'.[26] If Andrew's destruction of his wife's angelic space may be said to possess 'an attractiveness', the situation in the serious narrative which it parallels – Eugene's abuse of Isabelle – certainly cannot, at least in a feminist reading, be made to yield such a saving grace. This is because much of the Le Marc marriage drama constitutes a remarkably precise dramatization of the Lambian picture of the dominantly organized middle-class

---

[26] Simon Shepherd and Peter Womack, *English Drama: A Cultural History* (Oxford: Blackwell, 1996), p. 210.

home, a picture in which conventional masculinity is far from charming.

As soon as the curtain rises upon Act Two it is clear that Eugene has remained 'strange and variable'. Isabelle's anxious vigil beside a clock showing 'the hour of two' and the sleeping forms of her infant and of Sophie, now her maid, visually communicates her loneliness before she laments it verbally, intimating that Eugene's being 'still from home' at such an hour is nothing unusual: 'Since his diplomatic appointment here, I rarely see him … ambition is a sad foe to domestic peace' (2:1 p. 8). By the end of the heroine's first picture and first speech as 'The Wife', then, the fact that conventional masculinity has a detrimental effect upon supposedly sacred 'domestic peace' has been firmly established. In what follows a detailed explanation of how and why is offered through both dialogue and action, but just before this the drama dissolves for a moment into a vignette of distinctly anti-patriarchal female friendship. When the heroine wakens Sophie from a distressing dream she endeavours to rouse the love-struck young girl from a mental slumber much more debilitating. Isabelle advises Sophie not to sigh for Andrew, who is currently 'away in the country'; the danger is, she warns, that she will follow so many other young women – as, she implies, did she – into the folly of believing in the romantic myth of masculinity and all its 'imaginary excellencies': 'should you be reconciled … you are miserably disappointed at finding the reality fall so far beneath the creation of your dreams' (2:1 p. 8).[27] Isabelle then debunks for the girl the other supporting myth of domestic ideology, that of the ever radiant wife and mother. She articulates the fact that she is 'so grave' as an inevitable condition of those subject-positions: 'Ah, Sophie! When we become wives and mothers, so many new cares and thoughts spring up daily, that they sometimes make the merriest heart thoughtful, if not sad' (2:1 p. 9).

There can be no doubt that Isabelle is justified in her implicitly and explicitly expressed dissatisfaction with her lot once the 'loud knocking' of Eugene is heard, a brief but critical bit of stage business which effectively confirms his selfishness and insensitivity. 'I wish the General wouldn't startle one so', Sophie complains, 'There, now, the baby has woke up' (2:1 p. 9). As Sophie exits and Eugene enters, Isabelle's function shifts from exposer of the saddening 'cares and thoughts' of wifehood to sufferer of them, the position from which her feminist message is most powerfully conveyed. The dialogue that takes place between Isabelle and her husband at this point is worth quoting at length:

---

[27]   Isabelle might be seen as a dramatization of Lamb and her ilk at this point. Lamb's text opens with the claim that its warnings are those of women 'who have experienced some of the realities of life, its difficulties and perplexities … those who have felt how different is actual existence to the fairy dream of youthful and glowing imagination' (Lamb, p. 2).

Isabelle. What is the matter, Eugene? You seem excited – angry.

Eugene. Don't ask me questions, you know I hate them. You women cannot comprehend all the annoyances to which men, circumstanced as I am, are daily and hourly exposed. I know you mean well, that you wish to advise and console, but that which appears light and of no moment to women, is sometimes a serious matter with us.

Isabelle. Yet, Eugene, you must allow –

Eugene. *Do* be silent! I don't require advice. Nothing is so annoying as being advised upon points that one knows the adviser cannot understand – cannot follow through their various ramifications.

Isabelle. Permit me to speak, Eugene!

Eugene. Well, well, commence.

Isabelle. Women, you must allow, are sometimes quick-sighted, and, not being mystified by the various ramifications that you speak of, are often apt to take a clear and straightforward view of a question, that at least enables them to give a serviceable hint or two.

Eugene. Now you are going to argue. Nothing on earth is so ridiculous as a disputative woman. Go to your room. I have letters to write.

Isabelle. Do not fatigue yourself too much. You forget the fête that you give to some of your officers tomorrow.

Eugene. Tut, tut! Don't stand chattering there; but do as I request. Leave me. I must be alone for a few minutes. (2:1 p. 9)

Isabelle, then, is shown to be denied purpose as well as life. In the course of this exchange she attempts to fulfil each of the higher duties allotted to wives by the discourse of woman's influence: she tries to sympathize with her husband, then to correct the patently unjust view he expresses, and finally to offer him advice. But, in the context of what contemporary feminists claimed was actually the role of the wife, each of Isabelle's endeavours is withered by anger or by scorn on the part of Eugene. As he shouts her down he represents her in that role, as a child out of her depth (uncomprehending, interfering, 'chattering'). The radical irony is, of course, that it is Eugene who emerges as the naughty child. He demonstrates peevishness, cruelty, and an utter lack of comprehension (it is obvious from what his wife says here and earlier in this act that she is only too 'quick-sighted'), while Isabelle, in spite of her understandable annoyance ('Permit me to speak, Eugene!'), is a model of dignified composure and sense. Indeed, as she defends female intelligence she casts it as 'clear and straightforward' rationality rather than as the product of some mystical or instinctive capacity, thereby strengthening the impression that were women like her allowed to see 'all the annoyances' of men and to contemplate the 'various ramifications' of serious arguments, 'a serviceable hint or two' would be the least that they could give.[28]   Thus it is implied that what is 'ridiculous' is the denial of 'disputative women', a message which is reinforced when we discover that petulant domestic despotism is not the only flaw of men like Eugene.   After the dialogue quoted above a moment of action occurs which is significant for more than its intensification of sympathy for Isabelle, who bears throughout it 'an expression of sorrow' which she 'appears to struggle against' (2:1 p. 9).   When she 'offers her hand' with the words, 'Good night, love!', Eugene takes it 'with indifference' and shows that conventionally masculine men can love no more than they can respect their wives.   *Isabelle*'s radical project now goes still further, illustrating the feminist thesis that such men, being completely closed to any form of wifely influence, are divorced from 'the principle of self-regulation'.   Far from worrying about some great public dilemma, Eugene is revealed to be vexed at missing a *rendezvous* with his latest mistress.   He actually confides to the audience that "'tis the way with us all.   Let ambition be once satisfied, indolence or something worse is sure to follow' (2:1 p. 9).   It is this 'something worse' that further establishes Eugene's proximity to Scipio, who, we hear soon after, has 'indulged in a plurality of wives' (2:1 p. 10).

At the end of Act Two Eugene's childishness and villainy are pointed up against his wife's superior moral subjectivity in a tableau which literally enlarges and empowers her, suggesting in a single visual moment the relationship that should subsist between them.   With his villainy marked upon his body (the gunshot wound signals his dark secret in that it is the product of his inability to defend himself against Scipio's attack – 'Can silence follow that word [liar] given to my husband?', Isabelle cries as she listens to their offstage argument), 'Eugene sinks at the feet of Isabelle, who raises his head and regards him with alarm and astonishment' (2:5 p. 15).   This tableau, however, does not register the start of a happier marital dynamic for the couple.   Isabelle's 'trial' as 'The Mother' is shown in Act Three (which occurs fifteen years later) to have been that of the deserted – she is led to believe widowed – wife raising her children alone.   Unable to endure the disgrace that followed Scipio's revelation of his crime (he had gambled away his regiment's pay and then 'forged a lie of having been plundered by a party of the enemy'), Eugene fled from France (3:2 p. 19).   The colour of Isabelle's Act Three costume, which includes a 'dark cotton dress' and 'dark toque', immediately conveys the consequent intensification of her suffering, which is then evinced on aural and verbal levels too (costume list, p. 2).   Her costume, sighs and lamentations are admonitory, of course, as her words to Eugene upon his return make clear: 'I have mourned you dead – as lost to me for ever; and my only wish

---

[28]   Lamb makes the same distinction regarding female intelligence, imploring in her conclusion that woman 'no longer be considered a mere instinctive, but ... a rational being' (ibid., p. 166).

would have been for death, but for our boy' (3:4 p. 21).

But there is a problem here. Isabelle reproaches Eugene with her misery, but that misery represents a life of passive endurance. Isabelle's passivity constitutes one of the sites at which the play's sexist project claims her, as she herself makes clear at the final curtain (appropriately after a joyous fit of 'falling' about Eugene). Isabelle delivers a direct ideological address upon her enactment of girlhood, wifehood, and motherhood to the '[m]any that ornament those stations ... now before me', advising them to use her narrative only to endure sexist injustice:

> Dear girls, may your bright hopes never be shadowed by disappointment. And when you become wives and mothers, think sometimes of Isabelle; and let her story teach you the best of all life's lessons – patience, fortitude, and a strong trust in all that is good. Believe me, you will then find happiness when you least expect it. (3:4 p. 22)

It should be noted that the feminist spectator has an option apart from that of simply rejecting Isabelle's climactic 'hour of happiness' and forgiveness (3:4 p. 21). What has gone before can be brought to bear against the episode with the help of Sophie. Though portrayed as happily married at the beginning of Act Three, the comic couple are not shown to be reconciled after Andrew destroys their parlour. Sophie watches the serious couple's reconciliation without him, bizarrely indulging in 'an immoderate fit of laughter' (3:4 p. 21). She claims that she is happy because all will now be happy, but is she really laughing at the ludicrous suggestion that such brutally selfish men should be so easily forgiven by their sorely abused wives? If we believe that she is then we are in a position to make the heroine herself say what she does not say in her curtain address to the 'Gentlemen' in the audience – 'if any portion of our Woman's Life has touched *your hearts*, all that we can ask of *you* in return is your approving *hand*' – namely that the hero, however penitent he may ultimately have appeared, constitutes a model of masculinity not to be emulated (3:4 p. 22).

Before the finale, though, there are a number of stubbornly antifeminist moments for the spectator of that persuasion to seize upon. When, for example, a maid offers Isabelle proof of her husband's infidelity in the form of a love letter addressed to him from the Marquise she is furious with the girl, crying, 'You do not know me, Marie. A wife never thanks the woman that appears as a tale-bearer against the man she loves' (2:5 p. 14). The heroine's blind refusal to believe in what the audience knows to be the truth of Marie's claim is plainly meant to be applauded, for it is fortified with class interest ('Curiosity in a domestic is a vice equally as mean as dishonesty', she tells the maid) and with a prolonged display of integrity overcoming temptation (after 'stoop[ing] to pick up the letter with great agitation', she 'suddenly springs up' with the words, 'No, no, I'll die first!'). Isabelle again works to quell the feminist questioning that she encourages elsewhere when, shortly after the letter episode, she is seen to be happy to submit to her husband's sexist view of women. Eugene shows that he can be pleased with her only when she embodies the most superficial femininity as she emerges 'splendidly dressed' for the fête (2:5 pp. 13–14). But instead of responding to his threatening remark that 'Our ladies must look to their attractions, or they may be eclipsed' with dismay, as she might have done had he spoken thus during their earlier exchange, Isabelle merely says, 'My only desire is to please you, Eugene'. Later in the play she even denies that Eugene is to blame for her suffering as she tries to redraw the hopelessly blurred line between the hero and the villain. Unconvincingly contradicting the evidence that has been so powerfully presented to the audience through the drama, Isabelle confronts the dying Scipio with the words, 'Help *you*? *You*, the destroyer of my happiness, the disgracer of my husband, the source of all my misery?' (3:2 p. 20). As an ideal woman she does eventually try to help him, but she persists in ascribing to him what are in fact her husband's crimes.

Isabelle was a hugely successful melodrama, enjoying revivals until 1851. The playbill of 1837 referred to earlier stated that it had 'been received with the greatest approbation and applause in London and the principal Country Theatres'. The first half of this report is confirmed by reviews of the original production in its first week. These clearly attribute a significant part of the 'approbation and applause' to the comic capers of Apollo and Andrew. *The Times* reviewer noted that '[Reeve's] drunken scene with Buckstone shook the house with laughter', which indicates that the mindless misogynistic vandalism of the actors' characters here was either endorsed or overlooked for the purpose of relishing the moment's 'joyous muckiness'. The destructive masculinity of the serious narrative, however, does not seem to have enjoyed such favour, for the reviewer reported that as Isabelle Mrs Yates 'excited a degree of interest almost painfully real'.[29] The *Literary Gazette* man actually stated that Isabelle's story caused weeping, concluding that it was the play's leaping 'between crying and laughing' that enabled him to say 'Woman's Life ... is likely to *last very long*'.[30] This 'crying' can be construed as a radical response since it registers sympathy with Isabelle's anguish, which was, as we have seen, a feminist quality. The positive nature of the tears is pointed up by the negative reaction of an audience member who clearly did not cry. The reviewer for the *Spectator* felt that Isabelle's unhappy story was boring and that she was 'a personage of secondary importance, in whose character and fate we take

---

[29]   Review of *Isabelle*, *The Times*, 28 January 1834, p. 3. Presumably he meant that Isabelle's plight stirred sympathy that bordered on genuine sorrow.
[30]   Review of *Isabelle*, *Literary Gazette*, 1 February 1834, p .84.

comparatively little interest'.[31]   Significantly, he saw Eugene as 'the principal character' and concentrated upon him at the expense of Isabelle (who is not mentioned at all) in his description of the narrative.[32]   The dominant nature of his response becomes clear in the praise he does grant to the Isabelle drama:

> Mrs Yates read a most impressive lesson on 'curiosity in servants'; shows an edifying example of forbearance in a wife not peeping into her husband's *billets*; and at the conclusion addresses a pretty little sermonet, and bestows a stage blessing upon the fair portion of the audience – which is rapturously received; and we daresay will attract many a sentimental mother and daughter to see *Isabelle*.[33]

The last comment shows that the reviewer was not alone in constructing the heroine as an 'edifying' figure of feminine conservatism. What is more, it seems that he was in female company. But his use of the word 'sentimental' is important and not only for its intensification of the sense that he may have shared his view of women with Eugene; it implies that there were *un*sentimental mothers and daughters who were not inclined to give the 'pretty little sermonet' a rapturous reception.

'A Pattern of Diligence and Prudence': Feminist Discourse in *A Woman of Business*

In the 1850s middle-class feminists began to act as well as write against the imprisonment of women in domestic infantilism and servitude.   The birth of organized feminism occurred in 1855, when Barbara Leigh Smith commenced her campaign for the introduction of a Parliamentary Bill granting women the right to hold and acquire property after marriage.[34] Four years later the feminists who had gathered under Leigh Smith established the Society for Promoting the Employment of Women, an organization which assisted would-be women workers by providing training schemes and encouraging employers to hire women, particularly in the expanding retail and clerical areas.[35]   In 1858 the *Englishwoman's Journal* was

---

[31]   Review of *Isabelle*, *Spectator*, 1 February 1834, p. 103.

[32]   Ibid.

[33]   Ibid., p. 104.

[34]   This and the following developments are succinctly discussed in Caine, ch 3, and Bolt, ch 3.   Under common law a husband assumed legal possession and control of any property belonging to his wife upon, and of any that came to her after, marriage.

[35]   New economic opportunities for women were required independently of feminist demands.   A significant number of middle-class women were desperately in need of training

founded, carrying searching feminist analysis of women's educational, legal, and economic inequality. Over the next decade the feminists and their journal, located in Langham Place in London, spearheaded a burgeoning women's movement which attacked male privilege in every sphere, public and private. There were campaigns to open up the professions and higher education to women, the latter achieving the creation of two women's colleges at Cambridge (Girton and Newnham) by 1873. The battle for married women's property rights continued unrelentingly after the failure of the Bill provoked by Leigh Smith in 1857, securing reform in 1870 and 1882. And in 1866 the struggle for women's right to vote began as the first female suffragist organization was founded.

It fell to comedy, with its plucky and self-assertive heroine, to represent this rebellion on the 'domestic' stage. Webster's *A Woman of Business*, which was first performed on 29 August 1864 at the Adelphi, uses the comic heroine's vigour to carry something of the contemporary feminist drive to attain women's rights to rationality and professional labour; more specifically, the play appears to dramatize some of the claims and goals articulated by Leigh Smith in her book *Women and Work* (1857). Here Leigh Smith attacked the injustice of the enforced idleness of middle-class women, arguing that it made them 'frivolous, ignorant, weak, and sickly'.[36] She offered this degeneracy as proof of the unnaturalness of their domestic immurement and stated that 'women are God's children equally with men'.[37] Consequently, she went on, 'Adult women must not be supported by men, if they are to stand as dignified, rational beings before God'; they all required and were perfectly capable of 'a science, art, or profession'.[38] This was a particularly radical belief, for in advocating the right of wives to such occupations Leigh Smith went further than many of her fellow campaigners.[39]

So too, then, did the feminist dimension of Webster's play, for the heroine Annie Hall is a married 'Woman of Business'. Moreover, she is a completely

---

and employment simply because dependent domesticity was not available to them. In 1851 there was a surplus of single women to single men of 72,000, rising to 125,000 in 1871 (a 72.7 per cent increase). These figures are supplied in Martha Vicinus, 'Introduction', in Vicinus (ed.), *A Widening Sphere: Changing Roles of Victorian Women* (Bloomington and London: Indiana University Press, 1977), p. xvi.

[36]   Barbara Leigh Smith, *Women and Work* (London: Bosworth and Harrison, 1857), p. 18.

[37]   Ibid., p. 6.

[38]   Ibid., pp. 11–12.

[39]   For example, in her *Hints on Self-Help: A Book For Young Women* (London: S.W. Partridge, 1863), p. 53, Jessie Boucherett, another leading Langham Place feminist, wrote the following: 'The first prize in life is a happy marriage, the second a life of independence ... The pursuit of the second prize in no way prevents the winning of the first, for the second best can at any time be exchanged for the best whenever the opportunity occurs'.

independent one whose fitness for the masculine world simply cannot be denied as she runs her wine-merchant husband's company without professional assistance from him or from any other man. The play makes it easy for feminist spectators to champion the character, who is clearly, as another says of her, 'to be both respected and admired'; she is in no way a shrew or an adventuress, being 'a thoroughly good woman' (f. 5).[40] In addition, she is shown to be capable and intelligent (she is the only intelligent major character in the play), 'doing a spanking trade' and saving the day without once requiring her husband's help (f. 14). Indeed, it is he who is desperately in need of hers. The couple are surrounded by men whom he regards as friends but whom she knows to be villains who would break up their marriage, make off with their fortune, and ensnare their niece. As Annie deals with these various perils we see how the comic heroine's plot as well as character is utilized to support the play's feminist project. In Annie's flawless and amusing schemes to send villainy flying (some of which involve such masculine operations as the hiring of a private detective and the movement of funds) inheres a dramatic demonstration of the legitimacy of her elevated position.

The play even appropriates patriarchalism to legitimize Annie's position. Hostile reaction to the unconventional marriage of the Halls is voiced throughout, but it is put into the mouths of villains and oafs and, perhaps symbolically, cast as a dishonest means to dark and selfish ends. Thus Hall's cousin Simon says to him, 'you're a naught in your own house' and warns, 'your wife will go on from one thing to another, and have a game of blindman's buff all to herself – you'll be the blind man, old son', but he wants Hall to be 'lord and master' in order that he may override Annie's objection to his marrying their wealthy niece (ff. 16–17). Again, Hall only insists upon being 'lord and master' and seriously articulates patriarchal sentiments ('the dignity of my manly nature has been outraged', 'look after your servants and your dresses') when he is drunk and under the malicious influence of Simon (ff. 29–39). Crucially, in his rational moments he not only endorses Annie's being in charge of the business, but also expresses the rightness of that state of affairs: 'I don't know what I should do without her ... I'm quite satisfied, and I am not ashamed to own it' (f. 12). As soon as he banishes her from the office the ludicrousness of his action is manifested: he 'upsets letters on floor' and tries to hand ten thousand pounds to a swindler (f. 31). In yet another delightfully ironic invocation of patriarchalism Annie here plays the idle, frivolous, and ignorant ideal woman lamented by Leigh Smith. 'It is clearly understood', she tells her newly assertive husband, 'I have nothing else to do but sit in the drawing room and look interesting' (f. 30). As she flirts with her would-be seducer and responds to her husband's resolve to strike a deal with the swindler with the words, 'Everything

---

[40] All quotations are taken from Benjamin Webster, *A Woman of Business* (1864), British Library, Lord Chamberlain's Collection, Add MSS 53034, ff. 1–47.

you do is for the best of course, and I have no business to interfere', the tone is primarily comic, for she is actually punishing both men (she exposes the former's insincerity and lets the latter think himself ruined – she has, of course, already emptied the account upon which he drew) (f. 36). But there is a serious inflection here and it subsists not only in the fact that Annie's brilliance is demonstrated once again; for a moment the audience gets a glimpse of how disastrous things would have been for the Halls, both maritally and financially, had Annie been an 'ideal' woman.

It is not just here and in this manner that Leigh Smith's feminist criticism is mobilized in Annie. Earlier in the play the heroine delivers a direct feminist attack upon the enforcement of female idleness. When Hall puts the dominant view to her – 'The drawing room is your proper place' – Annie says 'Nonsense' and argues the following:

> A business woman is no loss to society, whilst the want of something to do has made many a place vacant which would otherwise have been honourably filled. There is no idea of you men relative to our sex; and you have an enormous number of silly ones, goodness knows, so injurious to us, as that of stupidly supposing that every woman should sit all day long with her hands in her lap.[41]

Here Annie asserts that the *lack* of businesswomen is 'a loss to society', not enough men being able to carry out the professional labour it requires; her assumption is that together the sexes constitute a potentially even and adequate resource. But she does not stop at stressing the 'injurious' effect upon society in general of the fact that 'there is no idea of men relative to her sex'; like Leigh Smith, she points up the damaging and ridiculous consequence for women of their immobilization.

---

[41]   Interestingly, the licensing copy of *A Woman of Business* was not exactly the script that was performed. This speech is in the published version of the play, which I have been unable to obtain; Margo Mellick uses this text and cites this speech in her discussion of the play, which can be found in her 'Divergent Melodramatic Heroines of the Mid-Victorian Play; or, The Woman Who Doesn't Faint', unpublished PhD thesis, Ohio State University, 1976, pp. 214–18 (speech cited p. 215). The speech in question is present in the licensing copy, but it is drastically reduced and softened: '[A] business woman is no loss to society, and I don't like sitting all day long with my hands in my lap' (f. 10). Annie's final implication that 'every woman' is oppressed is replaced by the very much narrower suggestion that *she* would be if made to 'sit all day'. This apparent evasion of the censor's law, of course, adds another layer of daring opposition to the play's feminist project. Mellick, it should be noted, holds *A Woman of Business* up as a perfect example of a 'role reversal' play. She conceives of this type ahistorically, and so does not read the play in relation to its period's feminism; nor does she perceive the play's serious conservative dimension, which is discussed below.

It is worth noting at this point that Annie's attractiveness and dynamism appear to have been well served by Fanny Stirling, the actress who played her. Stirling was a much-loved and very talented comic actress in the early and mid-Victorian period. In 1862 one critic remarked that '[n]o living actress can approach her in comedy ... she combines every qualification to produce a matchless embodiment of the piquant, the high-bred, the witty heroines of the old drama'.[42] He went on to praise her for being 'capable at once of sweetness and acerbity' and for 'know[ing] how to give point to the wit of her author' and 'emphasis to his satire'.[43] Annie may not be 'high-bred' and Webster's play was not 'old drama', but Stirling's skill in realizing the other qualities listed was called for and by all accounts delivered.[44] The reviewer for the *Athenaeum* reported that '[t]he drama ... exhibit[s] to the best advantage the talents of Mrs Stirling', who, he went on, played a character of 'great energy' with 'great spirit'; the reviewer for the *Illustrated London News* also felt Annie was perfect for Stirling, whose 'acting in this character', he wrote, 'is admirable, one might add inimitable'.[45]

It seems safe to assume, then, that *A Woman of Business* would have given feminists and those in sympathy with feminist aspirations considerable pleasure. But, just as *Isabelle* does, the play also provides a route through its action for sexist spectators, and this is no less significant or powerful than that from which it diverges. After we have seen Annie at work in the office and heard her speak of woman's right to work, for example, our attention is drawn to her equally grand capacity for housekeeping: 'she's just suited to this place', says Simon, 'look at the paper on the wall, and the carpet all over the room, and this ain't your best room neither' (f. 13). Roughly half way through the play Annie herself fortifies this suggestion that she is naturally 'just suited' to the role of 'angel in the house', explaining her motives to her clerk as follows:

> It was not a very long time after I was married that I discovered my husband was one of those men who chooses rather to be led than to lead. I determined that if anyone was to be his guide and friend, it should be his wife, who would have nothing but his good in view ...

[42]   Cited in Donald Mullin (ed.), *Victorian Actors and Actresses in Review: A Dictionary of Contemporary Views of Representative British and American Actors and Actresses 1837-1901* (Westport and London: Greenwood, 1983), p. 424.

[43]   Ibid.

[44]   Annie was 'a poor governess' before her marriage to the aristocratic Hall (f.24). The radical message, incidentally, seems to be that a woman can climb in this way and not be another Lady Audley.

[45]   Reviews of *A Woman of Business*, *Athenaeum*, 3 September 1864, p. 315, *Illustrated London News*, 3 September 1864, p. 246. Further quotations are from these pages.

> The estate which today will see Mr Hall its owner is that on which he
> was reared. It was his till the negligence of others deprived him of it;
> it will again be his. I have arranged it all, we shall live in the country
> leaving you in charge of the business. Julia will make you a capital
> housekeeper. I shall have done with business; Harry will be happy for
> ever and a day. (ff. 25–26)

Long before closure, then, Annie's behaviour is rooted in the period's angelic
femininity: she has worked for 'nothing but [Hall's] good', her end has been the
purchase of his beloved aristocratic childhood home. In direct contrast to the
sentiments she articulates elsewhere, Annie says that she works *only* in order to be
a proper wife to Hall. Moreover, she seems to believe that she will best realize that
subject-position when she 'shall have done with business' – her current productive
state is merely the means of facilitating an ideal future state divorced from such
production. And not, it is implied, from *re*production: the play insinuates that
female labour destroys the maternal capacity for the Halls are childless. Indeed,
when Simon remarks that there is 'no chick or child' the lack is expressed as
acutely felt: 'That's the only thing we need wish for', Hall replies (f. 14). Clearly
non-feminist impulses are also evident in Annie's suggestion that she is a
businesswoman because her husband 'chose' for her to be and in her imposition of
entirely conventional domestic femininity upon her niece Julia, whom she promises
as a wife and 'capital housekeeper' to her clerk and successor Tylney (Julia is a
manipulated object neither seen nor heard in the play). *A Woman of Business*, then,
promises that beyond the final curtain its world will see women realizing only
conventional domestic femininity. But, as is the case with *Isabelle*, the play does
offer feminist spectators an opportunity to problematize its dominant climactic
meaning. Annie may be about to 'have done with business', but the last words of
the play suggest that this is a lamentable or even temporary affair. '[I]f our friends
before us should feel inclined to do the same', says Simon, 'we'll drink success to
Mrs Hall as a woman of business' (f. 47).

Reviews of the play give little away regarding what those before the stage felt
about Simon's proposal, but they do record that, to quote the *Athenaeum* man,
'[t]he curtain fell to much applause; the new piece, indeed, was decidedly
successful'. The *Illustrated London News* critic went so far as to predict 'a
lengthened run, and a place permanently in the repertoire of the theatre' for the
play.[46] His review suggests that he at least enjoyed the feminist dimension of the
drama. He writes that 'The strong-minded woman is now familiar enough on our

---

[46]   The play ran for at least 23 nights, for 'the Highly Successful NEW
COMEDIETTA' was advertised as running for a further five nights on 19 September
(playbill in the Theatre Museum, Covent Garden).

boards, but we know not that she has been more attractively presented than in this production'.[47] He praises 'the clever woman' highly, carefully detailing all 'proofs of her shrewdness and especial capacity for business' and even holding her up as a model for real women: 'Mrs Hall ... is a pattern of diligence and prudence, and should be imitated by all wives who have partners who are liable to be led by other people'.

As we have seen, both *Isabelle* and *A Woman of Business* engage in framebreaking at their final curtains. Isabelle and Simon step outside of their fictional worlds to ask for the approbation of their audiences, and in doing so they remind those audiences that what they have been watching are people earning their livings, people who are hoping to receive applause that will enable them to go on stage again with their current parts and with new ones. For the spectator who was happy with the period's patriarchal division of the sexes into public and private spheres of labour, such moments must have been unsettling, for they exposed the fact that when characters like Isabelle and Annie generate the message that women should exist only in a state of domestic passivity, their very mediums simultaneously constituted powerful examples of a directly opposite female state.[48] For the feminist spectator, however, climactic frame-breaking moments must have been satisfying, even – perhaps especially – when they required actresses to deliver 'pretty little sermonets' like Isabelle's. In being reminded that independent and successful working women stood before them, the feminist spectators of *Isabelle* and *A Woman of Business* could have augmented their readings of the plays, seeing in Elizabeth Yates a possible solution to Isabelle's predicament and in Fanny Stirling a living justification of Annie's advocacy of female professional labour. As Powell, Marshall, and others have shown, the nineteenth-century actress did not enjoy complete freedom from the ideological restrictions that were suffered by her domestic sisters, experiencing sexism socially and professionally. But she may have been able to say of her life what Bianca Pazzi, the actress heroine of Geraldine Jewsbury's novel *The Half Sisters* (1848), was able to say of hers:

I have had a definite employment all my life; when I rose in the morning my work lay before me, and I had a clear, definite channel in

---

[47]   The term 'strong-minded woman' was used to denote feminists in the 1850s and 1860s, just as the term 'New Woman' was used to denote feminists in the 1890s.

[48]   In her *Actresses as Working Women: Their Social Identity in Victorian Culture* (London: Routledge, 1991), pp. 105–106, Tracy C. Davis argues that such spectators 'were required to separate the defeminized actress from her roles', which then in a sense *became* her. Davis points to the case of Ellen Terry: 'Even with several ill-fated marriages, a succession of lovers, and two illegitimate children, Ellen Terry still evoked the consummation of "womanliness" in her roles and could command universal respect and admiration in the practice of her art'.

which all my energies might flow ... I was kept clear of ENNUI, which eats like a leprosy into the life of women. I was leading a life of my own, and was able to acquire a full control over my own faculties; and I have always had a sense of freedom, of enjoyment of my existence, which has rendered all my vexations easy to be borne ... I have had work to do, and I have done it. I have had a purpose, and have endeavoured to work it out.[49]

---

[49]   Geraldine Jewsbury, *The Half Sisters* (1848; Oxford: World's Classics, 1994), pp. 249–50.

Chapter 9

Women's Playwriting and the Popular Theatre in the Late Victorian Era, 1870–1900

Kate Newey[1]

What would our picture of the London theatre of the late nineteenth century look like if we took account of plays written by women for the popular theatre? How might these two marginalised categories – popular entertainment and women's writing – act as filters through which to review the history of English theatre and drama of this period? In this chapter, I will examine the work of a selection of women who wrote for the London stage at the end of the nineteenth century, challenging both the standard narrative of the development of English drama, and the tendencies of current feminist literary criticism to focus principally on women's writing which fulfils paradigms of transgression or subversion.[2] I will argue that an examination of the cultural work done by women writing for the popular stage is central to both an accurate account of late-nineteenth-century theatre and an inclusive feminist critical practice. The women on whom I have chosen to focus – Florence Marryat, Lucy Clifford, and Florence Bell – are representative of the many women who wrote mostly for the commercial London stage at the end of the nineteenth century. They are only a selection of women playwrights active at the end of the nineteenth century; others who might also be covered by this discussion include Pearl Craigie ('John Oliver Hobbes'), Jeanie Adams-Acton, Aimee Beringer, Rosina Filippi, Constance Fletcher ('George Fleming'), Clo Graves (later 'Richard Dehan'), Frances Hodgson-Burnett, Harriet Jay ('Charles Marlowe'), Ellen Lancaster-Wallis, Madeleine Lucette Ryley, Janet Steer, Netta Syrett, and Florence Warden (*née* Alice Price). They

[1]   Research for this chapter was supported by the Australian Research Council. My thanks to Margaret Leask and Tiffany Unwin for their research assistance.
[2]   At this point in my argument, I realise that this is a brief summation – some may argue caricature – of an array of complex arguments within feminist literary criticism. I also recognise the multiplicities of feminist theory and practice – feminisms – and am using the term here in the broadest possible sense of a critical practice which seeks to value the work produced by women.

were variously involved with specifically feminist or political projects, either
for the reform of the position of women or the English stage, but in the work I
am discussing, these were not their principal concerns. In this chapter, I am
interested in looking at plays written by women for the unashamedly popular –
that is, commercial – theatre. Neither standard theatre histories nor feminist
literary history have entirely accommodated such work so I shall provide an
introductory (and thus, necessarily partial) map of that unexplored territory.[3]

The Politics of Theatre History

The story that is usually told about English drama and theatre in the nineteenth
century is developmental, evolutionary and teleological, where English drama
moves inexorably towards the goals of psychological realism and
representational naturalism. This narrative was shaped through a series of
binary oppositions which constructed an evolutionary progression from
primitive to sophisticated dramatic forms, from popular performance to
literary text, and from the feminised excess of melodrama to the masculine
scientific realm of realism. In the latter part of the nineteenth century, this
account of English drama became a campaign for its reform, carried on by
critics and historians of the drama, and it was this group which laid down the
patterns of the emergence of the modern drama in English which is still a
powerful story today.

To sample a range of middle-class and middle-brow periodical articles on
the state of the English theatre in the 1860s to the 1880s is to trace the
formation of theatre history in these terms. This comment in 1863 from the
Cornhill is typical: 'That our drama is extinct as literature, and our stage is in
a deplorable condition of decline, no one will venture to dispute.'[4] In 1869,
Macmillan's Magazine opines that 'It is in England only that the glory of the
drama has gone down, and it is a fact much to be deplored, for it coincides
with an undeniable degeneracy of taste, and it suppresses the noblest form of

---

[3]   Feminist critical and theatre historical work in this field which is not concerned
primarily with 'New Woman' theatre and fiction is indeed sparse; for the most focussed
discussion, see Susan Carlson, 'Conflicted Politics and Circumspect Comedy: Women's
Comic Playwriting in the 1890s' in Tracy C. Davis and Ellen Donkin (eds), *Women and
Playwriting in Nineteenth-Century Britain* (Cambridge: Cambridge University Press, 1999),
pp. 256–76.
[4]   'Foreign Actors and the English Drama' *Cornhill Magazine* 8 (1863), pp. 172–
9, (p. 172).

expression affected by the national tongue.'[5]   In the *Temple Bar*'s discussion of 'The Present State of the English Stage' in 1871 the degradation of the drama is attributed to just five causes: the influence of the lessees, the influence of the playwrights, the influence of actors, the influence of professional critics, and the influence of the audience.[6]   Although just what is left as a benign influence on the theatre is unclear.   In the course of this discussion the *Temple Bar* makes an observation which pinpoints very neatly one of the central binary oppositions in the historiography of the period.

> A lessee is entitled to look to a safe and decent livelihood ... but the more ardently he professes to honour and be enamoured of his art, the smaller, comparatively, should be the return that contents him.[7]

This opposition between art and commerce is a familiar one in the late nineteenth century, and underpins critical articulations of the oppositions between art and entertainment, and drama and theatre.   G. H. Lewes, for example, writes that: 'The drama has an immediate and an ulterior aim.   Its immediate aim is to delight an audience; its ulterior aim is the ennobling and enlarging of the mind through the sympathies –'[8]   However, according to most contemporary commentators, enlarging managers' accounts rarely resulted in ennobling the audiences' minds.

These sets of oppositions are even more marked in the contemporary and retrospective commentaries of Henry Arthur Jones, whose work as a proselytiser for a particular vision of English drama now appears at least as influential as his plays.   In his introduction to his first collection of polemical pieces, *The Renascence of the English Drama*, Jones states that he has been fighting for 'a recognition of the distinction between the art of the drama on the one hand and popular amusement on the other, and of the greater pleasure to be derived from the art of the drama.'[9]   The problem with contemporary English drama is that:

> It is a hybrid, an unwieldy Siamese Twin, with two bodies, two heads, two minds, two dispositions, all of them, for the present, vitally connected.   And one of these two bodies, dramatic art, is lean

---

[5]   'A Word on the Drama in England and France,' *Macmillan's Magazine* 20 (1869), p. 70.

[6]   'The Present State of the English Stage,' *Temple Bar* 33 (1871), p. 458.

[7]   Ibid., pp. 460–61.

[8]   G. H. Lewes, 'Shakespeare in France,' *Cornhill Magazine* 11 (1865), p. 35.

[9]   Henry Arthur Jones, *The Renascence of the English Drama* (London: Macmillan, 1895), p. vii.

and pinched and starving, and has to drag about with it, wherever it goes, its fat, puffy, unwholesome, dropsical brother, popular amusement.[10]

Indeed in a later lecture at Harvard, Jones argued that one of the 'Corner Stones of Modern Drama' is 'The severance of the drama from popular entertainment: the recognition of it as a fine art which, though its lower ranges must always compound with mere popular entertainment, and be confused with it, is yet essentially something different from popular entertainment, transcends it, and in its higher ranges is in marked and eternal antagonism to popular entertainment.'[11]

By the end of the century this polemic had solidified into an orthodoxy which valued drama over theatre, art over entertainment, individual genius over collective industry, and Englishness over foreignness. The influential critics Clement Scott and William Archer presented models of English dramatic development which linked epochal moments with individual playwrights, Scott focussing on the 'landmark' of Marie Wilton's 'discovery' of Tom Robertson,[12] and Archer charting the peaks of English drama through a series of male playwrights, Tom Robertson, Arthur Wing Pinero, and George Bernard Shaw.

> The first two movements came from within the theatre itself ... But the third movement proceeded from without. It was an intellectual movement and a movement of intellectuals. Its leaders, with one exception, were men of letters before they became men of the theatre. Economically, it was at first, and has continued to be in some measure, an endowed movement ... if the Shaw drama had been forced to pay its way, as were the Robertson drama and the Pinero drama, it would long ago have died of starvation.[13]

Elsewhere, Archer distinguishes between the literary and the non-literary drama, continuing Jones' argument that until the English drama is read as well as performed, 'our drama will remain unliterary, frivolous, non-moral, unworthy of its past and of our present stage of advancement in other branches

---

[10]   Ibid., p. 11.
[11]   Henry Arthur Jones, *The Foundations of a National Drama* (London: Chapman and Hall, [nd]), pp. 37–8.
[12]   Clement Scott, *The Drama of Yesterday and Today* (London: Macmillan, 1899; 2 vols), vol 1, p. 471.
[13]   William Archer, *The Old Drama and the New* (London: William Heinemann, 1923), p. 338.

of literature and art.'[14]   Archer, Jones, and Scott replicate and renew old debates about the superiority of the literary drama over the popular theatre, even though the evidence of audiences, managements, and performers throughout the nineteenth century suggests that the popular theatre, no matter how frivolous or non-moral, is the great survivor.

Simply as an account of plays written and produced in England in the late nineteenth century, this model leaves out more than it includes.   Yet it still wields a powerful influence.   The same hierarchy of value is reproduced in twentieth-century histories of the theatre, where moral and aesthetic judgements are merged in apparently objective critical histories which actually operate as tools to preserve cultural hegemony.   Allardyce Nicoll's magisterial history of English drama, for example, schematises an evolutionary model of progress towards realism in chapter headings which announce Robertson as the 'reformer' of the theatre, and position Henry Arthur Jones and Pinero as the playwrights at 'The Turn of the Tide' with Wilde and Shaw indicating 'The Success of the Reformers.'[15]   Even recuperative studies such as Michael Booth's ground-breaking study of popular theatre, *English Melodrama*, reproduce this model, linking progress and modernity with realism and a gradual sloughing off of the sensationalism of Gothic and romantic melodrama, discussing the opposition between 'serious drama' and melodrama in terms which, as Shepherd and Womack point out, 'not only Archer but Robertson and even Lewes would have recognised.'[16]

In all these histories women playwrights in the popular theatre have been rendered doubly invisible.   Like their male peers, their work has been overlooked in critical canons of English literature because of their choice of popular medium and genres; but unlike their male peers, women playwrights are also marginalised by attitudes to playwriting which assume that it is a preserve of masculinity in both its aesthetic and professional structures.[17]

---

[14]   William Archer, *English Dramatists of To-Day* (London: Sampson Low, Marston, Searle, and Rivington, 1882), p. 7.

[15]   Allardyce Nicoll, *A History of the English Drama, 1660–1900*, vol V, *Late Nineteenth Century Drama, 1850–1900* (Cambridge: Cambridge University Press, 1959).

[16]   Michael R. Booth, *English Melodrama* (London: Herbert Jenkins, 1965), and Simon Shepherd and Peter Womack, *English Drama: A Cultural History* (Oxford: Blackwell, 1996), p. 227.

[17]   Note that John Russell Stephens's important study, *The Profession of the Playwright: British Theatre 1800–1900*, (Cambridge: Cambridge University Press, 1992), contains little more than two paragraphs discussion of women playwrights (p. 3). For an extended argument about the long-term impact of such a gendered definition of 'playwright' see Ellen Donkin, *Getting into the Act: Women Playwrights in London, 1776–1829* (London and New York: Routledge, 1995).

Women attempting to write for the popular stage needed to operate within the predominantly masculine and patriarchal hierarchy of the London theatre as a business sector. As playwrights, they worked hard to have their plays read, accepted, produced, and received well in the London theatre industry. While they faced inescapable difficulties in gaining acceptance as professional 'women of letters,' these women were successful and active, and exercised a remarkable degree of agency and autonomy in a profession which still presented barriers to female participation. Looking back at them now, we can see how the women who did write plays faced up to many of the taboos contested by the figure of the 'New Woman'. Unlike historical and fictional New Women, who challenged these openly, even scandalously, Marryat, Bell, and Clifford wrote plays about femininity from within its traps and freedoms.

Theatre from the Drawing-Room

Of the women I discuss here, all but Florence Marryat were most active in the theatre in the 1890s and beyond, working as writers alongside their more notorious and visible New Women sisters. As part of this public visibility of women, the 1890s was the most productive decade of the century for women playwrights. Almost 270 women produced over 650 dramatic works, including plays for children, translations, and closet dramas by women writers better known as poets such as 'Michael Field' (Katherine Bradley and Edith Cooper) and Augusta Webster. While women's writing was still only a small part of the total dramatic and theatrical output of the period – over the whole century women's theatrical and para-theatrical writing constituted some 12 per cent of all such writing – work in the 1890s makes up just over half the total of women's writing for the theatre in the nineteenth century.[18] Thus for women writers, the 1890s can be seen as epoch-making simply in the sheer volume of their dramatic work made public.

---

[18]   Over 500 women wrote some 1,200 titles for the theatre or in para-theatrical forms between 1800 and 1900. These figures are based on my tabulations of 'Appendix A' identifying women playwrights in James Ellis and Joseph Donohue (eds), *English Drama of the Nineteenth Century, An Index and Finding Guide* (New Canaan: Readex Books, 1985), Allardyce Nicoll, 'Hand-Lists' and 'Alphabetical Catalogue of Plays' in *A History of English Drama 1660–1900*, vol VI (Cambridge: Cambridge University Press, 1959–70), Donald Mullin, *Victorian Plays. A Record of Significant Productions on the London Stage, 1837–1901* (Westport: Greenwood Press, 1987) and indexes to the Pettingell Collection, University of Kent at Canterbury. As my study is not primarily a statistical one, and contemporary records (let alone our modern indexes of them) are not always accurate, these figures are necessarily approximate, but as near to accurate as I can be.

However, women's theatre work of the 1890s represented more than just visibility, although this was in itself not insignificant. As Tracy C. Davis notes, census returns from 1841 to 1911 show a steady increase of women coming into the acting profession.[19] In the last third of the century, women also started to move into the theatrical trades in significant numbers: for example, from the 1870s, '[M]ore than half of the new costumier outlets were established by women under their own names'.[20] These substantial moves into professional careers across the range of theatrical activities (as women moved away from theatre work just as actress/commodity) had a specific and deliberate political meaning for some women. In the 1890s, women started to use their positions in the theatre as actresses, writers, critics, and managers to make connections between their work and their proto-feminist politics.[21] Julie Holledge recounts how in the 1890s a group of actresses (pre-eminently Elizabeth Robins) moved into the performance, production and management of plays with a feminist agenda, particularly those by Henrik Ibsen, led by their 'belief that Ibsen's characters could speak to all women [which] inspired them to devote their energies to productions of his plays.'[22] Elizabeth Robins' championing of Ibsen on the London stage was a way of introducing better roles for women, by promoting better plays *about* women. Kerry Powell goes so far as to cast Robins' campaign for a 'Theatre of the Future' as a potential revolutionary moment when 'it appeared that masculine control of the theatre as an institution might be overthrown by the efforts of women and a few male allies.'[23] Thus, the conventional pattern of nineteenth-century theatre history, which casts the end of the century as a watershed when the tired and old-fashioned aesthetic of the popular stage is overthrown, is replicated in these accounts of women's theatre work.

Yet we might argue that it is the role of feminist historians to question such periodisations and patterns, rather than attempting simply to fit women's histories into established historical narratives. As Thomas Postlewait reminds

---

[19]   Tracy C. Davis, *Actresses as Working Women: Their Social Identity in Victorian Culture* (London and New York: Routledge, 1991), p. 10.

[20]   Tracy C. Davis, 'Laborers of the Nineteenth-Century Theater: The Economies of Gender and Theatrical Organization', *Journal of British Studies* 33 (1994), pp. 50–51.

[21]   See, for example, Sheila Stowell's study of women playwrights of the suffrage era: the 'self-consciously feminist playwrights who used the overtly "public" forum of drama as a point of entry to the debate.' *A Stage of Their Own: Feminist Playwrights of the Suffrage Era* (Manchester: Manchester University Press, 1992), p. 1.

[22]   Julie Holledge, *Innocent Flowers. Women in the Edwardian Theatre* (London: Virago Press, 1981), p. 27.

[23]   Kerry Powell, *Women and Victorian Theatre* (Cambridge: Cambridge University Press, 1997), p. 149.

us, theatrical revolutions do not happen in isolated places and moments, but occur on several fronts over time.[24] And while Robins' work is crucial in focussing attention on the theatre as a place for active female participation and even leadership, our understanding of Robins' use of the theatre as a fruitful site for a feminist campaign cannot be separated from the work of those who came before her. As Viv Gardner points out, an investigation of the relationship between the 'Woman Question' and the theatre of the 1890s requires a look 'backwards to the elder sisters of the New Woman' as well as forward to her metaphorical daughters.[25] But these 'elder sisters' were not necessarily concerned with what we recognise now as feminist issues. Their work calls for a more nuanced understanding of aspects of popular entertainment produced and consumed by women. We need to be sensitive to the negotiations that they made between the obstacles presented by late Victorian ideologies of femininity, and the ways in which they used the very same socially constructed models of femininity to empower and articulate women's points of view.

The work of Florence Marryat (1838–99) provides a potent example of the necessary delicacies of interpretation involved in understanding both her work and the conditions in which she worked. Florence Marryat was the youngest of the eleven children of novelist Frederick Marryat, and like him, a prolific writer and family woman: she published over seventy novels and bore eight children.[26] Literary and biological fecundity is routinely noted in accounts of Captain Marryat, but her productivity was probably far more significant a shaper of Florence Marryat's life than her father's. In a pattern familiar in the histories of professional women writers, Marryat was required to earn her living because the ideals of Victorian marriage failed her in practical terms. Like many other women writers, she turned to writing and performing to support her family and husband as she could not rely on her husband to support her. By 1893, when Helen Black interviewed her, she had lost the fortune she earned by her writing: 'Others have spent it for me ... and I do not

---

[24]   Thomas Postlewait, *Prophet of the New Drama: William Archer and the Ibsen Campaign* (Westport, Conn.: Greenwood Press, 1986), p. 50, and 'From Melodrama to Realism: the Suspect History of American Drama' in Michael Hays and Anastasia Nikolopoulou (eds), *Melodrama: The Cultural Emergence of a Genre* (London: Macmillan, 1996), p. 41.

[25]   Viv Gardner, 'Introduction', in Viv Gardner and Susan Rutherford (eds), *The New Woman and Her Sisters: Feminism and Theatre, 1850–1914* (Hemel Hempstead: Harvester Wheatsheaf, 1992), p. 2.

[26]   Elaine Showalter notes the influence Captain Marryat may have had on Florence Marryat's career, *A Literature of Their Own: from Charlotte Brontë to Doris Lessing* (1977; London: Virago, 1978), p. 62.

grudge it to them.'[27]   The chief impression one gains of Marryat is of her versatility and energy, and the professionalism and ease with which she wrote, performed, edited and conducted a career as 'a woman of letters.' This latter pursuit required her to be tough: letters to her agent Mr Colles at the Authors' Syndicate are constantly enquiring about payments and arrangements for publication: 'I write to remind you that the 18th of this month is the date for handing over the royalties on "At Heart a Rake" & I hope you will ask Mr Cox not to delay making up his books, as I shall be leaving Torquay shortly. Hutchinson's are to be made up I believe every 3 months. He told me there would be something due over the advance at the end of the first three.'[28] Marryat's attention to detail here is at odds with her publicly indulgent attitude towards others spending her fortune, an inkling perhaps of the determination with which Marryat constructed herself in a socially acceptable – but also profitable – model of femininity.

Marryat's novels are generally classified as sensation fiction,[29] which she maintained that she wrote quickly and did not revise; her plays, usually adapted by Marryat from her novels, were melodramas and comedies in the sensational style. Helen Black writes admiringly: 'at one time nine of these plays were running simultaneously in the provinces. She wrote a play called "Her World Against a Lie" (from her own novel), which was produced at the Prince of Wales' Theatre, and in which she played the chief comedy part ... with so much skill and *aplomb*, that the *Era*, *Figaro*, *Morning Post*, and other papers, criticised her performances most favourably.'[30] Marryat collaborated with Sir Charles Young in dramatising two of her novels, *Miss Chester* and *Charmyon*. *Miss Chester*[31] is a full-blooded domestic melodrama of the upper classes (and in this respect different from the melodramas of working-class life prevalent in the 1820s and 30s), in the mould of *East Lynne* and *Lady Audley's Secret*. Although Marryat's work lacks the explicit political dimension of her near contemporary 'New Woman' writers, her dramatisation of the feeling woman as a passionate and powerful speaking subject challenges the ideological quarantine of emotion into the private sphere, and is

---

[27]   Helen Black, *Notable Women Authors of the Day* (Glasgow: David Bryce and Son, 1893), p. 87.

[28]   14 July 1896, Authors' Syndicate collection, Humanities Research Centre, University of Texas (Austin).

[29]   Showalter, p. 28; Janet Todd (ed.), *Dictionary of British Women Writers* (London: Routledge, 1989), p. 448.

[30]   Black, p. 90.

[31]   All quotations are taken from Florence Marryat and Sir Charles Young, *Miss Chester* (London: Samuel French, [nd]), first performed at the Holborn Theatre, 6 October 1872.

all the more significant for its location in the popular theatre, rather than the emerging 'fringe' of private theatres, clubs, and experimental venues in the late nineteenth century where the work of Ibsen and his school tended to be produced.

The plot of *Miss Chester* brings the past history of the complicated relationships of an aristocratic family to work on the present situation of the characters, ending, in the convention of melodrama, with a series of public confessions of wrongdoing and contrition, and the public vindication of the virtuous and the victimised. It is concerned with revealing the true identities of Miss Chester, her husband Sir Arthur Ashton (who first appears as the Bohemian drinker and gambler Michael Fortescue), and their son Rupert (who first appears as the second son of the Earl of Montressor). At the start of the play Miss Chester is the companion of the juvenile heroine, Isabel Montressor, and she appears to be hardened against the claims of love and sympathy. Of course, the audience is quickly shown that Miss Chester's bitterness is a facade to cover her extreme despair over the lost loves of her life – her husband and her son. These men are revealed through a series of sensational incidents which begin with the family solicitor's revelation that Rupert was actually the illegitimate son of the Earl of Montressor's sister, who had been married against her family's wishes to a man who had a first wife already living. Rupert leaves the Montressors, intent on living the Bohemian life of drinking and gambling. But he is involved in a duel with his drinking and gambling companion, Michael Fortescue, over Fortescue's plan to ruin the eldest son of Montressor, and when Rupert is apparently mortally wounded, Miss Chester's speech to Fortescue brings down the act curtain:

> As surely as we three shall stand before the judgement seat of God, the boy your guilty hand has now struck down, *is your own son!* (p. 29)

The ending of the play unravels the complicated relationships of the Montressors, revealing Miss Chester to be Lady Gertrude, the Earl of Montressor's lost sister, Rupert to be her son, and Michael Fortescue to be the errant Sir Arthur Ashton and husband of Lady Gertrude, who has recently inherited his father's title and estate, which lies next to that of the Montressors. The apparent irregularity of his marriage to Lady Gertrude is duly explained, and its legitimacy publicly reinstated, and Rupert is free to marry Isabel Montressor. This ending demonstrates a concern with the complicated nature of family relationships, and a dramatisation of the ways in which legal, economic, and emotional elements are entangled in the construction of personal identity and relationships. The play is of interest for the way that it shifts the focus from the plot of the love triangle between the juvenile lead characters – Rupert, Michael (the Earl of Montressor's eldest son), and his cousin Isabel – to a searing dramatisation of the pain of an older woman, the abandoned Miss Chester. It is her voice which is dominant in the play, whether it be her feigned stance of anti-romanticism, in which she tells her charge, Isabel, that 'if you wish to fight successfully the battle of the world, you must ignore the very existence of a heart' (p. 7), or her private voice of pain, revealed only to the audience. The sense of a female authorial voice is strong here, and read this way, to some extent counters Kerry Powell's argument that the numbers of adaptations of women's novels (principally by male playwrights) 'represent a massive assault against women writers that is both textual and sexual in nature.'[32]   The recognition of Miss Chester as the central voice of the play is reflected in contemporary reviews of the first production, which generally criticised *Miss Chester* for being an improbable melodrama[33] constructed 'on a totally wrong principle,'[34] but noted that it was received enthusiastically by audiences[35] due principally to the performance of Mrs Herman Vezin as Miss Chester.

Despite its conventional happy ending, *Miss Chester* does not offer an uncomplicated celebration of regularised marriage. The strength of Miss Chester's sufferings, and her deliberate articulation of them in the course of the action undercut the satisfaction to be felt over the pairing of characters at the final curtain. In theory, this melodramatic ending is constructed so as to admit of little doubt or ambivalence about the moral and emotional resolution of the plot, whatever plot complications, moral or ideological ambiguities may have been raised in the play. But what if all meaning cannot be contained within this structure? And what if we want to interrogate the structure for what it represses, or for what it does with the excess of feeling it generates? These questions, and the possibilities for multiple readings offered by *Miss Chester*, are a common feature of popular plays by women playwrights. In *Miss Chester*, the audience is forced to listen to the voice of the apparently outcast and redundant woman, who is barred from the conventional feminine roles of wife, lover, and mother. Although the play makes no explicit feminist claims, this performance of an aspect of female experience calls into question contemporary ideals of femininity, and significantly, does so from within those very conventions. Such miniature revolutions from within might even

32   Powell, p. 101.
33   'Holborn Theatre', *Athenaeum*, 12 October 1872, p. 476.
34   'Holborn Theatre', *Daily Telegraph*, 7 October 1872, [np].
35   'Holborn Theatre,' *The Era*, 13 October 1872.

be seen as more subversive than the overt critiques by later Victorian feminists of the position of women.

The theatre writing of Lucy Clifford (1853–1929) is a further example of this critique of femininity from within popular melodrama of the late nineteenth century. Clifford's melodramas, together with the comedies of Florence Bell, are all the more interesting because they appear at the same time as the explicitly political proto-feminist theatre work of the New Women. Although Clifford and Bell were involved in progressive intellectual and feminist movements, their theatre writing is not programmatically political, but this does not mean that their work cannot be read for its political insights. Like Marryat and Bell, extant evidence of Lucy Clifford's life reveals her to be determinedly professional in her pursuit of a literary career including writing for the stage. Her marriage to William Kingdon Clifford, Professor of Applied Mathematics at University College, London, connected her with an élite intellectual circle including Elizabeth Robins, T. H. Huxley, Leslie Stephen, the Pollocks, Grant Allen, Eliza Lynn Linton, and Thomas Hardy,[36] most of whom she stayed in contact with after her husband's early death in 1879. But in contrast to this intellectual élite, Clifford's work was resolutely popular. Her first novel *Mrs Keith's Crime* (1885), is about a dying woman who is told by her doctor that she will not live to see her daughter die. In an act represented as extreme maternal devotion, Mrs Keith kills her daughter Molly before she herself dies so that she is with Molly as she dies. Such was the impact of this book that Clifford was thought to be the author of *Alan's Wife* when that play was produced eight years later by Elizabeth Robins at J. T. Grein's Independent Theatre and then published anonymously. With its twist on the plot of maternal devotion established by Ellen Wood's *East Lynne* (a plot echoed at the end of the century by Oscar Wilde in *Lady Windermere's Fan*), *Mrs Keith's Crime* represents a late development of the sensation novel of the 1860s. Clifford combines the elements of sensation melodrama – a crime arising from extreme emotion, the focus on the high passions of middle-class domestic life – with some of the intellectual currents and fashions of the period: in this case, the novel bears the influence of spiritualism, a movement Alex Owen links explicitly with the women's movement of the 1870s and 80s

---

[36]   Edward Clodd, *Memories* (London: Chapman and Hall, 1916), pp. 37–9. See also Marysa Demoor and Monty Chisholm's brief biography of Lucy Clifford in *"Bravest of women and finest of friends": Henry James's Letters to Lucy Clifford* (University of Victoria: English Literary Studies, 1999), pp. 11–16.

through spiritualism's 'potential, not always consciously realised, for subversion.'[37]

Lucy Clifford's most famous (or notorious) dramatic work, *The Likeness of the Night*, began as a story 'The End of Her Journey' in *Temple Bar* in 1887, and was then adapted by Clifford as a play which ran for 63 performances at St James's Theatre in 1900.[38] The play's reputation endured throughout the early twentieth century: in 1913, *Evening News* columnist Percy Cross Standing called it 'One of the most remarkable plays ever written by a woman,'[39] and in 1921 it was adapted into a film by producer Percy Nash. The dramatic version of *The Likeness of the Night* is a reworking of the classic love triangle, where Bernard Archerson, a barrister, has married Mildred for her money, forsaking his true love, Mary. After a few years of marriage, Bernard and Mary meet again, and eventually Bernard maintains Mary and their son as his lawful family in a villa in Hampstead. The play begins with Mildred's suspicions that all is not right with her marriage: she loves Bernard passionately, but suspects that he feels no more than friendly affection for her. The first act culminates in Mildred's discovery of another Mrs Archerson, living in Finchley Road, Hampstead; in the second act, Mildred visits Mary, the other Mrs Archerson and sees the closeness of the relationship between her husband and his mistress. Mildred goes on a cruise with friends, and disappears in a storm – as her friend Mrs Carew speculates:

> Oh! she was the sort of woman of whom an unlucky chance is apt to take advantage, and I think that, as she sat there dreaming on through the twilight with the wild winds all about her, and the waves mounting higher and higher, that somehow she went forward to meet them – and they just folded her in. (p. 120)

The sub-text for the audience is, of course, that Mildred has committed suicide, while making it look like an accident, so her husband can marry his true love. However, when Mary, the second wife, finds out about her predecessor's sacrifice she ends the relationship. The curtain falls on a typical melodramatic tableau, made all the more powerful by Mary's use of the water imagery which had been connected with Mildred throughout the rest of the play:

---

[37]   Alex Owen, *The Darkened Room: Women, Power and Spiritualism in Late Victorian England* (London: Virago, 1989), p. 4.

[38]   All quotations are taken from Lucy Clifford, *The Likeness of the Night. A Modern Play in Four Acts* (London: Adam and Charles Black, 1900).

[39]   'Our Women Dramatists', *Evening News*, 31 December 1913.

Mary. [*Putting out her hands again with a gesture of despair.*]
Keep back! Keep back! Between us flows the sea –
[*He* [Bernard] *half staggers; they stand looking at each other aghast.*
(p. 146)

While this brief plot summary sounds like a masochistic romantic fantasy, the representation of the self-centred man, content to ruin two lives because of his desire for material and worldly comforts, is scathing. We are left in no doubt about Clifford's view of the evils of the system of selling women into marriage, and their powerlessness to resist such usage through their investment in a romantic ideal, at odds with the pragmatic views of love and marriage apparently held by those who become their husbands.

Clifford's plays continued to be demanding and challenging while remaining within the generic conventions of melodrama. Her drama *The Latch*, produced by Lena Ashwell at the Kingsway in a matinee programme of one-act plays in 1908, was seen as 'a harrowing theme of a tragic domestic complication, powerful in a grim way.'[40] *A Woman Alone*, first performed in 1914, about a mis-matched husband and wife who decide to part, shows how frustrating such a marriage is for a woman with 'brains, energy, interests', but how 'unsatisfactory in the long run so-called freedom is for a woman.'[41] The entrapment of women in marriages with dominating, even brutal men, is the theme of *The Searchlight*, another sensation melodrama set in the milieu of the comfortable middle and upper classes.[42] The play dramatises the afterlife of Miss Williamson (formerly Mrs Waylett) who has been tried and acquitted for the murder of her husband. She seeks refuge from the 'searchlight' of public disapproval in a quiet hotel in the Austrian lakes where she is thrown into the company of an assortment of English visitors, including the self-made wealthy Rigby, who guesses her secret, and the invalid Major Travers, with whom she develops an intense relationship. The idle gossip of the hotel guests speculates over the Waylett case, causing Miss Williamson increasing alarm, which is brought to a head when her aunt, Mrs Lawson, appears. Mrs Lawson accuses Miss Williamson of infamous behaviour (p. 14) in presuming to mix with respectable people, to which Miss Williamson replies in a set-piece speech of justification central to the argument of the play:

The receiver is as base as the thief, the tempter is worse than the tempted. Think – think of the life you led us – my two sisters and

---

40   *Sheffield Daily Telegraph*, 20 May 1908.
41   *The Era*, 22 July 1914, p. 12.
42   All quotations are taken from *The Searchlight* (London: Samuel French, 1904).

me ... But think of the price *I* paid, the *years* I spent with that man shuddering at his touch, dreading the sound of his voice, a man who insulted me when he was sober, and ill-treated me when he was drunk – I went to him because I was frightened, forced, and ignorant of everything. You *knew* ... That deed – if, in a moment of madness I *did* do it, is one of which you, as well as I, should pay the penalty, for you drove me to it on the awful day of my marriage. (p. 15)

Here, Clifford's indictment of what Cicely Hamilton was later to write about as *Marriage as a Trade* (1909) does not stint in its apportioning of blame to the older women who collude in the process instead of protecting their charges. The second part of the play shows the developing attachment between Travers and Miss Williamson, which eventually forces Miss Williamson to confess to Travers that she is Mrs Waylett. A quick curtain obscures her exit, but the implication is that she has committed suicide by throwing herself under a train. Clifford's presentation of the problem of marriage for women is not a theoretical critique of patriarchy which might analyse the inequalities of power in the structures of class and gender, but in its exploration and representation of the emotional truth of a cruel marriage, it is no less feminist in intent. Even Clifford's comedies, such as *The Hamilton's Second Marriage* and *A Honeymoon Tragedy*[43] have an edge of social commentary. Like her melodramas, Clifford's comedies are firmly located within the drawing rooms and holiday resorts of the affluent and powerful, and use that vantage point to make sharp observations of the consequences of unequal power relations between the sexes.

The work of Florence Bell (1851–1930) is a prime example of the way that even recuperative feminist literary histories can have blind spots about the popular and the non-feminist. However, as I will argue, feminist approaches also offer the most effective ways of reading Bell's work. Bell is perhaps now best known as Elizabeth Robins' collaborator on *Alan's Wife*, a key text in theatrical feminism of the late nineteenth century. However, when Bell collaborated with Robins on an adaptation of Elin Ameen's story as the play *Alan's Wife* (first performed in 1893), she was already in the middle of a successful career as playwright and essayist. Bell was an energetic and busy woman, doing the unpaid work of running a large household which included several relatives of her husband, the industrialist, Hugh Bell, as well as maintaining that public position of 'lady' required as part of her husband's business and social position, and maintaining a steady output of writing across

---

[43]   *The Hamilton's Second Marriage*, in *Plays* (London: Duckworth, 1909), and *A Honeymoon Tragedy* (London: Samuel French, 1904).

a wide variety of genres. The range of Bell's work reveals her to be a truly professional writer – a woman of letters – able to move from translations and adaptations of French plays, to children's literature, to editing her step-daughter Gertrude Bell's letters, to sociological essays for the French journal *La science sociale* and English journals on a variety of topics, from personal memoirs to informed and detailed studies of working-class reading habits. *Alan's Wife* was produced and published anonymously, but during her lifetime, Bell's claim to 'serious' literary attention is derived from her pioneering observational work of sociology, *At the Works* (first published in 1907); her close observation of and engagement with working-class life in Middlesbrough is also evident in her earlier essay 'What People Read' (1905) on working-class reading practices,[44] and her play *The Way the Money Goes*, published in 1910, and produced by the Stage Society in 1911.[45]

While *Alan's Wife* has been recently anthologised, revived, and discussed in terms of its proto-feminist themes and Naturalist aesthetics,[46] Bell's other work has been marginalised, if not made completely invisible in conventional theatre history and its feminist revisionings (note for example, Catherine Wiley's erasure of Bell in the title of her essay about *Alan's Wife*). There is, it seems, a continuing difficulty in discussing Bell, an upper-class woman who became increasingly anti-suffragette,[47] whose work revels in the apparently trivial, comic and often woman-hating aspects of feminine lives lived in the drawing-rooms of the comfortably off. However, the feminist project of recognising and naming these aspects of the construction of late-Victorian femininity through fictional or theatrical representation can also offer us a way to place in Bell's drawing-room comedies alongside *Alan's Wife*. Bell's one-act comedy, *A Joint Household*, for example, playfully explores the battles between women in domestic culture, but paradoxically, the conditions of production of the play itself remind us of Bell's place in a collaborative female network of professional and personal relationships.

---

[44]   Reprinted in Florence Bell, *Landmarks: A Reprint of some Essays and other Pieces Published Between the Year 1894 and 1922* (London: Ernest Benn, 1929).

[45]   Florence Bell, *The Way the Money Goes* (London: Sidgwick and Jackson, 1910).

[46]   For example, Vivien Gardner and Linda Fitzsimmons (eds), *The New Woman*, (London: Methuen, 1994), Elin Diamond, *Unmaking Mimesis* (London and New York: Routledge, 1997), and Catherine Wiley, 'Staging Infanticide: The Refusal of Representation in Elizabeth Robins's *Alan's Wife*', *Theatre Journal* 42 (1990), pp. 432–46.

[47]   See, for example, Wiley's assumption that Bell's class position 'must have prevented real communication between her and her [working-class] subjects,' in ibid., fn 21, p. 438.

A Joint Household was first performed at Steinway Hall, London, on 13 March 1891, with Henrietta Cowen (who also wrote plays in this period) as the overbearing Mrs Smithers, and Elizabeth Robins playing her hapless friend, Mrs Tallett. The play is an inconsequential commedietta which makes a joke of a bossy and hypocritical woman, Mrs Smithers, who ruins her husband's plans for a joint household by the seaside for the summer, with his friends, the Talletts, by her overbearing and suspicious behaviour. There is a delight, however, in the awfulness of Mrs Smithers, and the sweet and ladylike revenge that Mrs Tallett wreaks, (accidentally on purpose?) by handing Mrs Smithers a letter to Mrs Tallett. The letter is from Mr Smithers, asking Mrs Tallett not to mention to Mrs Smithers that he, Mr Smithers, had once proposed to Mrs Tallett before either of them was married. This is the sort of farcical situation bordering on the risqué upon which English drawing-room comedy is founded. But what is noteworthy in this piece is that, like so many other plays of this sort by women playwrights, the apparently trivial parts of life – marriage, children, household arrangements, meals and so on – are given weight as central experiences of women's lives, so that the objectified and fetishised female body on the nineteenth-century stage is given the opportunity to assert her subjectivity and speaking power. It might be a power exercised through domestic tyranny, and it might not be a subject position that twenty-first century feminist critics are complacent or comfortable about, but in this domestic world we see women without men taking the stage. And in an account of women's popular playwriting these domestic female bodies need to be 'excavated', to use Elin Diamond's term[48] and interpreted just as much as the subversive body of Jean Creyke in *Alan's Wife*.

Like many other of Bell's one-act comedies, such as *Time is Money, In a Telegraph Office, Between the Posts,* and *An Underground Journey, A Joint Household* had repeat performances, including a performance with two other of Bell's one-act plays, *In a Telegraph Office,* and *Between the Posts,* at the Sloane Square Parish Hall, on 11 May 1893, less than a month after the premiere of *Alan's Wife.* Of these plays, and the difficulty of doing them justice, the *Era* writes that they are 'like most of Mrs Hugh Bell's pieces ... slight, sketchy, and amusing. Indeed, a mere outline description gives but a poor idea of one of these smart *saynetes.*'[49] One of the other plays in this bill, *Between the Posts,* was first produced as *L'Indecis,* and was well-known as the play in which the fashionable French actor Coquelin played. *The Theatre*

---

[48]   Diamond, p. 8.
[49]   *The Era,* 13 May 1893, p. 11.

called it 'an exquisite piece of comedy' at its first performance in 1887.[50]
Dramatic Notes commented that, 'It was no small compliment to our
countrywoman that her little play was so brightly written, and contained such
lively sallies of wit, that M. Coquelin accepted it to play the title *role*;' the
review going on to note 'the call for the author at its close'.[51] The neatness
and entertainment value of Bell's one-act comedies is acknowledged in a
review of *An Underground Journey*, also first produced in February 1893, a
month before *Alan's Wife*:

> Mrs Hugh Bell has no need to rush all over the earth, after the
> fashion of most writers for the stage, before she can find a subject to
> treat. Her dramas lie practically ready-made in drawing-rooms,
> offices, where men and women congregate, and observation finds
> material to work upon ... The trifle [*An Underground Journey*] has
> all the light wit and naturalness which Mrs Bell's commediettas
> generally possess, [52]

Like Lucy Clifford, Florence Bell was actively writing and involved in the
theatre from the 1880s through to the 1910s, her plays were widely reviewed
and well-received, but a century later, she has disappeared from the critical
stories we tell about the popular theatre and women's writing.

Feminist Literary Histories and the Popular Theatre

How can we place the work of these three women, representative of so many
more? This chapter is as much about the ways these women's careers and
their plays have been categorised, interpreted, and placed, as it is about the
plays themselves: that is, I am as concerned with literary historiography as
with literary history. Like other feminist literary critics, I find that my
interpretations of these women's work and careers oscillates between a desire
to find a recuperative and triumphalist history of the proto-feminist Modernist
and suffragette drama, and a perplexed concern that, as Susan Carlson puts it,
some of the most active and prolific women playwrights at the end of the
nineteenth century were 'not literary heroines with progressive agendas.'[53]
For this reason, it seems, we have a lot of information about Elizabeth Robins

---

50   *The Theatre*, 1 December 1887, p. 331.
51   *Dramatic Notes* (1887), p. 120.
52   *The Theatre*, 1 March 1893, pp. 160–61.
53   Carlson, p. 273.

as a playwright, because she wrote plays we can name as broadly 'feminist', and her life was one of lived feminist heroism; this is, of course, no bad thing. But it is time to reinscribe into feminist criticism the work of Robins' less considered sisters: those women writers who were not 'notorious and self-consciously transgressive' in their writing.[54]

I want to propose a model which allows us to read these women's plays, and hundreds like them, in such a way as to begin to answer the questions I posed at the beginning of this chapter. In recovering women's playwriting for the popular stage, we need to see their work as that which necessarily takes place within a patriarchal masculinist culture. Popular women playwrights negotiated the challenges of the late-nineteenth-century theatre as a workplace in which part of their role was a stereotypically feminine one: to please male managers, enact shining womanhood, and entertain and seduce audiences. The nature of their work and their ambitions for it meant that they could not afford *not* to participate in this masculinist arena. As I have argued elsewhere, when women become involved in theatrical activity, even of the most apparently private and domestic, the ideological and physical separation of the 'separate spheres' of men's and women's lives begin to dissolve and interpenetrate.[55] Ann Game and Rosemary Pringle offer a theoretical explanation of women's work which seems to replicate sexist or patriarchal power relations (their focus of study is the female secretary). Women, they argue, live in two cultures – 'a "heterosexual" culture in which they interact directly with men, and a "women's" culture.' These cultures do not occur in separate spaces, but 'occur simultaneously in the *same* social space.' Women's culture is 'a way of making sense of the heterosexual one, and the power relations in it. Although associated with "powerlessness", it is a means for constructing separate space.'[56] Thus, rather than construct an oppositional binary, in which one set of terms is always hierarchically subjugated to the other, Game and Pringle propose a model of intersecting and interacting spheres which operate relationally, each with the potential of making sense of the other.

---

[54]   Viv Gardner, 'Women and Writing at the *fin de siècle*' in Marian Shaw (ed.), *An Introduction to Women's Writing* (Hemel Hempstead: Prentice Hall, 1998), p. 180. Gardner acknowledges that her focus on these transgressive writers will lead to 'significant omissions.'

[55]   Katherine Newey, '*Home Plays for Ladies*: Women's Work in Home Theatricals', *Nineteenth Century Theatre Research* 26 (1998), pp. 93–111.

[56]   Ann Game and Rosemary Pringle, 'Beyond *Gender at Work*: Secretaries' in Norma Grieve and Ailsa Burns (eds), *Australian Women: New Feminist Perspectives* (Melbourne: Oxford University Press, 1986), pp. 286–8.

   This model allows us to see how the work of usually invisible women
playwrights – invisible in that they fit into neither a high cultural model of
literary drama, nor a feminist model of transgressive woman writer – can
make a substantial contribution to challenging patriarchal theatre history. We
do not need, for example, to write Florence Bell out of the argument of the
feminist challenge to realism to be found in *Alan's Wife*. In the model
suggested by Game and Pringle, Bell's occupation of the position of 'lady'
and her collaboration with Robins in proto-feminist work, might not be
contradictory. Instead what I note here is the way that Bell's work brings
together the women's cultures of domesticity and collaboration she inhabits in
her work with Robins, and the heterosexual culture which gives her a
privileged position (patriarchally derived nonetheless) from which to speak.
So that it is her apparently frivolous plays about drawing-rooms, or children's
plays about fairies, which constitute an important – even central – exploration
of women's culture, and an insertion of that culture, into the heterosexual
culture of the late nineteenth century theatre constitutes a politicised feminist
act. Florence Marryat's and Lucy Clifford's use of sensation melodrama to
place the private suffering woman centre stage are similarly important public
stagings of private emotion in a public arena, which challenge the relegation
of emotion to the private (and thus feminine) sphere. Marryat's and Clifford's
determination to have their plays produced in the commercial theatre, evident
in their letters and professional activities, could again be read as a political
practice. Furthermore, a recognition of women as producers and consumers of
popular entertainment goes some way, I would argue, to counter rather
simplistic interpretations of women as only oppressed objects of popular
culture.[57] The lessons here are salutary: perhaps more than any other critical
approach, a feminist reading of popular entertainment must be careful not to
make assumptions that the power relations involved in the production and
consumption of nineteenth-century popular culture inevitably oppressed
women.
   What emerges then, from bringing together a more detailed study of some
women writers of popular plays and a critique of the conventional
historiography of late-nineteenth-century English theatre? The apparently
simple act of pausing to examine these now obscure plays in their own terms,
paying particular attention to contemporary reviews, reminds us of the variety
of theatre in the late-nineteenth-century, and the very positive receptions now

---

[57]   See the work of Judith Mayne, *Private Novels, Public Films* (Athens, Ga.:
University of Georgia Press, 1988) and Jackie Stacey, *Star Gazing: Hollywood Cinema and
Female Spectatorship* (London: Routledge, 1994) for a development of this argument in terms
of women's roles as producers and consumers of Hollywood film.

forgotten plays often received on first production. Such knowledge undercuts conventional judgements of 'good' and 'bad' writing and judgements of plays that should endure as 'classic', to demonstrate the multiplicity and complexity of the theatre of the late nineteenth century. Focussing on *women's* plays, and asking questions about the cultural work they might do, irrespective of judgements of quality, or preconceptions about their political utility, foregrounds the inclusiveness of feminist critical practice and the new knowledges it can bring. As Helen Day argues, '[W]omen's theatre history ... is inclusive rather than exclusive and without imposed hierarchies. The high and the popular co-exist and have equal status.'[58] The knowledge liberated by this approach suggests that we need to recover a model of the late nineteenth century theatre as more successful, more various, and more buoyant than William Archer, Henry Arthur Jones, or Clement Scott would admit. In spite of the concerted critical campaign against it, popular theatre endured and endures still, although its role as mass entertainment has been replaced by film and television. An acknowledgement of the contemporary successes, however ephemeral, of playwrights in the popular theatre such as Marryat, Bell, and Clifford disrupts the standard model of modernity in the theatre as a revolt against the conventions of Victorian theatrical representation. Their work, if we are to take it seriously, by including it in an account of cultural production, rather than dismissing it as bad writing, suggests one of the *other* stories of modernity: a history of the complicated intertwining and circulation of plots, characters, emotions, and narrative techniques within popular culture in which women, as producers and consumers of popular entertainment, are central.

---

[58]   Helen Day, 'Female Daredevils', in Gardner and Rutherford, p. 137.

Bibliography

Theodor Adorno and Max Horkheimer, 'The Culture Industry: Enlightenment as Mass Deception' (1946) in Simon During (ed.), *The Cultural Studies Reader* (London and New York: Routledge, 1993).

R.D. Altick, *The English Common Reader: A Social History of the Mass Reading Public, 1800–1900* (Chicago: University of Chicago Press, 1957).

Isabel Armstrong, *Victorian Poetry: Poetry, Poetics and Politics* (London: Routledge, 1993).

Nancy Armstrong, *Desire and Domestic Fiction: A Political History of the Novel* (Oxford: Oxford University Press, 1987).

Bob Ashley, *The Study of Popular Fiction: A Source Book* (London: Pinter, 1989).

Owen Ashton and Stephen Roberts, *The Victorian Working-Class Writer* (London: Mansell, 1999).

Marie Axton and Raymond Williams (eds), *English Drama: Forms and Development* (Cambridge: Cambridge University Press, 1977).

Diana Basham, *The Trial of Woman: Feminism and the Occult Sciences in Victorian Literature and Society* (London: Macmillan, 1992).

Margaret Beetham, *A Magazine of her Own? Domesticity and Desire in the Woman's Magazine, 1800–1914* (London: Routledge, 1996).

Tony Bennett, Colin Mercer and Janet Woollacott (eds), *Popular Culture and Social Relations* (Milton Keynes and Philadelphia: Open University Press, 1986).

Virginia Blain et al (eds), *The Feminist Companion to Literature in English* (London: B.T. Batsford, 1990).

Michael R. Booth, Richard Southern, Frederick and Lise-Lone Marker, and Robertson Davies, *The Revels History of Drama in English, Vol. V, 1800 to the Present* (London: Methuen, 1975).

Michael R. Booth, *English Melodrama* (London: Herbert Jenkins, 1965).

Rachel Bowlby, *Just Looking: Consumer Culture in Dreiser, Gissing and Zola* (New York and London: Methuen, 1985).

Jacky Bratton, *Acts of Supremacy: The British Empire and the Stage* (Manchester: Manchester University Press, 1991).

Jacky Bratton, Jim Cook, and Christine Gledhill (eds), *Melodrama: Stage Picture Screen* (London: British Film Institute, 1994).

Mary Cadogan and Patricia Craig, *You're a Brick Angela! A New Look at Girls' Fiction from 1839 to 1975* (London: Gollancz, 1976).

Barbara Caine, *English Feminism, 1780–1980* (Oxford: Oxford University Press, 1997).

Janice Carlisle, 'Spectacle as Government: Dickens and the Working-Class Audience' in Sue-Ellen Case and Janelle Reinelt (eds), *The Performance of Power: Theatrical Discourse and Politics* (Iowa: University of Iowa Press, 1991).

Susan Carlson, 'Conflicted Politics and Circumspect Comedy: Women's Comic Playwriting in the 1890s' in Tracy C. Davis and Ellen Donkin (eds), *Women and Playwriting in Nineteenth-Century Britain* (Cambridge: Cambridge University Press, 1999).

Jennifer Carnell, *The Literary Lives of Mary Elizabeth Braddon* (Hastings: Sensation Press, 2000).

Gilbert B. Cross, *Next Week – 'East Lynne': Domestic Drama in Performance, 1820–1874* (London: Associated University Presses, 1977).

Ann Cvetkovich, *Mixed Feelings: Feminism, Mass Culture and Victorian Sensationalism* (New Brunswick: Rutgers University Press, 1992).

Leonore Davidoff and Catherine Hall, *Family Fortunes: Men and Women of the English Middle Class, 1780–1850* (London: Hutchinson, 1987).

Tracy C. Davis, *Actresses as Working Women: Their Social Identity in Victorian Culture* (London and New York: Routledge, 1991).

Tracy C. Davis, 'Laborers of the Nineteenth-Century Theatre: The Economies of Gender and Theatrical Organization', *Journal of British Studies* 33 (1994), pp. 50–51.

Tracy C. Davis and Ellen Donkin (eds), *Nineteenth-Century British Women Playwrights* (Cambridge: Cambridge University Press, 1999).

Daniel Duffy, 'Fiends instead of Men: Sarah Ellis, Anne Brontë and the Eclipse of the Early Victorian Masculine ideal' in Antony Rowland, Emma Liggins and Eriks Uskalis (eds), *Signs of Masculinity: Men in Literature 1700 to the Present* (Amsterdam: Rodopi, 1998).

Daniel Duffy, 'Heroic Mothers and Militant Lovers: Representations of Lower-Class Women in Melodrama of the 1830s and 1840s', *Nineteenth-Century Theatre* 27 (1999), pp. 41–65.

Gail Finney, *Women in Modern Drama: Freud, Feminism, and European Theater at the Turn of the Century* (Ithaca and London: Cornell University Press, 1989).

Leona W. Fisher, 'Mark Lemon's Farces on the Woman Question'. *Studies in English Literature 1500–1900* 28 (1988), pp. 648–70.

John Fiske, *Understanding Popular Culture* (London: Unwin Hyman, 1989).

Kate Flint, *The Woman Reader, 1837–1914* (Oxford: Oxford University Press, 1993).

Wendy Forrester, *Great-Grandmama's Weekly: A Celebration of the Girl's Own Paper, 1880–1901* (Guildford: Lutterworth Press, 1980).

Gill Frith, 'Transforming Features: Double Vision and the Female Reader', *New Formations* 15 (1991), pp. 67–81.

Viv Gardner and Susan Rutherford (eds), *The New Woman and her Sisters: Feminism and Theatre, 1850–1914* (Hemel Hempstead: Harvester Wheatsheaf, 1992).

Pamela K. Gilbert, *Disease, Desire and the Body in Victorian Women's Popular Novels* (Cambridge: Cambridge University Press, 1997).

Sandra M. Gilbert and Susan Gubar, *The Madwoman in the Attic: The Woman Writer and the Nineteenth-Century Literary Imagination* (New Haven and London: Yale University Press, 1984).

Catherine Hall, *White, Male and Middle-Class: Explorations in Feminism and History* (Cambridge: Polity Press, 1992).

A. James Hammerton, *Cruelty and Companionship: Conflict in Nineteenth-Century Married Life* (London: Routledge, 1992).

Michael Hays and Anastasia Nikolopoulou (eds), *Melodrama: The Cultural Emergence of a Genre* (London: Macmillan, 1996).

Julie Holledge, *Innocent Flowers: Women in the Edwardian Theatre* (London: Virago, 1981).

Winifred Hughes, *The Maniac in the Cellar: Sensation Novels of the 1860s* (Princeton: Princeton University Press, 1980).

Patricia Ingham, *The Language of Gender and Class: Transformations in the Victorian Novel* (London: Routledge, 1996).

Fredric Jameson, 'Reification and Utopia in Mass Culture' (1979) in *Signatures of the Visible* (London and New York: Routledge, 1990).

Anthony Jenkins, *The Making of Victorian Drama* (Cambridge: Cambridge University Press, 1991).

E. Ann Kaplan, *Motherhood and Representation: The Mother in Popular Culture and Melodrama* (London and New York: Routledge, 1992).

Elizabeth Langland, *Nobody's Angels: Middle-Class Women and Domestic Ideology in Victorian Culture* (Ithaca and London: Cornell University Press, 1995).

Jane Lewis (ed.), *Labour and Love: Women's Experience of Home and Family, 1880–1940* (Oxford: Basil Blackwell, 1989).

Emma Liggins, 'The Evil Days of the Female Murderer: Subverted Marriage Plots and the Avoidance of Scandal in the Victorian Sensation Novel', *Journal of Victorian Culture* 2:1 (1997), pp. 27–41.

Harriet Kramer Linkin and Stephen C. Behrendt (eds), *Romanticism and Women Poets: Opening the Doors of Reception* (Lexington, Kentucky: University Press of Kentucky, 1999).

Brian Maidment, *The Poorhouse Fugitives* (Manchester: Carcanet, 1992).

Gail Marshall, 'Ibsen and Actresses on the English Stage', in Inga-Stina Ewbank, Olav Lausund and Bjørn Tysdahl (eds), *Anglo-Scandinavian Cross-Currents* (Norwich: Norvik Press, 1999).

Gail Marshall, *Actresses on the Victorian Stage: Feminine Performance and the Galatea Myth* (Cambridge: Cambridge University Press, 1998).

Judith Mayne, *Cinema and Spectatorship* (London and New York: Routledge, 1993).

Donald Mullin, *Victorian Plays: A Record of Significant Productions on the London Stage, 1837–1901* (Westport: Greenwood Press, 1987).

Lynda Nead, *Myths of Sexuality: Representations of Women in Victorian Britain* (Oxford: Blackwell, 1988).

Victor E. Neuberg, *Popular Literature: A History and Guide* (Harmondsworth: Penguin, 1977).

Katherine Newey, '*Home Plays for Ladies*: Women's Work in Home Theatricals', *Nineteenth Century Theatre Research* 26 (1998), pp. 93–111.

Katherine Newey, 'Climbing Boys and Factory Girls: Popular Melodramas of Working Life', *Journal of Victorian Culture* 5:1 (2000), pp. 28–44.

Allardyce Nicoll, *A History of the English Drama, 1660–1900, Vol.V, Late Nineteenth-Century Drama, 1850–1900* (Cambridge: Cambridge University Press, 1959).

Carol Polsgrave, 'They made it Pay: British Short Fiction Writing 1820–1840', *Studies in Short Fiction* 11 (1974), pp. 417–21.

Kerry Powell, *Women and Victorian Theatre* (Cambridge: Cambridge University Press, 1997).

E. Deirdre Pribram (ed.), *Female Spectators: Looking at Film and Television* (London and New York: Verso, 1988).

David Punter, *The Literature of Terror: A History of Gothic Fictions from 1765 to the Present Day* 2nd edition, 2 vols (London: Longman, 1996).

Lyn Pykett, *The 'Improper Feminine': The Woman's Sensation Novel and the New Woman Writing* (London: Routledge, 1992).

Lyn Pykett, *The Sensation Novel: from The Woman in White to The Moonstone* (Plymouth: Northcote House, 1994).

Kimberley Reynolds, *Girls Only? Gender and Popular Children's Fiction in Britain, 1880–1910* (Hemel Hempstead: Harvester Wheatsheaf, 1990).

Judith Rowbotham, *Good Girls make Good Wives: Guidance for Girls in Victorian Fiction* (Oxford: Basil Blackwell, 1989).

Mary Lyndon Shanley, *Feminism, Marriage and the Law in Victorian England, 1850–1895* (London: I.B. Tauris, 1989).

Marion Shaw (ed.), *An Introduction to Women's Writing: from the Middle Ages to the Present* (Hemel Hempstead: Prentice Hall, 1998).

Simon Shepherd and Peter Womack, *English Drama: A Cultural History* (Oxford: Blackwell, 1996).

Elaine Showalter, *A Literature of their Own: from Charlotte Brontë to Doris Lessing* (London: Virago, 1977; reprinted 1982).

Jackie Stacey, *Star Gazing: Hollywood Cinema and Female Spectatorship* (London and New York: Routledge, 1994).

John Russell Stephens, *The Censorship of English Drama, 1824–1900* (Cambridge: Cambridge University Press, 1980).

Glennis Stephenson, *Letitia Landon: The Woman behind L.E.L.* (Manchester and New York: Manchester University Press, 1995).

Sheila Stowell, *A Stage of their Own: Feminist Playwrights of the Suffrage Era* (Manchester: Manchester University Press, 1992).

Jenny Bourne Taylor, *In the Secret Theatre of Home: Wilkie Collins, Sensation Narrative and Nineteenth-Century Psychology* (London: Routledge, 1988).

R.C. Terry, *Victorian Popular Fiction, 1860–1880* (London: Macmillan, 1983).

Nicola Diane Thompson, *Reviewing Sex: Gender and the Reception of Victorian Novels* (London: Macmillan, 1996).

Janet Todd (ed.), *Dictionary of British Women Writers* (London: Routledge, 1989).

D.J. Trela (ed.), *Margaret Oliphant: Critical Essays on a Gentle Subversive* (London: Associated University Presses, 1995).

Marlene Tromp, Pamela K. Gilbert and Aeron Haynie (eds), *Beyond Sensation: Mary Elizabeth Braddon in Context* (Albany: State University of New York Press, 2000).

Gaye Tuchman, with Nina E. Fortin, *Edging Women Out: Victorian Novelists, Publishers, and Social Change* (London: Routledge, 1989).

Martha Vicinus, '"Helpless and Unfriended": Nineteenth-Century Domestic Melodrama' in Judith Fisher and Stephen Watts (eds), *When They Weren't Doing Shakespeare: Nineteenth-Century British and American Theatre* (Athens and London: University of Georgia Press, 1989).

Martha Vicinus, *The Industrial Muse* (London: Croom Helm, 1974).

Catherine Wiley, 'Staging Infanticide: The Refusal of Representation in Elizabeth Robins's *Alan's Wife*', *Theatre Journal* 42 (1990), pp. 432–46.

Robert Lee Wolff, *Sensational Victorian: The Life and Fiction of Mary Elizabeth Braddon* (New York: Garland, 1979).

Susan Zlotnick, '"A Thousand Times I'd be a Factory Girl": Dialect, Domesticity, and Working-Class Women's Poetry', *Victorian Studies* 35 (1991), pp. 20–42.

Index

Adorno, Theodor, xiii
advice literature, 53–9, 63, 97
The Age, 5
Aguiler, Grace
    'The Authoress', 108
Allen, Grant, 158
Amulet, 2
annuals, xvii, 1–17, 110
Argosy, 98
Armstrong, Nancy, 53, 96
Arnold, Matthew
    Culture and Anarchy, 94–6
Ashton, Owen, 19
Austen, Jane, 91, 121
autobiographies, 27–8

Basham, Diana, 109, 111
Bateson, Margaret, 54
Beetham, Margaret, xvii, 54
Beeton, Isabella, 53, 68
    Book of Household Management, 54–
    5, 56, 62, 66
Bell, Florence, 147, 152, 166
    comedies, 163
    Alan's Wife (with Elizabeth Robins),
    158, 161–2, 163
    A Joint Household, 162–4
    The Way the Money Goes, 162
Ben Brierley's Journal, 20
Bennett, Tony, xiv
Bijou, 2
Blackwood, Algernon
    'The Kit-Bag', 113
Bobo, Jacqueline, 128
Bolt, Christine, 127–8
Book of Beauty, 2, 4, 6
Booth, Michael, xiv, 151
Bourne Taylor, Jenny, 83
Bowlby, Rachel, 93
Boy's Own Paper, 37, 39–40
Braddon, Mary Elizabeth, ix, xvi, 59–60,
    69–70, 72–8, 90, 98, 101, 122

Hostages to Fortune, 71–2, 78–88
Lady Audley's Secret, 60, 70, 81, 89,
    105
Bratton, Jacky, xv, xxiii
Brontë, Anne
    The Tenant of Wildfell Hall, 64
Broughton, Rhoda, 112, 122
    'The Truth, the Whole Truth, and
    Nothing but the Truth', 111
Buckstone, J.B., 127, 138
    Isabelle; or, Woman's Life, 127–8,
    131–9, 144, 145
    The Green Bushes, xxiii

Cadogan, Mary, 36
Carey, Rosa Nouchette, 38, 47
    'Doctor Lutherell's First Patient', 38
Carlisle, Janice, xxii
Carlson, Susan, 164
Carnell, Jennifer, 72
Cassell's, 20
Clarke, John Stock, 110
Clifford, Lucy, 147, 152, 164, 166
    comedies, 161
    Mrs Keith's Crime, 158–9
    The Likeness of the Night, 159–60
    The Searchlight, 160–61
Coleridge, Samuel Taylor, 2
Collins, Wilkie, 90
    The Woman in White, 100, 101
comedy, xv, 127–8, 129–30, 140–45,
    162–4
conduct books, 3, 53, 99
Cook, Eliza, 18, 23, 26
    'Song of the Haymakers', 24
Cooper, Mrs Orman, 1–2, 44, 47
Countess of Blessington, *see* Gardiner,
    Marguerite
Craig, Patricia, 36
Cross, Gilbert, xiv–xv
Cross, Nigel, 98
Cvetkovich, Ann, xvi, 62–3, 66

Davidoff, Leonore, 56, 65
Davis, Jill, 127
Davis, Tracy, 153
Day, Helen, 167
Dickens, Charles, 7, 100
   Great Expectations, 91
   Martin Chuzzlewit, 104
Dilthey, Wihelm, 27–8
Duffy, Daniel, 64

Edwards, Amelia B., 109
Eliot, George, 90
   Middlemarch, 104–5
Ellis, Sarah, 53, 59, 61, 68
   The Wives of England, 54, 56, 57, 66–7
   The Women of England, 55–6, 62, 108
Engels, Friedrich
   Origin of the Family, Private Property and the State, 94
English Annual, 5, 10
Englishwoman's Domestic Magazine, 54
etiquette books, *see* conduct books

Falconer, Lanoe, 123
   Cecilia de Noël, 118–22
   Mademoiselle Ixe, 118, 119, 121, 122
farce, 129
'Field, Michael', 152
Finney, Gail, 126
Fisher, Leona, 129
Fisher's Drawing-Room Scrapbook, 5, 6, 12, 13, 14, 16
Fiske, John, xiv
Flint, Kate, xvi, xviii–ix, xxi
Forget-Me-Not, 2
Forrester, Fanny, 20, 24, 32, 34
   'The Lowly Bard', 25
Forrester, Wendy, 36
Forster, John, 7
Forty, Adrian, 106
Foucault, Michel, 92
Fox, W.J., 19
Friendship's Offering, 2
Frith, Gill, 98

Game, Ann, 165

Gardiner, Marguerite, 1, 4–5, 7–11
   Conversations of Lord Byron, 4
   'The Coquette', 9
   'Mary Lester: a Tale of Error', 8
   'Remorse: A Fragment', 8
   'Stock in Trade of Modern Poetesses', 9
Gardner, Viv, 154
Gaskell, Elizabeth, 90, 112
   'The Grey Woman', 111, 112
   'The Old Nurse's Story', 110, 111, 115
   Ruth, 111
Gem, 2
ghost stories, xx, 108–25
Gilbert, Susan, 78
Gilfillan, George, 31
Girl's Own Paper, 35–52
Glasgow Examiner, 20
Gledhill, Christine, 127
Gubar, Susan, 78

Hall, Anna Maria
   'La Femme Noir', 110
Hall, Catherine, 56, 59, 65
Hamer, Sarah Sharp, 44
Hamilton, Janet, 20, 31–2, 34
   'Lay of the Tambour Frame', 24–5
Hammerton, A. James, 56, 161
Hardy, Thomas, 158
Henkle, Roger B., 96
Holledge, Julie, 153
Horkheimer, Max, xiii
Huxley, T.H., 158

Ibsen, Henrik, 153
Ingham, Patricia, 26–7

Jacob, W.W.
   'The Monkey's Paw', 113
James, Henry
   The Tragic Muse, 80
   The Turn of the Screw, 113–14
James, M.R., 113
Jameson, Fredric, xiv, xviii
Jerdan, William, 6, 11
Jewsbury, Geraldine
   The Half Sisters, 145–6

Johnston, Ellen, 19, 20, 34
  Autobiography, Poems and Songs, 20,
    28–30, 32–3
  'The Factory Exile', 24
  'Lines to Isabel from the Factory
    Girl', 22
  'Lord Raglan's Address to the Allied
    Armies', 20
  'The Maid of Dundee to her
    Slumbering Muse', 22–3
  'The Maniac in the Greenwood', 33
  'The Pleasure Trip', 21
  'We've Parted', 21

Kaplan, E. Ann, 65, 66
Keepsake, 2, 4, 5, 9, 10, 13

Lamb, Charles, 2
Lamb, Ruth, 41–2, 44–5
  'Sackcloth and Ashes', 43
Landon, Letitia (L.E.L.), 1, 4, 6–7
  'The Chinese Pagoda', 12
  'Coniston Lake', 14
  'Experiments', 13
  'Grasmere Lake: By a Cockney', 13–
    14
  'The Head', 13
  Romance and Reality, 11–12, 16
  'Sefton Church', 13, 14–16
Langland, Elisabeth, 53–4, 56–7, 63
Lee, Vernon, 115, 117
  Hauntings, 112
  *Studies of the Eighteenth Century in
    Italy*, 116
Linton, Eliza Lynn, 89–90, 158
Literary Souvenir, 2
Loudon, John, 65
Lytton, Edward Bulwer, 6, 116
  'The Haunted and the Haunters', 113

magazines, xvii, 35–52
Maginn, William, 6
Maidment, Brian, 18–19, 21–2, 23, 27,
    30–31, 33
marketplace, the, ix–xx, xxi–xxii, 19, 37,
    97–101
Marryat, Florence, 147, 152, 154, 166
  Miss Chester, 155–8
Marryat, Frederick, 7

Marshall, Gail, 126, 145
Mayne, Judith, 128
Mayo, Isabella Fyvie
  'The Other Side of the World', 47
McRobbie, Angela, 51
Melodrama, xiv–xv, xx, xxiii–xxiv, 127–
    8, 129, 131–9, 155–61
Mill, John Stuart, 110
Mitchell, Sally, 98
Molesworth, Mary Louisa
  Four Ghost Stories, 123–4
Mulock, Dinah, 59
  'The Last House in C-Street', 111

Nead, Lynda, 24, 32
Neuberg, Victor, xii
New Juvenile Keepsake, 6
New Monthly Magazine, 97, 99–100
newspapers, 20, 22, 27, 33
Nicoll, Allardyce, 151
Norton, Caroline, 1, 4, 5–6, 23
  'The Departed Friend', 10–11
  *English Laws for Women in the
    Nineteenth Century*, 11
  'The Lost Election', 10
  'The Sorrows of Rosalie', 5
  'Voice from the Factories', 23–4

Oliphant, Margaret, 110, 112, 113
  'A Beleaguered City', 116
  'The Open Door', 109, 111, 113
  'Old Lady Mary', 112
Ouida, 101, 115–16
Owen, Alex, 158–9

periodicals, *see* magazines
Pinero, Arthur Wing, 150, 151
poetry, ix, 2, 5, 8, 9, 10, 12, 14, 18–34
popular culture, xii, xiv, xviii, xx–xxiv
Postlewait, Thomas, 154
Powell, Kerry, 126, 145, 153, 157
prefaces, 27–8, 33
Pringle, Rosemary, 165
Punter, David, 114
Pykett, Lyn, xvi, ix, 54, 59, 60, 61, 70

Reade, Charles, 90
Reynolds, Kimberley, 36
Richards, Thomas, 107

Riddell, Charlotte, 96
Roberts, Stephen, 19
Robertson, Tom, 150
Robins, Elizabeth, 153, 154, 161, 163,
    165, 166; see also Florence Bell
romance, 4, 30

The Satirist, 5, 6
Schloss's Bijou Almanac, 5
Scott, Sir Walter, 2, 38, 116
sensation fiction, xvi, ix, xxi–xxii, 53–88,
    89–107
Shanley, Mary Lyndon, 93
Shaw, George Bernard, 150, 151
Shelley, Mary, 1
Shepherd, Simon, xv, 133, 151
short stories, 1–3, 5, 8–9, 13, 14–16, 38,
    43, 47, 57–8; see also ghost stories
Showalter, Elaine, 60, 61
Stoker, Bram
    'The Judge's House', 113
Southey, Robert, 2

Terry, R.C., xiii
theatre history, 148–51, 166–7
Trollope, Anthony, 90
Tuchman, Gaye, ix, xxiv

Uglow, Jenny, 109

Varley, Isabella
    The Manchester Man, 22

Vicinus, Martha, 22

The Wasp, 11
Webster, Benjamin, 127
    A Woman of Business, 127–8, 140–45
Wilde, Oscar, 151
    Lady Windermere's Fan, 158
Wiley, Catherine, 162
Williams, Merryn, 110
Williams, Raymond, xiv–xv
Wollstonecraft, Mary, 1
Womack, Peter, xv, 133, 151
Wood, Mrs Henry, xvi–xvii, xx, 53–4, 59–
    60, 89–90, 96, 97–8, 105–7
    Danesbury House, 61–2, 66, 67
    East Lynne, 60–61, 64, 65, 66, 89, 97,
    99, 100–101, 105, 158
    Edina, 102
    Lord Oakburn's Daughters, 104
    The Master of Greylands, 97, 102
    Mrs Halliburton's Troubles, 101–2,
    103
    'Rushing Headlong into Marriage',
    57–8
    The Shadow of Ashlydyat, 62–5, 67–8
    St Martin's Eve, 91
    Verner's Pride, 92, 102, 103–4
Wordsworth, William, 2, 14

Yonge, Charlotte, 120

Zlotnick, Susan, 25, 29, 33